TRADE AND POLITICS IN ANCIENT GREECE

TRADE AND POLITICS IN ANCIENT GREECE

BY

JOHANNES HASEBROEK

PROFESSOR OF ANCIENT HISTORY IN THE
UNIVERSITY OF COLOGNE

TRANSLATED BY

L. M. FRASER AND D. C. MACGREGOR

FELLOW OF QUEEN'S COLLEGE   FELLOW OF BALLIOL COLLEGE

ARES PUBLISHERS INC.
CHICAGO   MCMLXXVIII

The English edition is dedicated to the memory of my grandfather

HERMAN JOHANNES HASEBROEK

Citizen of the United States of America

Born 1820 in Leyden, Holland.

Died 1866 in St Louis, Missouri, U.S.A.

Exact Reprint of the Edition:
London 1933
ARES PUBLISHERS INC.
612 N. Michigan Avenue
Chicago, Illinois 60611
Printed in the United States of America
International Standard Book Number:
0-89005-240-9

PREFACE

THE object of this book has been to define the relation of the classical Greek State to commerce in all its forms and activities, and to describe its commercial policy. Such a task could not be attempted, in the present state of these studies, without adopting a definite position in regard to the problems of Greek commerce and the Greek economy in general; for ancient economic history is still in its infancy. Of all the problems of ancient history, that of the material background has been the last to come within the range of the classical scholar; and even the economic historian, confronted by the difficulties of a very differently constituted body of evidence, has hesitated to go back beyond the beginnings of the Middle Ages. Thus the degree of economic development attained in antiquity is still one of the most disputed questions of history. To-day there is a reaction against the familiar idealisation of antiquity, and the theory that it had reached an advanced stage of economic development has found support.[1] The holders of this view regard the economic phenomena of the classical age as more or less closely comparable to those of to-day—as may be seen from their practice of projecting purely modern conceptions into the past. In particular they see in the fifth and fourth centuries before our era a period of national and world economy in which industry was the predominant feature. Opposed to this view there is the other, which insists upon the markedly primitive economic conditions of the ancient world, and in effect will not allow it to have passed beyond the stage of the independent 'household economy.'

On the whole it is coming to be recognised that the extreme modernising attitude, hitherto prevalent, can no longer be maintained. The household-economy theory of Rodbertus and Bücher was exaggerated; but there is no longer any reason

---

[1] This may be seen in the views expressed by so distinguished an authority as W. Otto in many parts of his *Kulturgeschichte des Altertums* (1925).

to doubt that Bücher was right in repudiating the conventional view, or that the economic conditions of the fifth and fourth centuries were relatively primitive. The old views of ancient industrialism have been largely modified,[1] and in particular the fantastic picture of an industrialised Greek world is beginning steadily to fade.

The problem of differentiating between historical epochs is one which cannot be shirked; and in the end even ancient history must face the discovery and statement of the vast differences between past and present and of the peculiar characteristics of ancient life. But its aim will not be attained without a further discrimination between period and period in the development of the ancient economy itself. The conventional picture was in no small degree due to the uncritical combination of evidence from widely separated centuries; and Bücher's serious underestimate of ancient economic development was in great part the result of confining his study to the period before Alexander and ignoring the Hellenistic age. The task of the future must be, I believe, to consider each period separately, and so to arrive at a real understanding of the economic conditions of each of the great epochs of historical development. Hitherto the evidence has been examined without even the most rudimentary understanding of the questions which must be asked and answered. A new and systematic review of the material is now indispensable, and for that the ordinary handbooks and collections are wholly insufficient. In particular, it has never been recognised, as it must be, that the great cleavage in ancient economic development comes with the beginning of the Hellenistic age. The importance of this *cæsura* is much greater than has been supposed; and the remarkable economic progress achieved by this age cannot be duly appreciated until it is recognised how many of its characteristics were still absent in the fourth century. No view which sees in the seventh and sixth centuries a more or less mature 'national' economy can do justice to the importance of the Hellenistic age.

[1] For example, by Francotte, Max Weber, Bolkestein, and Oertel.

Ancient trade has never been thoroughly and scientifically studied.   The following account,[1] which concerns itself with the classical, or pre-Hellenistic, period only, leads to the conclusion that trade in that period was relatively primitive, and that the current view is mistaken which takes trade to have been a preponderant factor in politics and political life.   This view, postulating a parallelism between modern and ancient conditions, has guilelessly accepted as a *datum* the doctrine that the ancient state had a commercial policy in the modern sense.   Yet there is in effect no foundation for such a doctrine. The interests of national production, or of a class of producers, never determined the policy of the autonomous Greek State.   At no time in the history of Greek independence did the State concern itself with the protection or development of citizen industry by a policy of capturing and maintaining markets at home or abroad.   The background and the basis of politics and economics in antiquity was *force*.   The rights of man had not found recognition.   The institution of slavery and, not less important, of that half-citizenship which implied the political degradation of free men, remained unassailable and almost unquestioned throughout.   The class of fully privileged citizens, which was sharply divided from the other inhabitants and which obstinately preserved its exclusiveness, must not be regarded as in any way representative of a national industry or trade.   The citizen of antiquity was a *rentier*, for whom trade was only one of many fields for the investment of his capital. The so-called commercial policy of the ancient state was not concerned with trade, but with the supply of necessaries, such as grain and timber, and with the enrichment of the treasury by means of tolls and duties.   This is another illustration of the difference which Max Weber insists upon between the modern and the ancient world: on the one hand the economic man, on the other the 'political' man.   And it is also a very notable illustration of the character of ancient aristocracy, an aristocracy which was based upon force and unrestrained

---

[1] See my articles on Greek trade and on Greek banking in *Hermes*, 1923, pp. 393 ff., and 1920, pp. 113 ff.

brutality, and which, remoulded to an ethical pattern, was to become the governing class of Plato's Ideal State. The economics of the *Republic* and the *Laws* appear much less Utopian, less divorced from contemporary fact, when the false assumptions of modern historians are cleared away.

I have only been concerned to determine the general type or character of the economic structure of the classical age, and the various forms in which this type has manifested itself. In spite of political changes and other special conditions these forms remained essentially the same throughout the centuries till Alexander and later. The scantiness of the evidence at our disposal has often made it impossible to trace developments in detail.

More space has been given to polemic than I should have liked. I hope I may find excuse in the present chaotic state of the subject and in my anxiety to contrast my conclusions as clearly as possible with the current views.

J. HASEBROEK

PREFACE TO THE ENGLISH EDITION

For the English edition I have preferred to leave the text of *Staat und Handel im alten Griechenland* (Tübingen, 1928) as it stood. On the advice of the publishers most of the extracts from Greek writers have been omitted, without, I hope, impairing the force or the clarity of the argument. But any other alteration whether of addition or excision would have altered the original character of the book; and in particular any attempt to deal with the many criticisms which it has received would merely have increased the perhaps already disproportionate measure of polemic. Moreover, these criticisms have not persuaded me to change my main position, though I need scarcely say that I make no claim to have spoken the last word on the intricate problems of detail which are involved. In a later book, *Griechische Wirtschafts- und Gesellschaftsgeschichte bis zur Perserzeit* (Tübingen, 1931), I have elaborated my conception of the course of Greek economic and social history from the beginnings until the time when the characteristic features of the fifth and fourth centuries had taken shape. I have there dealt more fully with certain questions; and have endeavoured to meet a charge which certain critics have brought against me, namely, of generalising (particularly in the matter of labour and of the metic system) from the peculiar conditions of the Athenian Empire, and of wrongly attributing these to earlier times.

I wish to thank Mr Fraser and Mr Macgregor for undertaking the work of translation. They have been good enough to verify the references to Greek writers, and have drawn my attention to a number of errors and misprints which are here corrected.

Cologne   J. H.
   May, 1933

TRANSLATORS' NOTE

References enclosed in square brackets have been added by us. Those following citations from Boeckh are to Sir George Cornewall Lewis's translation of the *Staatshaushaltung*. For the Lyric Poets reference has been made not to Bergk's *Poetae Lyrici* as in the original, but to the more easily accessible *Anthologia Lyrica* (fourth edition): references to Diehl have been added. The third edition of Dittenberger's *Sylloge* is cited throughout as *S.I.G.*; and Oertel's appendix to the third edition of Pöhlmann's *Geschichte der sozialen Frage* is cited as *Anhang*. Other references, though somewhat abbreviated from the German form, will explain themselves.

CONTENTS

xi

CHAPTER I
THE TRADER

I. *Types of Merchant*

IF we are to arrive at any proper appreciation of Greek economic life, and in particular of the attitude adopted by the Greek State towards trade and commerce, we must first of all get some clear understanding of the types of people by whom these activities were carried on, and of their precise social and economic significance. To do this is one of the most urgent tasks of ancient economic history.

Let us, then, begin by defining our terms.[1] At a period when the division of labour had been carried to considerable lengths, the Greek language recognised three distinct types of trader or middleman—the *kapelos*, the *naukleros*, and the *emporos*, and in addition two sub-types. The *kapelos* is the local dealer—the man who in general does not leave his own place of residence either for the purpose of importing or exporting, but confines himself to selling on the home market. Usage, however, makes a further distinction, according to the manner in which the commodities which he offers for sale are obtained. If he buys them directly from the producers he is a *kapelos* in the strict sense; if from another middleman—a merchant or importer—he is a 'dealer at second remove' (παλιγκάπηλος).[2] But in either case what he sells is not his own produce. The farmer or manufacturer who brings the

---

[1] For what follows readers are referred to the author's article, *Die Betriebsformen des Griechischen Handels im 4. Jahrhundert* in *Hermes*, 1923, pp. 393 ff., 423 ff., where the evidence is treated in greater detail.

[2] See the Schol. on Aristophanes, *Plutus*, 1156 ; Plato, *Sophistes*, 223c, 231d, where the αὐτοπώλης is classed with the κάπηλος, and both are contrasted with the ἔμπορος. In the *Politicus*, 260d, αὐτοπώλης and κάπηλος are opposed to one another. For παλιγκάπηλος and the corresponding verb see Demosthenes, xxv, § 46, and lvi, § 7, respectively, and compare Pollux, vii, 12, and Phot., *s.v.*

I

results of his own labour to market is not a dealer but a 'self-seller' (αὐτοπώλης). Plato, whose Ideal State embodies the principle of the division of labour in its extremest form—that each individual in the community shall have one occupation and one occupation alone—describes the work of the trader as a 'service' which he renders to the producer, in that he takes over his products as a whole and thereby saves him from the loss of time which he would have incurred, if he had had to dispose of them himself (*Rep.*, 371c, d).

Let us recognise, however, that the Greek *kapelos* is not, as such, a small trader or retailer. The correct Greek word, at the time of which we are speaking, for the man who sells his wares by the pennyworth is μεταβολεύς ('trafficker,' or small change man).[1] This, of course, does not mean that the *kapelos* was never as a matter of actual fact a petty tradesman, or huckster—that he never sat in the market-place displaying his goods for sale. In many cases, perhaps in most cases, that is precisely what he did. Indeed, κάπηλος sometimes comes to mean simply 'someone who sells goods'[2]—for the significance of terms of this kind is at all times more or less fluid. But in its essential meaning the word applies to the local dealer as opposed to the foreign dealer, and not to the retailer as opposed to the wholesaler. The local dealer might sometimes have to deal wholesale, because his customers might be not consumers but foreign merchants and buyers for resale—he might be acting as a local middleman between the exporter and the producer, or, if he were a 'dealer at second remove,' between the exporter and another dealer. It is at least conceivable, too, that in disposing of his goods for sale in his own district he might deal solely with small tradesmen, and so never come into direct relation with the consumer at all.

The special characteristic, then, of the *kapelos* is that he remains at home and confines himself to local trade. The other two types of dealer, the *naukleros* and the *emporos*, are both concerned with foreign trade—that is, with overseas

---

[1] Schol. Arist., *loc. cit.* ; Dem., xxv, § 46 ; Pollux, i, 50.
[2] Schol. Arist., *loc. cit., sub fin.*

trade, for in a region with the geographical features of the Greek world practically all traffic will be sea traffic. The *naukleros* is the merchant-shipowner—the man who transports his goods from place to place on his own ship (as a rule travelling with them himself). The *emporos*,[1] on the other hand, is the man who, not possessing a ship of his own, travels, and carries his wares, on a ship belonging to someone else—that is, to a merchant-shipowner. He is engaged in the activity of 'conveying' or 'accompanying' his goods (φορτηγία, Arist., *Pol.*, 1258b). But since the merchant who is not a shipowner is the normal type in Greek commerce, the word comes to be used generally of all foreign traders, whether shipowners or not, as opposed to local dealers.[2] In this wider sense, therefore, the *naukleros* is himself an *emporos*.

The foreign traders, of both types, like the local dealers, confine themselves to selling the goods of other people: they are not themselves producers. That is clear not merely from the actual examples of individual traders which the evidence affords us, but also from the definition which we have already quoted[3] of the *emporos*—'the man who buys goods from a producer or a local dealer and sells them in other countries.' Like the local dealers, they are middlemen—but middlemen between one district and another, not between the producers and consumers of the same district. This does not mean that they are necessarily wholesalers—even though they may commonly deal with other middlemen and not directly with the consumers. Naturally they will try as far as possible to dispose of their goods in large rather than in small quantities.[4]

---

[1] ἔμπορος originally means simply a passenger, or voyager. ἐπιβάτης, which can be used in the above sense, also began by having no specifically commercial significance but meant simply a person who ' embarks.'

[2] Similarly foreign trade in general is ἐμπορία, as opposed to καπηλεία, local trade. [3] See above, p. 1, n. 2.

[4] ' It is to the advantage of merchants not to retail (κοτυλίζειν) their wares, but to sell them wholesale (ἀθρόα πεπρᾶσθαι),' Ps.-Arist., *Econ.*, ii, 1347b 8 (for ἀθρόα=*en gros*, cf. 1350b 11). The same thing will of course be true of the local dealer and of the ' self-seller.' But foreign trade lends itself to wholesale dealings, whereas local trade will normally tend to be retail.

But in view of the fact that the Greek States, unlike the towns of the Middle Ages, placed no restrictions whatever on any form or class of retail activity on the part of merchants from another place, we may suppose that these merchants would be correspondingly ready to exhibit their wares for sale directly to consumers—in certain cases, no doubt (Xen. *Econ.*, viii, 11) on board the ship itself.[1] It is probable, in fact, that many merchants and merchant-shipowners were scarcely more than hawkers—that they sailed from port to port without any fixed destination, selling their goods whenever and wherever a favourable opportunity presented itself.[2] No doubt, too, in winter, when the ships were laid up, the Greek foreign trader would establish himself as a petty tradesman in his own town and sell off his imported goods on the home market. This does not imply, however, that foreign trade was merely subsidiary to home trade, or that the foreign merchant was just a local retailer and went abroad merely to bring back goods for sale at home. There can be no doubt whatever of the existence, in the fourth century at any rate, of a class of people who specialised in foreign commerce and for whom local business was of secondary importance only.

In ancient Greece, then, trade was a clearly defined and distinct form of economic activity, carried on by a class of whole-time professional traders. In this respect the Middle Ages were not so far advanced. The economic theories of the mediæval church demanded that producers and consumers must deal with one another directly, without the intervention of any middlemen; the result being that professional trading was everywhere suppressed, and producers were for the most part compelled to undertake for themselves the task of selling their goods. It is consequently a matter of some difficulty to know whether mediæval labour was of the 'custom' variety —whether, that is to say, the labourer was employed directly

---

[1] The word which is used by the Greeks for the disposal by a merchant of his goods is διατίθεσθαι—'arrange in order' or 'display.'

[2] We may cite for comparison the example of the mediæval merchants of the Hansa towns. They were primarily active in wholesale business, but did not for that reason refuse retail dealings—indeed, they made it their aim to combine the two (v. Below, *Probleme*, p. 342).

by the consumer, either working to his order or else selling him the product in the market.[1] For students of the economic conditions of fourth-century Greece these problems do not arise. By that time, if not earlier, the economic terms had become sufficiently crystallised for their meaning to be clear and certain. The trader of the classical period, though he might occasionally (as in the speech of Lysias against the corn dealers) be the object of bitter attack,[2] was not in general regarded with hostility. Even in the Ideal State his function, though it is as far as possible restricted, was not entirely abolished.[3] The types of trader with whom we have been dealing form a clear and well-developed class. They carried on the trade with other communities. They dealt both in food and the means of supporting life and also in manufactured articles. Even trade in produce seems to have been primarily in their hands and only secondarily (at least during the fourth century) in the hands of landowners and peasants with surplus produce for disposal. (It was never, as far as can be seen, under the control of millers and bakers in Greece, as it was in the Middle Ages.) How important a part was played in the trade of this period by manufactured goods cannot be ascertained. That problem is closely bound up with the whole question of the size of Greek industry in general. Of the existence of producers who sold direct from their workshops to the consumers there is for all periods abundant evidence. And we can further recognise the manufacturer who himself conveys his products to other districts and there disposes of them—if necessary hawking them from house to house.[4] (Even Pasion, who was a manufacturer on a large scale, appears to have used his ships only for the purpose of importing raw materials from abroad for his workshop and then of exporting his finished products for sale in other parts of the world.) But on the other hand the passage already quoted from Plato's *Republic* (371c), which describes the trader as rendering a 'service' to the producer with goods for sale, clearly includes under

---

[1] v. Below, *Probleme*, pp. 445 ff.   [2] See below, p. 12, n. 4.
[3] See below, p. 18.   [4] See below, p. 13.

the term 'producer' the manufacturer as well as the farmer or peasant; and even without this evidence no one could seriously dispute that all three types of trader—local dealers, merchants, and merchant-shipowners alike—were in the habit of dealing in manufactured goods as well as in agricultural produce.

II. *The Ownership of Capital*

'The traders of the Middle Ages' we are told [1] 'have been too readily described in modern and indeed twentieth-century terms. The interpretation of the past in the light of the present has on this point proved quite exceptionally dangerous and misleading.' What is said here of mediæval history may be said with equal force of ancient history. It is true that commercial intercourse was far more fully developed in classical Greece than in mediæval Germany; that in the fourth century B.C. (as we may see from the precision and differentiation of Greek economic terms) the division of labour had been carried, in the world of trade, to considerable lengths. But nevertheless the current view of the Greek commercial classes, which conceives of them as having the same social and economic character as the commercial classes of to-day, is wholly mistaken. The *kapelos* is usually regarded as having been a mere petty tradesman or huckster; and we have seen that this was not always or necessarily the case. Conversely the *naukleros* and *emporos* tend to be thought of as transport agents and capitalists, similar to the merchant princes of late mediæval and modern times. This too is an error. The Greek merchant-shipowner was not a transport agent. The function of such a person is to convey passengers and freight from one place to another; he uses his ship for the purpose of forwarding other people's goods, thereby relieving these people of the task of personally attending them. Forwarding businesses of this kind were wholly unknown in classical Greece.[2] The Greek

---

[1] v. Below, *Probleme*, p. 323.

[2] See *Hermes*, 1923, pp. 402 ff., and also, in agreement with the view here put forward, Oertel, *Anhang*, p. 524. W. Otto, on the other hand, holds the statement in the text to be 'not proven' (*Kulturgesch. d. Alt.*, 1925, p. 77, n. 150).

trader regularly conveyed his goods to their destination either in person, or by means of a personal representative. He did not entrust them to the care of the shipowner.[1] The latter was himself a merchant. He used his ships for his own commercial undertakings. If he had room to spare he might carry other traders with their goods, but that was something quite secondary to his main interests.

And if the *naukleros* was not a transport agent, neither was the *emporos* a big business man in the modern sense. There were no commercial magnates among the Greek merchants and shipowners; for commercial magnates must be capitalists, and the Greek foreign traders, in so far as trade was their only occupation, were as a rule wholly without capital of their own. Demosthenes tells us that 'neither ship nor shipowner nor merchant can put to sea without the assistance of the lenders.' [2] What was true, moreover, of foreign trade in Athens (and no doubt in Greece generally) must also have been largely true of local trade. Otherwise there would have been no need to provide special legal protection for those who lent money to local dealers to enable them to start in business.[3] Even the corndealers in Lysias (xxii, 13), who are, of course, *kapeloi*, plead poverty. Capitalists, indeed, existed; but they were entirely distinct from traders and took no part in commercial activities.[4] The merchants and shipowners, if we may judge from those of them who appear in the private speeches of the Athenian orators, were invariably without any capital worth mentioning of their own. They were always in difficulties, they had no reserves to fall back upon, they possessed nothing

---

[1] The same thing is true in the Middle Ages. The offices of shipmaster and supercargo remained distinct right up till the sixteenth century.

[2] xxxiv, § 51. This passage may be quoted against Otto's view that the thesis of the text (and of my article in *Hermes*, p. 424) rests merely on the inadequacy and onesidedness of the evidence which has been handed down to us in law court speeches. Otto is also mistaken as to the ownership of capital.

[3] See below, p. 172.

[4] It followed that the typical method of financing foreign trade was by speculative bottomry loans ; and the whole of Greek ' emporial law ' was directed towards the protection of these loans (see below, p. 169).

that might serve as security for a loan but their ship or the goods that borrowed money had enabled them to buy.

More important still, the Greeks themselves always regarded the occupation of sea commerce as essentially low-class and plebeian. This was true in all parts of the country; and it was evidently something more universal than a mere idealist reaction against the prevailing materialist philosophy of the later classical period. Aristotle [1] classes the merchants along with the local dealers as 'tradespeople', contrasting them with the wealthy and cultured nobles, or 'notables'; and a little later in the same passage describes trade in general as one of the occupations of the common people.[2] Diodorus [3] calls the merchant a 'craftsman' and Plato [4] speaks of the merchant's 'craft.' Xenophon [5] puts merchants and merchant-ship-owners on the same level as 'fullers and shoe-makers and builders and metal-workers and peasants and all the other classes of people who come to market to exchange their goods, and try to buy things cheap and sell them dear'; and Aristophanes [6] ranks them along with agricultural labourers and artisans. Plato, again, in the *Laws* [7] speaks of merchants (along with local traders and innkeepers) as being the objects of universal contempt, and in another passage in the same work [8] takes them as examples of people without any culture. The author of the *de Vectigalibus* [9] states that commerce, like local trade and petty speculation was the refuge of small husbandmen and vinegrowers whose land had ceased to yield them sufficient for their subsistence. Ephorus [10] tells us that in Ægina the barrenness of the soil led many people to take to foreign trade. And Aristotle in the *Politics* [11] holds it to be among the duties of the good democratic statesman to provide the poor out of public revenue with the means to buy a small piece of ground, or alternatively to 'make a beginning in commerce'—that is to say, with sufficient, in the latter case, to secure a ship and

[1] *Pol.*, 1289b, 1291a.   [2] *Pol.*, 1291b.   [3] i, 74, 7.
[4] *Euthyphro*, 14e.   [5] *Mem.*, iii, 7, 6 ; *cf.* Plut., *Pericles*, 12.
[6] *Plutus*, 904.   [7] 918d, *cf.* 919d.   [8] 643e.
[9] Xen., *Vect.*, iv, 6.   [10] In Strabo, viii, 6, 16.   [11] 1320a.

the other immediate necessities of overseas trade. Similarly Isocrates,[1] speaking of the benefits to Attica of the legislation of Solon, says 'the well-to-do helped the needy by leasing farmland to some of them on reasonable terms, by starting others in commerce, and by providing still others with capital to set up in industry'; and again,[2] 'the children of the poor were trained for working in agriculture or commerce.' And Xenophon in the *Cyropædia*[3] represents Cyrus as not merely encouraging the merchants who dealt with his soldiers by promises of gifts and honours, but as offering to supply them with money with which to buy their wares, on condition that they accompanied his army on its march.

Still further evidence of the lack of private means among the merchants of this period is to be found in the history of the Athenian orator and politician, Andocides. Andocides was of an old noble family and had been admiral of the Athenian navy, but he was driven from the country, and Lysias tells us how during his time of exile he turned his extensive foreign connections to good account by becoming a merchant-shipowner[4] and selling articles of various kinds at cost to the Athenian fleet at Samos—wood to be used as oars, for example (his friend Archelaus of Macedonia supplying him with as much timber as he desired)—and in addition grains and metals.[5] For a considerable time, in fact, he made his living by trade. But (like the poor peasants in the *de Vectigalibus*, mentioned above) he only did so because circumstances compelled him to—because he had 'fallen into great poverty and hardship.'[6] Examples like these suggest that the practice of commerce often yielded no profits over and above a bare subsistence revenue. On the contrary the richer classes, who would most readily have been able to carry on an extensive foreign trade, invested their capital in commercial undertakings, but did not take any personal part in them. They were ready to commission a professional merchant who acted more or less as their employee and with whom (perhaps along with other investors of capital

[1] vii, 32.   [2] vii, 44.   [3] vi, 2, 38 ff.
[4] vi, 19 ; vi, 49.   [5] Andoc., ii, 11.   [6] i, 144.

too) they divided the gains of the enterprise; but it never occurred to them to act themselves as merchants, or to use the wealth they had acquired or inherited, in the way a modern capitalist might use it, for owning and running a large scale commercial business of his own. In other words, what is true, as Sombart has maintained (how far correctly we need not discuss), of the earlier Middle Ages,[1] is also true of classical Greece. Those who owned capital did not take part in commerce. The commercial classes had to depend entirely upon borrowed funds for carrying on their business.

Furthermore, it is clear that the one object of the merchant is to be able to retire from commerce as soon as he possibly can. The merchant in the speech against Apaturius says:[2] 'For long I was a merchant and risked my own life at sea; but some seven years ago I left the sea to use my modest earnings in the bottomry business.' In the same way the creditor Nicobulus refers in the speech against Pantænetus[3] to his former profession, and declares that he had made a little money as a merchant and now lends it out to oblige others. Neither of these two ex-merchants had had the slightest intention of making use of any capital they could amass with a view to becoming commercial magnates or merchant capitalists. Indeed it is doubtful if they had the necessary training. We hear often of the account books and ledgers of the bankers of this period, but never of any merchant or merchant-shipowner who knew the art of book-keeping.[4] The trading classes must have been for the most part entirely without education. Just as in Italy up till the end of the thirteenth century, and in the rest of Europe right through the Middle Ages, so too in classical Greece reading and writing were accomplishments which

---

[1] *Der Moderne Kapitalismus*, i, 279 ff. H. Bolkestein (*Het economisch Leven in Griekenlands Bloeitijd*, 1923, p. 169) now holds with me that the great majority of *emporoi* 'were nothing more than small, hardworking tradesmen.'

[2] [Dem.], xxxiii, § 4 ff.   [3] xxxvii, § 54.

[4] For the book-keeping of the Greek banker see *Hermes*, 1920, pp. 130 ff. B. Laum (*Phil. Woch.*, 1922, col. 428) speaks nevertheless of the book-keeping of the Greek ' merchant.'

belonged to few of the ordinary traders, and the business world in general was quite untrained and illiterate.[1]

The merchants in the speeches against Apaturius and Pantænetus are also of interest in that they illustrate the possibility of a merchant's gaining at least a moderate competence from the pursuit of his profession. That foreign trade, and for that matter trade in general, yielded high returns is shown by the interest rates on bottomry loans; and it is in any case natural that the profits of commerce should vary directly with the hazards and difficulties of carrying it on. There is, however, no means of knowing what proportion of these profits was left over for the merchant after the moneylender had taken his share.[2] We can establish that the Greek merchant and merchant-shipowner, like the traders of the Middle Ages, took to petty moneylending as a subsidiary source of income. The sums lent might be 1000 drachmæ,[3] or in another case 4000 drachmæ [4]—though in these two instances, it is true, the money may have been borrowed originally by the trader from some other creditor. Again the merchant in the speech against Pantænetus tells us how his 'modest means' were sufficient to enable him to make loans on bottomry. The average amount of money lent to merchants by individual capitalists (as opposed to groups of capitalists) is about the figure of the Cyprian merchant's contribution and of the two loans mentioned above—sums like 2000, 3000, 4500 drachmæ.[5]

---

[1] *Hermes*, 1923, pp. 393 ff.

[2] In *S.I.G.*, 304 (330–325 B.C.), we learn of a merchant from Cyprian Salamis, who at a time when corn was cheap contributed 3000 drachmæ as a voluntary subscription for State purposes. This was regarded as very generous, and the State gave him great honour for it.

[3] [Dem.], xxxiv, § 6.   [4] [Dem.], lii, § 20.

[5] [Dem.], xxxiii, xxxiv, xxxv. We may obtain some idea of the significance of these 'modest competences' by comparing them with the amounts owned by people who were not regarded as exceptionally wealthy, like Stratocles (over 29,000 dr., Isaeus, xi, 42 ff.) ; Demosthenes' father (over 82,000 dr., Dem., xxviii, § 9 ff.) ; or Diogeiton (nearly 93,000 dr., Lys., xxxii) ; or still more with the large fortunes, of which we hear elsewhere in the fourth century of 40, 50, 60, 70, 100, even 200 talents. People with ' modest competences' included the father of Isocrates (*Vit. x Orat.*, 836e) and Solon (*Resp. Ath.*, v, 3).

Possibly, therefore, those people who were able to employ one or more agents in their undertakings, and so to build up a fairly extensive commercial business,[1] were simply merchants whose voyages had been more than usually profitable. Either skill or luck might lead, under the uncertain and hazardous conditions of Greek trade, to noteworthy gains, for merchants, local dealers, and manufacturers alike. For instance, Colæus, the Samian shipowner, made his fortune, Herodotus tells us,[2] through having been driven by storms out of his course and forced to put in at Tartessus, a port which was as yet unexploited and in which he could buy goods at very profitable prices. Again, we have the case of the Æginetan Sostratus, said by Herodotus to have been even wealthier than Colæus, and of another Æginetan, Lampis, who was said to own the largest ship of any Greek.[3]

But such examples as these are quite exceptional—indeed it is because they are exceptional that they have survived in tradition and we know about them—and they do not affect our general conclusion. The application to classical Greece of the modern distinction between commercial magnates on the one hand and petty dealers and hucksters on the other is wholly false and misleading.[4] Wholesale and retail trade were not sharply differentiated in the ancient world. The Greek trader could not confine himself solely to wholesale dealings. He was absolutely dependent on his capitalist creditor, and had to allow circumstances to decide for him whether to dispose of his wares in large or in small quantities.

Not all exchanges were effected through professional merchants and dealers. Right through the classical and post-

[1] *Hermes*, 1923, pp. 407 ff.
[2] iv, 152.
[3] Dem. xxiii, § 211. It is not certain, however, that Lampis was a trader by occupation. He may, like Pasion, have been primarily a manufacturer.
[4] In spite of Meyer (*Kl. Schr.*, i, 121 ff.) and Pohlmann (*Soz. Frage*, i, 171). Meyer considers (p. 125, n. 1) that Lysias' speech against the corn-dealers, especially §§ 17, 21, shows that the merchant in Athens felt himself superior to the local dealer. But of any *social* distinction there is not a trace in the speech. The Athenian local dealers 'stand together against the foreign merchants' in order to dictate the price of corn (§§ 17, 21).

classical periods a more primitive form of trade survived. The producer himself, a farmer or peasant, perhaps would take his surplus stock and sail with it to some other district where he could dispose of it. When trade was carried on in this way it could be combined with other occupations and interests. The peasants would convey their excess products to their foreign destinations at a time of year when they were not required at home to look after their land.[1] Or the purpose of the voyage might not be merely commercial. Sopæus, a rich landlord of Bosporus, for example (he was one of Satyrus I's governors, and a leader of his mercenaries), sent his son to Athens with two cargoes of corn, and also with a sufficiency of money,[2] partly for trade and partly for his education.[3] Similarly Aristotle says of Solon that his journey to Egypt was undertaken 'κατὰ ἐμπορίαν ἅμα καὶ θεωρίαν,'[4] and Plutarch speaks of his activities as merchant and shipowner.[5] It has been argued, indeed, from these statements, that Solon was by profession a merchant or commercial magnate.[6] But his travels were inspired purely by the desire for knowledge, and he carried goods with him for sale abroad simply because at a time when any money that existed was current only within a narrowly restricted area and trade between one district and another had to be carried out on a barter basis,[7] that was the only way in which he could support himself during his absence from home. For similar reasons Herodotus must have acted as a merchant during his voyages.

The brother of Sappho was not a trader, even though he

---

[1] Cf. the peasant in Hesiod, Erga, 630 ff. (cf. 1. 689). This type of trade might of course be carried on by land and not by sea.

[2] Hermes, 1920, p. 151.

[3] Isocrates tells us (Trapez., § 42) that he deposited the money (at interest) in Pasion's bank, and then later used it to finance a shipowner of Delos.

[4] Resp. Ath., ii, 6. On this 'seeing the world,' see the discussion in Plato's Laws, 951a ff.

[5] Plut., Solon, 5, 25. On the tradition see Busolt, G.G., ii, 297, n. 1.

[6] Busolt, op. cit., p. 255, also p. 187 ; Meyer, Kl. Schr., i, 110 ; Wilamowitz, Platon, i, 17.

[7] See below, pp. 84 and 157.

brought wine to Naucratis,[1] nor was his occupation 'sea commerce';[2] he was simply a large scale Lesbian farmer who sold off the produce of his vineyards in a foreign market. The shipowner in the speech against Lacritus[3] took on board with him a peasant from Panticapæum who had a supply of salt fish which he wanted to sell in Theodosia. Nor was this sort of 'side line' trade confined to agricultural producers. The manufacturer might do exactly the same thing. Hyperbolus, for instance, the lamp maker of Athens, hawked his wares round from place to place, probably on a ship which he himself owned.[4] Pasion, too, who besides being a banker was a manufacturer of shields, possessed ships of his own[5] and no doubt used them exclusively for importing raw materials for himself and exporting his finished articles. Clearly neither of these two examples, any more than the example mentioned above of Sopæus of Bosporus, can be held to prove the existence of a regular shipowning and transport business organised on a capitalist basis.

'Side line' trade might, finally, represent simply the importing by a private individual of goods for his own consumption.[6] No doubt the corn which Lysias' family used to obtain each year from the Chersonnese[7] was meant for its own use. Or the importer might be a philanthropist bringing in corn for public distribution.[8] Obviously these forms of trade, too, provide no evidence for any fully developed commercial businesses. How closely the corn trade in particular was bound up with the activities of non-professional merchants[9]

---

[1] Strabo, xvii, 1, 33 ; Athen., xiii, 596b ff. (Herod., ii, 135, only mentions his name Charaxus).

[2] Pöhlmann, *Soz. Frage*, i, 131.

[3] [Dem., xxxv], §§ 32, 34. See *Hermes*, 1923, p. 402.

[4] Arist., *Eq.*, 1315. See Bücher, *Beiträge*, 1922, p. 15.

[5] Dem., xlv, § 64.

[6] εἰς τὸν ἴδιον οἶκον and ἐπὶ κτήσει are the recognised formulas in decrees of *ateleia*, for goods imported by the consumers themselves. See below, p. 116.

[7] Lysias, xxxii, 15.   [8] See below, p. 146.

[9] Even in the Middle Ages corn was often brought into the towns by burghers who were not themselves merchants (v. Below, *Probleme*, p. 376).

is clearly shown by the history of the Athenian, Leocrates, who, having lived illegally as a metic in Megara for five years, used the money which he had brought to Megara with him to export corn from Epirus to Leucas and from there to Corinth.[1] It is clear, in fact, that a considerable proportion of Greek trade was carried on by producers or consumers themselves. And even the professional traders of the fifth and fourth centuries—the local dealers, the merchants and the merchant-shipowners—seem in many cases not to have specialised, as modern traders specialise, on one particular type of activity, but rather to have undertaken different forms of trade at different times according to circumstances.

The current interpretation of Greek economic history postulates the existence not merely of large scale shipping businesses and commercial houses [2] but also of commercial aristocracies. This is particularly important in the accounts of the early period immediately after the fall of the kingship. Historians have written as though during the eighth and seventh centuries B.C. the Greek oligarchs took an extensive and direct part in commercial and maritime activities of all sorts—as though they themselves acted as merchants, exporting and importing, and themselves travelling with their wares. Meyer states that the nobility were 'at the forefront of commercial development.' [3] Busolt similarly describes the Greek oligarchs as having turned their attention, in the larger cities, to sea trade,[4] and Wilamowitz speaks of the development from an oligarchy of landlords and knights to an oligarchy of shipowners and merchants.[5] In fact the whole political strength

---

[1] Lyc., c. Leocr., § 26 ff. (see § 55).

[2] For 'commercial houses' in Corinth and elsewhere, see Meyer, Kl. Schr., i, 119.

[3] G.A., ii, 366 ; cf. ibid., 553.

[4] Gr. St., i, 177 ; cf. G.G., ii, 186, as regards Corinth, Megara, and the cities of Ionia.

[5] Sitzb. Berl., 1906, p. 77. So, too, among economic writers, Max Weber (Wirtsch. u. Gesellsch., pp. 556, 558 ff.) is misled by current interpretations of the evidence that has come down to us into declaring that the city nobles took direct part in commerce and sea transport, no longer making casual profits by lending to merchants but rather becoming them-

of the nobility is currently regarded as having rested upon their commercial position—especially in states like Miletus, Ægina, Megara or Massilia, whose geographical position suited them specially for sea trade. With the development of money the oligarchs were able—'like the gilds of clothmakers in the towns of mediæval Germany'—to give employment to the lower classes. Their power was essentially economic and their culture commercial.[1]

We shall have to examine later on the general character and extent of early Greek commerce. For the present we are concerned only with the part played in it by the aristocrats. During the fifth and fourth centuries, clearly, when trade was regarded as a plebeian kind of occupation, they can have taken no personal share in it. But apart from that, it is surely obvious that if traders were not capitalists in the later period they cannot have been capitalists in the earlier. No doubt in all primitive societies the rulers and head men have control of commercial intercourse. They have the right of permitting foreign traders to carry on business within their territories, and naturally will try to secure as much profit as possible for themselves in the exercise of this right. But the mere fact that in this sense they keep the trade of the district in their own hands does not make them traders or the basis of their power commercial. The ruler of Cyrene is represented in the vivid picture on the Arcesilaus cylix as watching the weighing and packing of the silphium grown on his estates; but that does not make him a merchant, any more than landed aristocrats like Sappho's brother or Sopæus of Bosporus were merchants merely because they shipped their surplus produce for sale abroad. The wealth of the Greek nobles was derived in part from their agricultural land and their flocks and herds, in part also—particularly in the earliest period, and among the

selves professional merchants. Indeed, he speaks of Greek aristocracies, particularly in the colonies (for example, in Epidamnus) as having a specifically commercial character—though it is true that he has to limit this very considerably in order to make it fit with his account of the characteristics of ancient aristocracies in general.

[1] See Keil in *Gercke-Norden*, iii, pp. 357 ff.

most powerful of them—from piracy and plunder; it was not derived from trade. Their strength was the strength not of economic domination but of pure physical force.

The same sort of thing can be said of the later period. As wealth increased and the general level of prosperity was raised, the tendency was more and more for men to be ranked by wealth and not by birth.[1] Under these circumstances it was only to be expected that the nobility would begin to produce for profit rather than for direct private consumption. Their wealth could be substantially increased by the sale of their manufactured products and of the yield of their lands. Beyond this, economic motives would naturally prompt them to exact what revenue they could from the commerce in their territory, by means of market tolls, customs and so on. But there is no sufficient evidence for supposing that the competition of the lower orders drove them to adopt commerce as an occupation and career. As far as trade was concerned their position was that of a *rentier* not an *entrepreneur*.[2] They lent money to the merchant (as they did to the peasant), but they themselves took no part in the merchant's activities except occasionally and as a mere side line.[3] The view that the Greek aristocracy was a commercial aristocracy rests on a fundamental misunderstanding both of the whole Greek conception of aristocracy (and indeed of citizenship in general) on the one hand, and also of the psychological attitude of the ancient world towards all organised work for profit.

We have already argued that the commercial activities of Solon give no support to the current view of the Greek upper classes. We may proceed to test the value of this view by one or two further instances which are adduced as evidence in its favour.

(*a*) Meyer and Wilamowitz agree in stating that Menelaus

---

[1] χρήματ' ἀνήρ, Alc. fr. 59 [Diehl 101]; πλοῦτος ἔμειξε γένος, Theogn. 190.
[2] Max Weber, *Wirtsch. u. Gesellsch.*, pp. 554 ff.
[3] Their position was the same, *in fact*, as that of the Roman Senators, who were forbidden by law to enter on a commercial career, or to own any ship which was not exclusively devoted to the carrying of the surplus produce of his land (Liv., xxi, 63).

2

undertook expeditions for the sake of commerce.[1] But it is clear from *Odyssey*, iv, 77 ff., that these expeditions had one motive only, namely, piracy.   Piratical exploits—cattle stealing and the plundering of neighbouring territories—were common not merely then but also later in the feudal period; and they were regarded as the most honourable occupation a noble could have. [2]   There can be no doubt that the 'goodly subsistence' which Menelaus brought home with him from his expeditions [3]—fat cattle and meat, cheese and milk—were not commodities which he had bought abroad for resale at home, but plunder and booty.

(*b*) Again, in *Odyssey*, i, 185 ff., Athena is represented as appearing to Telemachus in the form of Mentes, the leader of the Taphians (whom Homer described as pirates), and telling him that she had sailed 'steering my course over the wine-coloured sea to men who speak a strange tongue, that in Temesa I might exchange my bronze for glittering iron.' This is merely a case of a petty corsair chief exchanging one kind of metal for another.   It cannot be seriously held to show that nobles in the Homeric period were personally active in sea commerce.[4]

(*c*) Meyer refers [5] to the commercial undertakings in which Odysseus shared, thinking presumably of the passage in the fourteenth book of the *Odyssey* where the Phœnician merchant entices him on board his ship 'to help him with his cargo.' [6] But Odysseus himself states that he only undertook the voyage 'of necessity.'   One cannot conclude that the poet pictured Odysseus and the nobles of his time as regularly taking part in commercial enterprise.   For him the trader is the Phœnician, not Odysseus.

(*d*) The question is finally settled, however, for the early period, by Homer's description of the stay of Odysseus in the land of the Phæacians.   One of the Phæacian nobles tells

[1] Meyer, *Kl. Schr.*, i, 104 ; Wilamowitz, *Staat u. Gesellsch.*, p. 69.
[2] *Cf.* Thuc., i, 5.   [3] *Od.*, iv, 90.
[4] As Pöhlmann tries to maintain (*Soz. Frage.*, i, 131).
[5] *Kl. Schr.*, i, 104.   [6] *Od.*, xiv, 296.

Odysseus (just before the beginning of the athletic contests) that he does not look like an athlete, but like a man who 'sails on a many-oared ship, a ruler of sailors, mindful of his cargo and of his wares and grasping after gains.' [1] This is treated by Odysseus as a great insult. Apart from this, however, the description given by Homer of the conditions in Phæacia cannot be meant [2] as a picture of the conditions actually existent in his time in a state like (for example) Miletus. Now Homer is never tired of emphasising their connection with the sea. They are 'oar-loving,' they wield long oars and are famous for their ships, they love mast and rudder and not weapons. Moreover, their town lies in a bay at the mouth of a stream and on either side of it lies a harbour; their market-place is close to the ships and in it equipment for ships is made available. And yet Homer expressly states that they have no dealings with other men. [3] There is not the slightest suggestion throughout the *Odyssey* that they ever took any part in trade or commerce. They have their land which supplies them with food. [4] Orchards and forests cover the shore. [5] Their task is to help shipwrecked sailors, and for that reason they have felt the wrath of Poseidon. [6] In other words they are simply a mythical race of sailors, living at the furthest end of the earth. The so constantly emphasised speed of their ships, moreover, suggests the pirate rather than the trader. Nausicaa's nurse, we may remark, had been kidnapped from Epirus. [7]

(*e*) We may pass on to a later period. Pöhlmann, speaking of the sixth-century poet Theognis of Megara, says: [8] 'Even Theognis, himself as extreme a spokesman of the aristocratic point of view as it is possible to imagine, paid his tribute to the spirit of the new era. Having invested his capital in a commercial enterprise which ended in disaster, he later tried to regain what he had lost through trade, both by land and by sea.' Now assuming that the passage referred to is not spurious, does it really say what it is here represented as

[1] *Od.*, viii, 159–164.　　　　[2] In spite of Meyer, *G.A.*, ii, 366.
[3] vi, 205. *Cf.* vi, 279, and vii, 32.　　　[4] vi, 259, 293.
[5] vii, 120 ff. ; v, 398.　　　　[6] viii, 557.
[7] vii, 9.　　　　[8] *Soz. Frage*, i, 131.

saying?[1] The poet complains that he is no longer able to cultivate his land ' because of the odious sailing.' Does that really mean that he had lost his money in an ill-fated commercial speculation? Let us observe what he writes elsewhere: 'Had I but my wealth, as formerly . . . but now I am dumb through poverty and am tossed about upon the sea.' 'On land and on the broad back of the sea must one find release from hard poverty.'[2] Seafaring is not the *cause*, it is the *result* of his losses and poverty. He loathes it and is driven to it only by the struggle to maintain life, exactly like Andocides, or the impoverished peasants in Xenophon's *de Vectigalibus*. In other words, his case really helps to show that trade was carried on by poor men in the sixth century as it was in the fifth and fourth.

(*f*) Pöhlmann further argues that the participation of the nobles in trade is shown by Theognis' advice that noblemen should enter into commercial partnerships only with members of their own class.[3] This is to make far too much of the passage. All Theognis is saying is 'Choose someone of your own class rather than anybody else.' The most this can prove is that there were other impoverished nobles as well as Theognis.

(*g*) Busolt deduces[4] that the nobles of Corcyra were merchants from the fact that they lived beside the market, and that according to Thucydides,[5] when the market was burned down, along with the neighbouring parts of the town, in 429 B.C., 'many commodities' were destroyed. But there is no evidence that these commodities belonged to the oligarchs, since Thucydides specifically says that the conflagration included 'houses belonging to other people'—*i.e.* to non-oligarchs.

(*h*) Busolt and Pöhlmann[6] maintain that the Bacchiads in Corinth participated in large scale shipping and commercial enterprises. The basis for this is Strabo's statement[7] that

---

[1] ll. 1197 ff., reading in l. 1202 τῆς μάλα μισητῆς εἵνεκα ναυτιλίης.
[2] 667 ff. and 179 ff.
[3] Theogn., 1165 ; Pöhlmann, *Soz. Frage*, i, 131, n. 5.
[4] *G.G.*, i, 444, 633.   [5] iii, 72, 3 ; 74, 2.
[6] Busolt, *op. cit.*, i, 633 ; Pöhlmann, *G.G.*, p. 46.
[7] Strabo, viii, 6, 20.

they 'drew a revenue from' (ἐκαρπώσαντο) the port of Corinth. In actual fact this merely means that they were able to exact considerable amounts in tolls and customs on goods passing between the Peloponnese and Central Greece. Beloch's contention [1] that they, and similarly, one may presume, the Hippobotæ in Chalcis, could never have kept their power for so long a time if they had remained mere landlords, is pure guess-work. The sea voyages which the noble families of Ægina undertook, and from which, according to Pindar, they acquired great renown,[2] were plundering expeditions, and had nothing to do with commerce at all. Similarly there is no solid foundation for the view of Busolt [3] and others that the ἀειναῦται in Miletus and Chalcis formed a commercial aristocracy. Plutarch [4] accounts for the name by the story that when they had to settle any matter of importance they went on board a ship, and did not return to land until they had arrived at a decision.

We have now examined all the evidence which has been used to support the 'commercial interpretation' of Greek history. And we have found that none of it will bear close scrutiny. Our conclusion must be, therefore, that all attempts to 'modernise' the economic history both of the fourth and fifth centuries and still more of the earlier period are false and misleading. The Greek culture was not a commercial culture, in the sense in which the cultures of Venice, or Holland or the Hansa towns were commercial cultures. In them trade was imbued with the aristocratic spirit—the spirit which makes a merchant's word his bond, and his signature a sure guarantee of good faith—and their aristocracies were true commercial aristocracies. How can one expect to find anything corresponding to that in ancient Greece, where even as late as the fourth century commerce was carried on without written records or accounts, where the merchants themselves were for the most part illiterate and uneducated, where the facilities for exchange were so few and the protection against fraud so inadequate?

[1] G.G., i, 1, 307.
[2] Nem., vi, 33.
[3] Busolt, Gr. St., i, 177, n. 4.
[4] Q.G., 32.

III. *The Status of the Trader*

Up to the present we have been concerned with the economic and financial position of the Greek traders. We must now pass on to consider the wider question of their social status and their relation to the State.

It has long been recognised that in Athens, at any rate, foreign trade was left entirely to metics—that is, to resident aliens.[1] None of the merchants and shipowners whom we encounter in the speeches of the Athenian orators, and whose disputes were dealt with by Athenian courts, were themselves Athenian citizens. But the full range and significance of this has not been adequately realised. Properly understood, it is the key to much that is otherwise mysterious and incomprehensible in Greek economic life—and particularly in the attitude of the Greek State towards commerce and industry.

Business in the Greek city, it is agreed, was in the hands of a body of people who, though permanently resident in the city, were foreigners, and did not possess full civic status or political rights: and these resident aliens, furthermore, were first and foremost traders and manufacturers. How, then, is it possible to believe that the citizens themselves took an active part in the commerce and industry of their cities? How, indeed, can it be supposed that external commerce played a large part at all in the life of the Greek State? Either trade was given over to foreigners or it was kept in the hands of citizens; it cannot have been both at once. The Greek citizen bodies were throughout their history highly exclusive, and they never allowed the participation of foreigners in their rights and privileges. If trade was in the hands of non-citizens that was because the citizens were not anxious to take an active part in it themselves.

---

[1] Clerc, *Les Métèques Athéniens*, pp. 396 ff.; Francotte, *l'Industrie dans la Grèce*, i, 192 ; Busolt, *Gr. St.*, i, 186 ; *cf.* Glotz, *Travail*, p. 214 ff. For the corn trade in particular, Gernet, *L'approvisionnement d'Athènes en Blé*, Bibl. de la Faculté des Lettres de l'Université de Paris, xxv, 328, n. 4 ; Premerstein, *Ath. Mitt.*, 1911, p. 73 (on *S.I.G.*, 640) ; Meyer, *Kl. Schr.*, i, 132. This seems to be true, indeed, not merely of the *importing* of corn, but also of the dealings in it in Athens itself. The spokesman of the corndealers in Lysias' speech against the corndealers was a metic (Lys., xxii, 5).

It is a well-known and universal phenomenon—one might almost call it a law of nature—that the friendliness of a state or city towards strangers is in inverse proportion to the ability of its own citizens to run their manufactures and their commerce for themselves. So long as its industries are still in their infancy and its trade is dependent on foreign assistance, so long it welcomes the settlement within its territory of craftsmen and merchants and bankers from other lands, and gladly gives them admission to civic and gild rights. But with the growth of its population and the development, through the immigration from abroad, of its technical skill and abilities, it sooner or later reaches the point at which it is able from among its own numbers to provide workers for all the forms of production which the limited markets at its disposal are able to support. And as soon as this stage has been reached it begins to discourage and repress further additions from outside to its members. It prevents in all sorts of ways (some of which have survived into modern times) the entry of outsiders into commercial and industrial occupations. Foreigners are not allowed to take part in retail trade—they are compelled to deal only with citizens, foreign craftsmen are forbidden to enter the employment of citizens, foreign merchants are excluded from the meeting-place of merchants who are citizens, citizen-dealers have various privileges as against foreign dealers (*e.g.* the right of first refusal of any article that is' offered for sale), and so on. The foreigner, in fact, is regarded as the intruder, the rival whose intolerable competition must be at all costs and as far as possible eliminated.

Now the Greek metic suffered from all sorts of disabilities as compared to the full citizen in legal and political matters. He commonly lacked the right of bringing lawsuits in his own name, and in general was at a disadvantage in both civil and criminal law. He was excluded from public offices and priesthoods, he had no voice or vote in public deliberations and elections, he was not legally entitled to enter into marriage with a citizen, he was even not allowed to derive an income from the ownership of land. And on the other hand he had to bear equally with the citizens all financial burdens, such as property taxes and 'liturgies,' and was equally liable for military service. But he was never put at any disadvantage in the pursuit of his trade or occupation. Rather the State seems to have guaranteed him, as some return for his other obligations and disabilities, free and unhindered rights to carry on whatever business he wished. He could deal retail or wholesale as he chose. In Athens he was entitled, on payment of a tax, to offer his goods for sale in the market like any citizen.[1] The idea that the competition of foreigners might be damaging to the economic interests of the citizens did not occur to any ancient writer—not even to Aristotle, though he was alive to dangers of other kinds which might arise from an excessive foreign population.[2]

Indeed, the ordinary Greek community, once it had ceased to be purely agricultural, so far from discouraging the immigration of foreign craftsmen and merchants, actively welcomed it. Foreign residents were widely held to be necessary and desirable to the State 'because of the multitude of crafts, and because of the bottomry business,'[3] and it was a recognised goal of public policy to induce as many of them as possible to settle in its territory and help to build up its urban life. This was true even in the sixth century. Plutarch says that Solon offered foreigners full citizen rights if they came to Athens with the intention of carrying on their craft there.[4] Polycrates, according to Athenæus,[5] attracted artizans to Samos by the

---

[1] Dem., lvii, §§ 31, 34. The passage cannot mean, in spite of Lipsius (*Att. Recht u. Rechtsverf.*, p. 94), that dealings in the market in Athens was reserved for Athenian citizens. The context makes it quite clear that the law quoted (a law of Solon re-enacted in the fourth century) prohibited retail market trade to foreigners—not absolutely, but—*except on payment of the tax*. As Francotte rightly points out (*Les Finances des Cités grecques*, p. 271), it is not certain from the passage in question that the metics as a class were liable to the tax. It may have been levied only on foreigners who were not enrolled as Athenian residents. In any case, its object (if it was levied at all, in fact) was purely financial.

[2] Ar., *Pol.*, 1327a.

[3] [Xen.] *Resp. Ath.*, i, 12. ναυτικὸν here does not mean 'maritime interests'—see Dem., xxvii, § 11.

[4] Plut., *Solon*, 24.   [5] xii, 540d (Alexis).

offer of high wages. Diodorus tells us [1] that Themistocles prevailed upon the Athenians to abolish the tax on metics 'in order that they may immigrate in large numbers from all parts and may increase and extend Athenian manufactures.'

The same point of view is adopted in the fourth-century pamphlet on the reform of the Athenian public revenues, the so-called *de Vectigalibus*, which has come down to us under the name of Xenophon. This work is one of the most important sources we possess for the economic history of the fourth century. It is usually regarded as fantastical nonsense. [2] But our knowledge of the economic conditions of the fourth century is far too slender for us to be able to pass sentence upon it, or to judge whether the various suggestions which it puts forward are sound or otherwise. The arguments of the writer only seem absurd if one judges them from the modern point of view and in the light of present-day conditions. It is our business rather to try to understand his proposals and his assertions, and to argue back from them to the actual conditions of the time at which he wrote. If we do this we shall recognise fairly clearly the peculiar features in the economic life of classical Greece, and the fruitlessness of analogies, in this respect, between ancient Greece and all other nations and eras. More important, we shall appreciate the naïveté of Greek economic thought, [3] and we shall realise the correspondence between this naïveté of thought and the simplicity of the facts of Greek industry and commerce.

The writer starts with a statement of the aim and goal of the policy he is advocating. 'The more foreigners come and settle down here, the more will goods be bought and sold, imported and exported, and the greater will be the public revenues from rents' (*i.e.* from the state-owned lodging-houses),

---

[1] xi, 43, 3.

[2] *E.g.*, by Boeckh, i, 698 ff. [599 ff.]. All later writers have followed him. Even Oertel does not do the pamphlet justice when he says (*Gnomon*, 1927, p. 95) that it 'cannot be used without question as evidence for the actual conditions.' The only just appreciation of the book is in Laqueur's *Hellenismus* (*Schr. d. Hess. Hochsch.*, 1925), pp. 33 ff.

[3] *Cf.* the second book of the Pseudo-Aristotelian *Economics*.

'taxes and customs.'[1] He then proceeds to enumerate his specific proposals. The first is the encouragement of immigration by raising the status and increasing the rights of metics.[2] 'This would be the best possible source of income for the State, for the metics do not draw their income from the State but obtain it for themselves—and they have to pay the State for protecting them.' He enumerates three lines along which concessions to the metics would be practicable: greater dignities, release from military service, and the granting of the right to own land. What he is concerned with in this is simply to increase the yield of the tax paid by resident foreigners. People from other places, he hopes, would be induced to migrate to Athens in increased numbers as a result of the new privileges they would be able to enjoy there. Similarly with his second proposal—the extension of Athenian overseas trade.[3] This can only be accomplished by providing all possible inducements to foreign merchants and shipowners to make Athens their base. Athens has good harbours and the best money in Greece, the procedure in the commercial law-courts could be quickened up, lodging-houses could be provided for merchants and shipowners and for their passengers, traders from abroad could be given places of honour and entertained at the public expense. If all this were done people 'would come in far larger numbers to Athens to carry on their commerce'— 'they would feel they were coming among friends.'

The writer is, of course, only concerned with the financial value of an increased foreign population, and not with its wider social and economic effects. But it is nevertheless noteworthy and significant that he does not consider the possibility that the competition of this foreign population might damage the interests of citizen traders and craftsmen.[4] The truth is that such a possibility was excluded by the actual conditions. In

---

[1] i, 1 ; cf. iv, 40, where the same thesis is repeated.

[2] Ibid., ii, 1–7.   [3] Ibid., iii, 1–5.

[4] Cf. Isocrates, de Pace, § 21 ; the city's revenues will be twice as great if peace is concluded ; in peace it will be 'full of merchants, strangers and metics.' He, too, is thinking of them as a source of income, not of competition. (On this see below, p. 159.)

Athens the citizens were not traders as they were in mediæval times and are now. Traders belonged to the lowest social and economic plane. Any citizen who turned to trade or commerce for a livelihood would have to spend his time among aliens and foreigners; and he would only do this if he was compelled to, by lack of means or owing to some other special circumstances—unless, indeed, he were himself originally an alien, and was already a trader when he received citizen rights. The enormous numbers of aliens in Athens,[1] and the fact that Athenian policy was always directed towards encouraging and attracting them—that they were thought of as a necessary and useful addition to the population of the State—shows clearly the inability of the Athenian citizens to run their industries for themselves. Even public works had to depend largely (as the inscriptions show) upon the labours of metics and slaves. There can be no doubt whatever that the industrial life of Athens was in the hands not of its citizens (apart from those of them who had been metics before they were citizens), but of foreigners and aliens.[2]

It has been argued [3] that so far as commerce and industry were concerned Athens was in an exceptional position and cannot be taken as typical of Greece in general. But Beloch has shown that there is no evidence to justify this distinction, particularly for the fourth century. During the period when Greek industry was flourishing—the period from which most of our evidence about it is derived—Athens was not receiving any tribute from her allies at all, and economic conditions there were in no way peculiarly or specifically Athenian.[4]

Metics were to be found in all Greek states, oligarchic and

---

[1] At the beginning of the Peloponnesian War there were about a third as many of them as there were citizens—at the end of the fourth century nearly a half (Busolt, *Gr. St.*, i, 294).

[2] No doubt large numbers of the citizens whom we find in industrial occupations were in this category. Andocides, for example (Schol. Ar., *Vesp.*, 1007), takes for granted that Hyperbolus, the lamp-maker, was a metic.

[3] Bücher, *Beiträge*, pp. 31 ff.

[4] Beloch, *G.G.*, iii, 2, 437, 444. (Beloch's purpose in establishing these points is, of course, quite different.) *Cf.* Oertel, *Anhang*, p. 519.

democratic, Æolian and Ionic, in the Peloponnese and in the North-West, provided that they had even the smallest commercial interests.[1] They were an essential part of the City-State. Citizenship in a Greek state was not compatible with commercial activities, and all inter-city trade had to be carried on by non-citizens.[2] In Delos, for example, as the inscriptions show, almost all traders were foreigners, Greek or barbarian. Delos was an important centre of commerce, but nevertheless neither the Delians themselves nor the Athenians —even when they were in control of the island—took more than a negligible part in its business life.[3] And similarly all over Greece. As Aristotle says, 'Formerly degrading (banausic) occupations were left entirely to slaves and foreigners, and in most states they are still.'[4] In the absence of direct evidence we must accept this as true not merely of Athens but of the whole of Greece.

Our conclusion, then, must be that modern scholars, while they are right in maintaining, as against the older view, that the craftsmen and handworkers of the typical Greek State were largely free men and not slaves, are wrong [5] in supposing that these free men (apart from the peasants and small farmers) were in any considerable proportion citizens. And if not many citizens were independent craftsmen, still fewer allowed themselves to enter into the employment of other people and work on their estates or in their workshops or mines. The discussion between Socrates and Aristarchus in Xenophon's *Memorabilia* illustrates clearly the attitude of the Greek citizen towards working in industrial occupations.[6] Aristarchus had lost all his possessions during the rule of the Thirty. His estates were in the hands of his political opponents, the city was so deserted that he could find no occupants for his houses,

---

[1] Clerc has collected evidence of their existence in no fewer than seventy cities (*Revue des Universités du Midi*, 1898, pp. 1 ff.).

[2] *Cf.* Laqueur, *loc. cit.* ' The citizens had nothing to do with commercial activities. That was left to the metics.' Hesychius, we may observe, gives μέτοικος as a definition of ἔμπορος.

[3] Homolle, *B.C.H.*, 1884, p. 75

[4] *Pol.*, 1278a.

[5] Meyer, in particular ; see *Kl. Schr.*, i, 127 ff.

[6] *Mem.*, ii, 7.

nobody would buy his personal property. These sources of revenue having failed him he could see no means of supporting himself and his dependents. Socrates suggests to him that he might start producing some useful commodity, but he replies that that is impossible because his household consists entirely of free citizens; and it requires the whole force of Socrates' dialectic to convince him that even a citizen can do productive work, and that (like local dealers without means of their own, or like the impoverished peasants who wanted to become merchant-shipowners [1]) he ought to go and borrow capital to set up a workshop. Aristarchus' assumption here is that manufacturing was not the kind of work which free people and citizens could be expected to do. And we may be certain that in fact industrial employees were largely slaves—indeed it would be surprising if this were not so, in view of the fact that in industrial cities such as Athens and Corinth, slaves, like metics, were continually increasing in numbers, and by the end of the fifth century must have constituted practically half of the total population. Moreover, those workers who were not slaves were almost entirely metics. There were, of course, citizen workers. Citizens sometimes acted as foremen or labourers in workshops, as independent farmers or citizens, as 'fullers, shoe-makers, carpenters, smiths, dealers or merchants.'[2] But of these, apart from the fact that they must have represented a very small proportion of the total of productive workers, some may really have been employers and not themselves workers—for example, Cleon is called a 'cobbler' by Aristophanes because he owned a tannery—some, like Hyperbolus, had been workers before they became citizens, and the remainder were driven to industrial employment by necessity (and in particular by the loss of their lands), and abandoned it at the first opportunity.[3]

---

[1] Above, pp. 7, 8.

[2] Xen., *Mem.*, iii, 7, 6. The craftsman mentioned in Lysias (xxiv, 6), and the charcoal-burners in Aristophanes' *Acharnians*, are citizens. Socrates came of a family of sculptors.

[3] *Cf.* the attitude of merchants to their occupation, above, p. 10. Diodorus speaks (i, 74, 7) of artisans who abandon their old trades. Oertel, though

The conditions here described contrast very strikingly with those of mediæval and modern times.[1] The citizens of the mediæval city—particularly the lowest classes—were primarily concerned with the peaceful pursuit of monetary profit in commerce or industry. The ideal citizen of the ancient world, on the other hand, was essentially a *rentier*. The income which he reserved for himself was not a labour income but a property income—the income, in particular, from the land. The mediæval citizen was, so to speak, an economic man; the ancient citizen, *qua* citizen, was a political man. That is why, on the one hand, the Greek State never interested itself in industry or developed any economic or commercial policies, and why, on the other hand, no gild system ever developed in Greece and all attempts at setting up monopolies in particular occupations were soon stifled out of existence.[2] No Greek citizen would dream of joining with non-citizens in a society which claimed for itself political rights. The economic man of the ancient world was politically a degraded man. In Rome commerce and industry were in the hands of freedmen, whose activities, just because they were freedmen and had practically no political rights and privileges, tended to develop along economic lines. In Greece the same thing is true of the metics. They were excluded from the ownership of land and from all other sources of unearned income; and they therefore turned their attention, like the burghers of the Middle Ages and the business men of to-day, to the pursuit of pecuniary gain, became the mainstay of industry and commerce,[3] and left the full citizens to live on their unearned incomes, on the rents of their lands or their houses, on the interest on their money

he recognises that the citizen population refused (' to a great extent,' ' in large part,' *Anhang*, pp. 545, 547) to pursue their crafts as employees of other people, yet holds that the crafts as such were largely carried on by citizens (and slaves), and makes only the scantiest references to the industrial significance of the metics. Indeed, his whole view of the position of the metics is in error. See his discussion in *Gnomon*, 1927, pp. 94 ff.

[1] As Max Weber has emphasised in his brilliant account of ancient and mediæval democracies (*Wirtsch. u. Gesellsch.*, pp. 582 ff.).

[2] *Loc. cit.*

[3] Though Weber does not expressly point this out.

investments, or on the payments they received from the State.

According to the ordinary view of Greek history not merely were the citizens actively interested in industry, but the rise of democracy was itself bound up with economic and industrial developments. With the extension of manufacturing and the growth of the use of money, the political power of the aristocrats came to be more and more challenged by the commercial and industrial lower classes. The advancing democracy was a democracy not merely of peasants and small farmers but also, where conditions were favourable, of traders and artisans. For the ancient as for the modern world, therefore, democracy meant the rise of the petty bourgeoisie as against the nobles on the one hand and the proletariat on the other.[1] In Athens, to take one instance, it is held that the 'third class,' which joined with the second class to establish itself on a footing of political equality with the aristocrats, was a class of business men and industrialists. Our previous discussion has shown the difficulties with which this view is faced. In the Middle Ages it is perfectly true that democracy received its first impetus from the distress of impoverished craftsmen and unemployed labourers, and its development meant the rise to power of a class of urban workers. In Greece, on the contrary, the proletarian was a man without political rights, a landowner who had become landless. Class struggles were concerned not with the control of industry but with the cancellation of debts. The lower classes were peasants who had borrowed from the nobles beyond their power to repay, and in accordance with the harsh laws of the period, had been enslaved by their creditors, and their objects were the repudiation of the loans, the redistribution of land, and, finally, the provision of incomes for themselves from the revenues of the State.[2] As they grew in numbers, and as at the same time the numbers of the nobles were reduced by wars, they were able to achieve these ends

[1] See, for example, Keil, in *Gercke-Norden*, iii, 356.

[2] The agrarian character of the reforms of Cleisthenes is shown by the importance he attached to rural and local units like the deme and the tribe (see Weber, *Wirtsch. u. Gesellsch.*, p. 584).

more and more. The increase of population in the early period (which received its clearest expression in the sending out of colonies) was an increase of the lower orders; but the lower orders meant primarily the small peasants and farmers and only to a much smaller degree the small artisans and labourers. Industry and trade at that time was far too little developed for these urban classes to play any decisive part in the movement towards democracy.

And if we have to revise our views as to the relation between democracy and the growth of industry in Greece, we must also reconsider the question of socialism in the ancient world. The conclusions at which we have arrived show the erroneousness of the current view [1] as to both its nature and its extent. The working classes were composed, as we have seen, largely of serfs, slaves, and half-citizens.[2] The compulsion of economic forces and the extension of slavery did, indeed, bring into existence a class of proletarian citizens; and no doubt the growth of large scale capitalists helped to add to their number, not so much directly (except in agriculture), as by increasing the gulf between the rich and the poor, between those who had, and those who had not, to work for their living. But this citizen proletariat was essentially a proletariat of consumers, or else, perhaps, farm labourers. The social and economic structure of Greek industry prevented its members from having (as in the Middle Ages) common interests as producers. That is why the industrial labourers never combined as such against the nobility.[3] The aim of the revolutionary classes in Greece, in so far as they were not merely agricultural labourers demanding a cancellation of their debts and a repartition of the large estates, was the securing of an unearned income, either from the State or from the ownership of land.

Now the nature of this rising of the lower orders against the

---

[1] As expressed, *e.g.*, by Pöhlmann.

[2] *Cf.* Oertel, *Anhang*, pp. 542 ff.

[3] The shore dwellers, who appear as a clearly marked political party in Peisistratean Athens, were not sailors and traders and artisans, as Pöhlmann declares (*G.G.*, p. 85). Aristotle explicitly declares them to be peasants (*Resp. Ath.*, xiii, 5).

nobles has often been seriously misrepresented. It has been regarded, for instance, as a kind of socialist upheaval, inspired from the first (and increasingly as time passed) by revolutionary ideals, and leading to the passage of socialist legislation designed to establish full economic equality.[1] This interpretation, apart from the fact that it exaggerates the extent and importance of the movement,[2] wholly misunderstands the structure of the Greek City-State and the character of its citizenship. The doctrine that it was the duty of the State not merely to secure for its citizens political rights but also to provide for their economic needs, was not the mere slogan of a mob lusting for power, it was part of the whole Greek conception of citizenship.[3] Without a secure income, either from the State or from his own landed possessions, the citizen could not play his proper part in the life of the State—in so far as he had to think of earning his own living he must act as an 'economic' man, and to that extent could not be a 'political' man. 'In some cities,' we are told, 'particularly those whose interests are primarily military, citizens are forbidden to undertake any handicraft,' lest they should be unable to devote themselves adequately to public affairs.[4] This expresses the point in a nutshell. The right of the citizen to an income for which he did not have to work was 'both natural and conventional'— just as much as the right of parents to support, in their old age, from their children—and a stoppage of this income was equivalent to an overthrow of the constitution.[5] This doctrine did, indeed, lead in Athens to all sorts of abuses and extravagances, and so roused the forces of reaction—the oligarchs and with them the philosophers—at first to criticism and satire, and

---

[1] Even Oertel adopts this view (*Anhang*, pp. 554 ff.), in spite of the fact that a few pages later he indicates that the revolutionaries were merely fighting for 'an ancient civic right which was inherent in the very nature of democracy' (*ibid.*, p. 558 ; *cf.* Pöhlmann, *Soz. Frage*, i, 266).

[2] As Oertel has rightly insisted.

[3] Pöhlmann has described this, most unfortunately, as the 'social welfare' policy of the Greek State (particularly of the democratic State) (*Soz. Frage*, i, 117 ff. ; Oertel, *op. cit.*, p. 558).

[4] Xenophon, *Econ.*, iv, 3.

[5] Demosthenes, x, § 40 ff. ; xxiv, § 99 ff.

later, with the general decline of political life, to active opposition. But the excesses of the democracy in Athens were due to the exceptional power which Athens possessed and to the enormous revenues which it drew from its allies and subjects. They cannot rightly be compared with the excesses of modern socialism or criticised and attacked as a conservative of to-day might attack the demands of the present-day proletariat: indeed to describe the Greek *demos* as a proletariat or 'rabble'[1] is itself a quite misleading modernisation and is calculated to prejudice our understanding of Greek political history and to distort our view of Greek democracy.[2]

According to the doctrine which we have been discussing, the citizens had the right to share in any excess revenues which flowed into the public treasury.[3] Thus in Athens the income from the state-owned mines was from the earliest times distributed among the whole citizen population, and Themistocles had considerable difficulty in persuading the Assembly to devote some of this income to the building of a fleet.[4] In the middle of the fourth century a special treasury was established, and fed from State revenues, from which to provide the citizens with the means of sustenance. These doles took the form not merely of frequent and regular public banquets but also, shortly before the downfall of the Athenian empire, of a daily payment to each citizen of two obols. The result was that in the fourth century all full citizens were in receipt of a sufficient amount of food and money to secure them their livelihood; and the orators of the period assumed that to be the normal and proper state of affairs. Again the financial operations of the demagogue Demades led to the State spending on the citizen body an amount equal to fifty drachmæ per head.[5] And Pericles' building policy tended in the same direction. 'Pericles'

[1] As Pöhlmann does.

[2] Max Weber (*Wirtsch. u. Gesellsch.*, p. 583) has already shown that such occasional distributions of State surpluses to members of the community as are met with in the Middle Ages, or at the present time, are not comparable to those of classical times, as Meyer claims (*Kl. Schr.*, i, 195, n. 1).

[3] See Pöhlmann, *Soz. Frage*, i, 266 ff.

[4] Arist., *Resp. Ath.*, xxii, 7.

[5] Plut., *Præc. reip. ger.*, xxv, 818 ff.

intention,' Plutarch tells us,[1] 'was not merely to provide those who were fit for military service with maintenance from the public revenues, but also to give some share in this largesse to the degraded mob which stayed at home . . . in order that those who remained in Athens, no less than those who saw service in the navy, in garrisons, and on the field, should have the opportunity of having their part in the advantages to be drawn from the State treasury.' Similarly the parcelling out of captured territories in the form of cleruchies furnished many thousands with a secure annual income. Nor must we forget the special distributions, the theatre allowances, and the whole system of payments for political and judicial services. These payments were an essential part of Greek democracy, not merely in Athens, though it is in Athens that we are able to see most clearly how the system worked, but also in other places where democracy had established itself sufficiently firmly.[2]

We have here the fundamental explanation of the unparalleled exclusiveness of the citizen bodies in the Greek States, both towards citizens of other communities [3] and also towards the half-citizens within the states themselves. These resident aliens, as we have seen, enjoyed the right of domicile, but they were politically degraded; they supported themselves; they were highly useful to the State but they drew no income from the public funds, and actually paid to the State the aliens' tax.[4] The fundamental cleavage in the Greek State was between the *rentiers* who lived at the expense of the State or on the proceeds of their own property and investments and the 'cityless' mass of aliens (as they are described in the *de Vectigalibus*). These aliens might be domiciled within the territory for a long or a short time: they might be wealthy, free

---

[1] *Pericles*, 12.

[2] Pöhlmann, *Soz. Frage*, i, 278. *Cf.* Arist., *Pol.*, 1304*b*, and Strabo, xiv, 2, 5 (Rhodes); Polyb., xx, 6 (Bœotia). Further references in Büchsenschütz, *Bes. u. Erw.*, pp. 280 ff. In particular see Glotz, *Travail*, pp. 178 ff., for μισθοφορία as the basis of democracy.

[3] As expressed most clearly in the attitude of the Greek law towards aliens—for instance, in the prohibition of marriage outside the citizen body.

[4] Xen., *Vect.*, ii, 1.

born and of Greek descent: they might (with the slaves) comprise a great part, or perhaps the greater part, of the total population: but they nevertheless remained permanently outside the political pale. The Greeks never believed that men had rights as men—the existence of slavery made the acceptance of that principle impossible—and even the most radical Greek democracy was really an unconcealed oligarchy. The possession of citizenship was more to be prized in the city-state of antiquity than in any other period or type of state that the world has yet seen. This explains the efforts made, particularly in the extreme democracies, to guard against any dilution of the citizen body from without (*e.g.* by confining citizenship to the children of full and natural citizens). It explains also why the Greeks desired to keep the number of citizen families as far as possible constant, and why, therefore, they laid so much stress on family rights, and in particular on the inheritance rights of daughters. It is, indeed, not surprising that when philosophers came to build up their Utopias— so much less utopian, in many ways, than is usually admitted— they should found them on the principles which they observed in the states actually existing round them.

Furthermore, we can now understand how it came about that only grave necessity could compel citizens to resort to manual labour as a means of maintaining themselves. They (or their ancestors) might have lost their landed possessions, and so having no means of employing themselves have been forced to enter the employment of others—and if so, they were likely to be economically as well as socially degraded. Or if the causes which drove them to work for their living were not quite so pressing as this, yet nevertheless they were in the position of having to associate to a greater or less extent with aliens and metics, instead of with full citizens. The number of such citizen labourers, and the nature of their work, would, of course, be different in different places. In Ægina, Ephorus tells us,[1] the poverty of the soil forced the inhabitants to become merchants; and Aristotle mentions both Ægina and Chios as

[1] Strabo, viii, 6, 16.

states in which the full citizens took part in trade.[1]   Again the
citizens of Tarentum and of Byzantium acted in unusually
large numbers as fishermen, those of Tenedos as ferrymen.[2]
But these places are all referred to primarily because they were
exceptions to the general rule.   Similarly with Megara.
Xenophon says that the majority of the Megarians earned their
living by making vests.[3]   We learn the reason of this from
Isocrates.   'Their natural resources were small and poor,
they possessed neither land nor harbours nor mines, and they
had nothing but rocks to cultivate.'[4]   Xenophon adds, moreover, that the labourers in their workshops were exclusively
'bought barbarians.'   In other words, Megara was peculiar
in that a considerable number of its citizens owned manufacturing establishments, and were in that sense industrial producers.   The implication in these passages is that conditions
there were exceptional and had led to exceptional results.
Corinth, again, was another exception.   Its soil was poor, like
that of Megara.[5]   Not merely that, but in Corinth unusual
respect was paid to the arts and crafts.   The Corinthians had
exceptional inventive powers, and their aptitude for all forms
of artistic production had a most stimulating effect upon the
rest of Greece.[6]   It is not to be wondered at, therefore, that,
as we learn from Herodotus,[7] manual labour was less looked
down upon there than anywhere else.

We must agree, therefore, with Francotte that 'industry in
Greece, whether carried on in small workshops or in large
establishments and factories, depended on the work of slaves
and foreigners.'[8]   All the evidence shows how mistaken it is
to suppose[9] that it was only in Athens that the metics formed
a considerable proportion of the population.   No doubt other
states as well as Ægina and Chios may have had an unusually

---

[1] *Pol.*, 1291*b* ; see following note.
[2] We may remark that in all these examples Aristotle is speaking only
of the *demos*, not of the nobility.
[3] Xen., *Mem.*, ii, 7, 6 (*cf.* below, p. 79).   [4] viii, 117.
[5] Strabo, viii, 6, 23.   [6] See below, p. 55.
[7] ii, 167.   [8] *L'Industrie*, i, 214.
[9] Kahrstedt, *Handw. d. Staatswiss.*, ii, 657.

large number of citizens who devoted themselves to trade. No doubt, too, in the many small towns and villages which dotted the coasts of Greece many or most of the citizens were sailors.[1] But the general rule still holds. Only necessity—either the barrenness of soil or political weakness (that source of all physical need)—could force these tiny communities to take to trade or to the sea. The true and normal type of maritime city was Athens.

There were, indeed, cases in which even full citizens who entered upon an industrial occupation might achieve considerable wealth. 'Many craftsmen are rich,' Aristotle declares.[2] Plato says the same of the potters [3] and Xenophon of the bakers and tailors.[4] But the ordinary good-class citizen looked down even on rich manufacturers (as may be seen from the comedies —whose audiences were composed of good-class citizens). The tendency was for traders and industrialists to retire from their business as soon as they had secured for themselves even a modest income;[5] and this tendency was entirely in accordance with the demands of public opinion.[6] It is worthy of note that even Plutarch found it necessary to excuse Solon's commercial activities to his readers by saying that 'at that time commerce was not looked down upon.'[7] And Pericles' employ-

---

[1] For example, in Phaselis (Dem., xxxv, § 1).

[2] *Pol.*, 1278a πλουτοῦσι γὰρ καὶ πολλοὶ τῶν τεχνιτῶν. This is the only possible reading, in spite of Bolkestein; see his *Fabrieken en fabriekanten in Griekenland*, p. 16 (*Tijdschr. voor Geschiedenis*, 1923). It is not permissible, however, to weaken the word πλουτεῖν, as Bolkestein would do, and make it mean simply 'to be comfortably off'; for Aristotle speaks expressly in the sentence before of τιμήματα μακρά. There were, then, craftsmen who rose to wealth, perhaps by running *ergasteria*. But the point which Bolkestein has missed is that such men became *rentiers* when they had made their money; we must not speak of rich *manufacturers*. When Bolkestein further maintains that no manufacturer could be classed as 'banausic,' because the βάναυσος was universally despised, he merely betrays ignorance of the facts.

[3] *Rep.*, 421d.   [4] *Mem.*, ii, 7, 6.   [5] See above, p. 10.

[6] Cicero expresses the point of view that was prevalent among Greek citizen bodies when he praises the merchant who 'satiated, or rather contented, with his profits leaves the harbour for landed estates, as he used to leave the sea for harbour' (*de Off.*, i, 42).

[7] Plut., *Solon*, 2.

ment of citizen workers of all kinds upon his public buildings—as 'carpenters, sculptors, bronze-founders, stonemasons, dyers, goldsmiths, ivory-workers, painters, embroiderers, engravers, wheelwrights, ropemakers, weavers, leatherworkers, roadmakers and miners' [1]—was merely designed to enable him to support those citizens at the public expense. They would not have accepted employment even with the State had they had any other means of maintaining themselves.

Now it has been argued that the contempt of the Greeks for industry, as it is displayed in so much of their literature, is really an aristocratic prejudice (like the prejudice of the upper classes of the present day), which was taken over and given a precise formulation by anti-democratic moralists and philosophers—in particular Plato and Aristotle.[2] But it was really far more profound and widespread than that. Even in Homer workmen are not regarded as being worthy of respect or consideration; and what was true in Homer's time was true right through the classical period. Herodotus, for example, says: 'The Egyptians are not permitted to follow any craft; the craft of war is the only one that is held to be honourable among them. Whether the Greeks learnt this point of view from them I do not know, for it is also to be found among Thracians, Scythians, Persians, Lydians, and other nations. At any rate it is common to all the Greeks except the Corinthians.' [3] We learn from Xenophon that in some states citizens were forbidden to take part in industry or trade,[4] and Aristotle tells us that in Thebes no one could enter upon any political office who had at any time during the previous ten years engaged in trade.[5] 'The best state,' Aristotle goes on to say, 'will not give low-class people citizen-

---

[1] Plut., *Per.*, 12, and the Erechtheum building accounts.

[2] Meyer, *Kl. Schr.*, i, 124 ff.

[3] *Hdt.*, ii, 167.

[4] *Econ.*, iv, 3 (quoted above, p. 33).

[5] *Pol.*, 1278a. *Cf.* the disqualification of industrial workers for public positions in Rome (Mommsen, *Staatsrecht*, i, 497). See also, for a just appreciation of the Roman contempt for manual labour, F. Cauer, *N. Jahrb. f. d. Klass. Altert. u. Pädag.*, 1899, and *Wochenschr. f. klass. Philol.*, 1913, p. 1399.

ship'; and in this he has the support of both Xenophon and Plato.[1]

Socrates, of course, questioned this, like every other, doctrine. 'Do you consider,' he is reported as having asked Aristarchus, an obstinate believer in the unworthiness of manual labour, 'that because a man is free born he ought to do nothing but eat and sleep?'[2] But then Socrates was well known for his fantastic views. Aristarchus was merely upholding the orthodox and commonly accepted belief.

Nor was the contempt for trade and industry merely academic. It might be highly practical. Local traders, for instance, had to be protected by law from scornful remarks about their occupation, and from the economic losses they might thereby incur [3]—and it is to be observed that small traders and merchants suffered no more at the hands of the writers of comedies than did workshop owners like Cleon and Hyperbolus.[4]

Pericles, indeed, declares in his funeral oration [5] that in Athens the poor are not despised, but only the idle poor. But that does not prove that the contempt for manual labour was not to be found in democratic states like Athens.[6] In democracies, it is true, poor men were not disqualified for citizenship, in virtue of their poverty, as they were in oligarchies; they were rather given public protection and support.[7] The democratic statesman tried, in the public interest, to eliminate idleness among the poor by laws against idleness,[8] and sought to secure that all citizens should have been taught some craft by their parents.[9] But the cause of this was not the belief that

[1] Xen., *Econ.*, iv, 2 ff. ; *cf.* vi, 5.   Plato, *Laws*, p. 741e.

[2] Xen., *Mem.*, ii, 7, 7.

[3] See below, p. 174.

[4] Arist., *Plut.*, 904.

[5] Thuc., ii, 40.

[6] As Meyer tries to maintain, *Kl. Schr.*, i, 124 ff.

[7] In Athens, indeed, during the later period, we are justified in describing the poor-relief policy as amounting to state assistance for all who were unable to earn their living (Ar., *Resp. Ath.*, xlix, 4).

[8] *Cf.* Ar., *Pol.*, 1320a (above, p. 8).

[9] Viz., by excusing any children whose parents had failed to train their children properly from the duty of supporting them in their old age (Plut., *Solon*, 22).

work was in itself good and leisure bad. On the contrary, Socrates himself declared that idleness is 'the sister of freedom,' and leisure the most noble of possessions.[1] What Thucydides is thinking of as disgraceful is not idleness as such, but the idleness of the poor—of those who could only spend their time loitering round the streets and begging. Similarly when Hesiod says that 'work is no disgrace, but idleness is a disgrace,' he is clearly thinking not of commercial and industrial labour, but of the work of the small debt-ridden peasant; and in any case the emphasis with which he makes the statement shows that it is in opposition to the commonly accepted view. We cannot, therefore, agree with Wilamowitz [2] that the citizens of the ancient world held essentially the same opinions about industry as the people of to-day—that the acceptance of any other view is 'an intolerable generalisation from the postulates of ancient philosophy, an unhistorical vision of the ideal Greek, happy in his leisure and basking in beauty.' To say this, we must insist, is to misunderstand the true conditions.[3] The Greeks were as deeply imbued as other nations with the acquisitive instinct, with the desire for limitless

---

[1] Ælian, *Var. Hist.*, x, 14 ; Diog. Laert., ii, 5, 31.

[2] *Staat u. Gesellsch.*, 2nd ed., p. 199. Meyer takes the same views (*Kl. Schr.*, i, 125, ' The ancient and the modern world think alike on this point '). See also Neurath in *Jahrb. f. Nat. u. Stat.*, iii, 32 (1906), pp. 577 ff. ; 34 (1907), pp. 145 ff. All these scholars forget that in the ancient world not merely handicraftsmen but also large scale merchants, manufacturers, and bankers were βάναυσοι.

[3] Oertel is also one of those who holds that there can be no question of a general contempt for labour (*Anhang*, p. 543). But he limits this assertion by admitting the existence of 'marked local and temporal divergencies' in this respect, and by speaking of a general 'workshyness' (p. 549). Laqueur, as before, comes far nearer the correct view in emphasising (with Max Weber) the *rentier* ideals of the Greek citizen (*op. cit.*). He rightly quotes Periander's prohibition against slave-owning (Nic. Dam., fr. 57) as significant ; for the result of that was a rebellion on the part of the citizens of Corinth, who evidently claimed the right to build up a life of leisure for themselves on a basis of slave labour. See also Büchsenschütz, *Bes. u. Erw.*, p. 261, on the 'dislike and contempt for economically productive work which characterised the Greeks practically throughout the whole of historical times' ; and *cf.* Kaerst, *Hellenismus*[2], i, pp. 122 ff. ; Glotz, *Travail*, pp. 193 ff. ; Boeckh, i, 57 ; Burckhardt, *Gr. Kulturgesch.*[3], pp. 4, 69, 87 ff., 123 ff.

gains beyond the immediate needs of life,[1] but in them it was primarily developed and found its fullest expression along non-economic lines. It could not be properly satisfied in the labours of industry and commerce, for these labours were degrading and fit only for the lowest classes. That being so, we need not be surprised that the Greek world never saw the development of a commercial aristocracy.

What, then, was the position of these large bodies of foreign merchants and craftsmen in the various cities in which they lived?

The Greeks divided the foreigners in their cities into three classes: those who came for a short time as visitors, those who made a temporary stay, and those who settled down in permanent residence.[2] All three types were 'cityless,'[3] and they were, furthermore, largely, if not predominantly, of non-Greek extraction.[4] The description suggests that, as a matter of fact, these foreigners were highly mobile—that they passed readily from place to place, attracted by the chance of work and the prospects of subsistence and profits. This conclusion is, indeed, just what one would expect from Greek industrial conditions. It is only after a long course of development that either men or industries and traders become really settled. And the Greeks, we may observe, never achieved this immobile state. The whole of their history is marked with the establishment of new settlements in different parts of the Mediterranean world, and with the end of the fourth century and the opening up of the Orient by Alexander, they entered upon their third great colonising period. It was not to be expected, therefore, that their industries or labourers should be centred permanently in particular localities. As in Homeric times when one had to send abroad for 'craftsmen, prophets, physicians, carpenters, and minstrels,'[5] so throughout the classical period—and for

---

[1] For the presence (which cannot seriously be disputed) of the capitalist spirit in the Greek world, see Max Weber, *Handw. d. Staatswiss.*[3], i, 59 ; Riezler, *Finanzen u. Monopole*, p. 96 ; Oertel, *Anhang*, pp. 514 ff.

[2] Busolt, *Gr. St.*, i, 292.   [3] Xen., *Vect.*, ii, 7.

[4] 'Lydians, Phrygians, Syrians and other barbarians,' *ibid.*, ii, 3. *Cf.* Dem., xxxv, § 2.   [5] *Od.*, xvii, 382.

that matter right on into the Middle Ages [1]—merchants and craftsmen of all types wandered from one city to another as opportunity called them, and refused to make any place their permanent home.[2]

This conclusion will help us to understand the Greek prejudice against trade and industry. To be a merchant one had to be homeless, and free from all local or patriotic ties. This was true of the metics, just as it was true of the Jews in the Middle Ages. But the citizen of a City-State had a home and a country, which demanded his whole energies and attentions, and to leave it was to abandon all the things that made life worth living. No commercial or industrial gains could compensate for the loss of home and citizenship.

What the above comes to, then, is simply this: that industry and trade, and in particular overseas commerce, really lay right outside the theoretical province of the State. The State existed for the citizens, not for the metics or slaves. It had no interest in trade, and it is quite misleading to talk [3] about its having a national mercantile marine, or a national industry. In so far as trade existed at all for the citizens (other than the very lowest class), it was merely as a field for the investment of their capital, and a source of their income.

[1] See especially Bücher, *Entstehung* (11th ed.), pp. 416, 430 ff.

[2] We may point out here the relevance of this conclusion for the student of Greek art. If the artist or craftsman (the Greeks did not distinquish between the two) had no fixed place of residence, then clearly there can be no question of local variations and peculiarities in art forms. The belief prevalent at present that different districts had their distinctive types of art product is but one more of the results of conceiving ancient industrial conditions in modern terms.

[3] As do Wilamowitz (*Platon*, i, 15), Meyer (*Kl. Schr.*, i, 128), and Pöhlmann (*G.G.*, p. 126).

CHAPTER II

COMMERCE IN ANCIENT GREECE

I. *The Archaic Period*

WE shall try in the following chapter to arrive at some conception of Greek trade in the classical period, and to determine as accurately as may be its volume and the stages in its development. This investigation will be essentially an attempt to discover (in so far as we have not already done so) the structure of the Greek economy as a whole. For the sake of avoiding confusions between different epochs we shall confine ourselves first to the period before the Persian Wars, reserving a study of the classical period to a later section.

The leading historians of to-day place the industrial and commercial awakening of Greece in the eighth and seventh centuries B.C.[1] According to their accounts this was the period, more than two hundred years before the Persian Wars, when money came into general use, and manufacturers and traders at home and abroad first began to flourish and prosper. The newly founded colonies required goods of all sorts, agricultural and industrial, and their demands created an extensive and growing market for the surplus products of the mother country. Wine, clay, bronze, and wool were all exported in large quantities, in exchange for articles of everyday need. Chalcis, Corinth, Megara, Athens, Ægina, Rhodes, Cyrene and other maritime cities became large and wealthy manufacturing centres, and exported articles for mass consumption in wholesale quantities, penetrating into foreign countries and dispossessing the Phœnician manufacturers of markets which they had hitherto monopolised. Miletus developed an

[1] Meyer, *Kl. Schr.*, i, 104. The following statements of the current view are given almost word for word from the relevant passages in Pöhlmann, *Soz. Frage* and *G.G.*, Beloch, *G.G.*, and Meyer, *Kl. Schr.*

extensive and large scale textile industry.   Corinth, the city of traders and manufacturers, built up a colonial empire and waged colonial wars for commercial ends.   All these cities received from their colonies raw materials, ores, agricultural produce, livestock, slaves, and so on in return for the manufactured goods they exported; indeed they depended upon this trade for the necessities of life.   Smiths and potters began to work more and more for the growing export market.   Large fortunes were piled up by merchants and manufacturers. Money flowed to large scale commerce, commercial interests became the predominant factor in public policy, the commercial states took the lead in the Greek world, a brilliant new commercial aristocracy at first intermingled with and ultimately displaced and overthrew the old landed gentry.

It will be our business to examine somewhat closely the historical basis of this generally accepted account of early Greek economic conditions.   But before we proceed to this, let us observe the evidence of Thucydides, the classical authority for the primitive period in Greek history.   Thucydides in the archæological introduction to his History of the Peloponnesian War described the development of Greece, as he conceived it, from its rude beginnings up to the time of its maturity.   This development is a progress from weakness (i, 3.1,4; 11.2) to power and strength (2.2, 4; 3.2; 9.1; 13.1).   The earliest Greeks were weak because they were isolated.   They had no trade or personal intercourse with one another, but kept absolutely apart (2.2; 3.4; 5.1); partly because they were not accustomed to sailing (7.1; 8.2; 13.1), and partly because owing to the general lack of security from invaders and pirates they 'took each enough for his own subsistence and did not cultivate the land.'   The result and symptom of this 'weakness' is lack of possessions.   It passes over to strength and an 'abundance of possessions' (2.2; 7.1; 8.3; 9.2; 13.1; 15.1) when people join in securing the mutual advantages of trade, and turn to cultivating their land, rearing livestock, growing fruit and olives and wines, not only for consumption but also for sale.   The source of their 'strength' is the earth.   But at the same time that their agricultural interests are developing and becoming a source of profit to them they also learn to venture more readily upon the sea, and seek additional gains from piracy (5.1). This adds still more to their strength. Their cities become larger (2.2) and are fortified against one another (8.3), or else they 'occupied isthmuses both for the sake of commerce and for strength against their neighbours' (7.1). But this leads to wars in which the stronger communities overthrow the weaker (8.3). Some individuals come to be outstanding rulers—like Agamemnon (9.1)—and sea powers come into being (13.1). These rulers drew to themselves ever-increasing revenues (13.1) from the territories which their fleets have enabled them to subjugate. Minos is the first (4.1). He acquires a fleet, rules the sea, occupies the Cyclades, setting up his son as ruler there, and puts down piracy, in order to consolidate his power and 'increase his revenues.' And in general (15.1) 'those who turned to the sea derived the greatest strength, both by the revenues they received and the peoples they conquered; for those whose own territories were insufficient for their support descended upon the islands and conquered them.' The power of Agamemnon was essentially power of this kind. It was through fear and not of their own free will that his army followed him on his wars (9.3).

'The Corinthians,' Thucydides tells us further, 'are said to have been the first to interest themselves in the sea after the present-day fashion, and to have built the first triremes; and it appears that Ameinocles, a Corinthian, built four such ships for the Samians. Moreover, the earliest sea battle of which we know was between the Corinthians and the Corcyreans.' However, in all this there was no question of commercial interests or aims. The ships were warships, and they were used for purely imperialist purposes. 'For the Corinthians occupied the isthmus, and their town was always a trading centre, since the earliest Greeks traded for the most part by land rather than by sea, and those within and without the Peloponnese if they wanted to have dealings with one another had to pass through Corinthian territory. . . . And as sea-faring increased in Greece the Corinthians got ships and drove away pirates, and made their city a centre for sea trade as well, whereby it became strong and drew in large revenues' (13.5). In other words the Corinthians, like cities which occupied strategic sites during the Middle Ages, took advantage of their favourable situation to exact taxes from merchants who wished to cross their territory or make use of their market.[1]

After speaking of Corinth, Thucydides goes on to tell of the sea power of the Ionians (who when warring with Cyrus 'obtained control for a time of the surrounding sea'), of Polycrates (who 'had a strong fleet and subjugated the neighbouring islands'), and of the Phocæans of Massilia (who beat the Carthaginians in a sea fight). In the following chapter (c. 14) he goes on to discuss the various types of vessel in use at this time.

According to Thucydides, then, as the Greek world developed it tended to focus itself round a number of strong naval powers. These powers had been able to reduce neighbouring communities to dependence and received tribute from them. Some, moreover, were well situated for commercial purposes and were able to add to their revenues by tolls upon merchants and traders. In all this there is no word of large scale industrial enterprises. The progress of Greece is held by him to have depended on two things: the increased cultivation of the land and the development of production for sale instead of for consumption—we have seen how this practice grew up not merely among peasants like those to whom Hesiod's poem is addressed, but also among nobles like Sappho's brother and Arcesilaus of Cyrene; and, secondly, the growth of naval imperialism. Even of commerce we are only told (a) that in the earliest times communities were isolated and trade between them non-existent; (b) that in the succeeding period people 'occupied isthmuses for the sake of commerce and for strength against their neighbours'; and (c) that Corinth derived considerable revenues from being an important trading centre. Trade is

---

[1] As Strabo says (viii, 6, 20) the Bacchiads did (above, p. 20).

regarded solely as a source of income. It is never for a moment suggested that the rulers themselves took an active part in it, or that the general progress was bound up with the development of their commercial interests. We hear nothing of the growth of a body of professional traders among the citizens— indeed the only traders mentioned are the farmers and landlords, who see to the selling of their produce themselves. Of the volume of the commerce of this time Thucydides indicates only that it was sufficient to provide a revenue to the State, through tolls and dues.

Having now observed the testimony of Thucydides we may turn to the positive evidence which is adduced in support of the prevailing theories. Let us take the industries first. It is held that in the various 'industrial centres commodities were produced in large establishments or factories and in wholesale quantities.' To this we may reply that all references to the production of goods in these 'ergasteria' (properly translated 'workshops' and not 'factories') come from a later period. There is no single case in which we have evidence of their existence in the centuries which we are now considering. It is of course admitted that as in agricultural so in manufactured commodities production for sale had replaced production for direct use, and that all sorts of goods were produced, and services rendered, by professional craftsmen and artisans.[1] But we must demand some further proof before we believe that production was carried on at this time in large industrial units and by mass methods.

Such a proof has been sought for in the fact that certain manufactured articles appear to have been sold over a very large area outside the territory of the state in which they were made. Now we may remark that in any case this does not prove the point. Chinese porcelain and Persian carpets, as has been pointed out,[2] are both the products of small work-

---

[1] This was true even in Homeric times. The *Iliad* and the *Odyssey* are both full of references to δημιουργοί of all kinds. (δημιουργός, we may note, means literally a man who works for the people, *i.e.* not for his own immediate use.)

[2] Bolkestein, *Het economisch Leven*, p. 65.

shops; but they have reached markets all over the world. And we need only refer to the textile monopoly under the Ptolemies to show that in the ancient as in the modern world cottage industries might go along with a large export trade.[1]

But, furthermore, the evidence for the wide circulation of manufactured goods in Ancient Greece is itself none too strong. It is partly literary and partly archæological. In the first place it is pointed out that many manufactured goods were called by the names of particular places. Expressions such as 'Chalcidian swords' and 'Chalcidian cups', 'Corinthian bronzes', 'Milesian woollens and carpets', 'Amorgian garments', 'Argive weapons', are perpetually used by Greek writers. These articles must have been produced, it is held, in the cities after which they were named—the cities must have been the centres of the industries with which they are in this way associated. But it is to be noticed that the articles in question are practically none of them articles of everyday need. They are either valuable raw materials or else they are luxury and art products—metal-work, fine cloths, and wools, and so on. We cannot suppose that there can have been a wide popular demand for goods of this type. The wants of the masses even in the fifth and fourth centuries were very limited indeed, and even in colonial towns men must have depended upon local handicraft (whether the craftsmen were themselves foreigners or not) to supply them with those simple articles—however named—which they required for the maintenance of life.[2]

Again, only a few of the expressions in question date from the period with which we are at present concerned.[3] Many of them belong to Hellenistic and Roman times, and may be the reflection of large scale industries and extensive export businesses as they existed then. There is no justification

---

[1] See Wilcken in *Schmollers Jahrbuch*, xlv, 2 (1921), p. 108.

[2] See on this Bücher, *Beiträge*, p. 95.

[3] They have been laboriously collected and set out without regard to date or locality by Blümner (*Die gewerbliche Tätigkeit d. Völker d. klass. Altert.*, 1869), and Büchsenschütz (*Bes. u. Erw.*, 1869, and *Die Hauptstätten d. Gewerbefleisses im kl. Altert.*, 1869).

4

whatever for supposing this of the centuries preceding the Persian Wars.

And, finally, to say that an article is called by the name of a particular place does not prove that it was manufactured in that place. It may have got its name from its form or quality;[1] or from the origin of the material out of which it was made; or from the nationality of the traders who dealt in it.[2]

Little light can be shed, therefore, upon early Greek industry by the evidence we have just been examining. Let us turn to the second line of argument. Painted earthenware, we are told, which seems to have been made in Corinth, and which dates from about the years 650–550 B.C., is to be found in all parts of the Mediterranean, from the shores of the Black Sea to Carthage and Etruria; and Attic pottery—the other main type of this period—is equally widely distributed (though it is more plentiful in Italy than elsewhere). This is held to indicate very clearly the size of industry in general at the time, and the extent of the markets.

Now we have already seen that large scale production is not a necessary corollary of a wide distribution of the product; and there is every reason for supposing that even in the later period the making of vases was exclusively in the hands of small producers.[3] But apart from this Bücher has proved conclusively how useless it is to try to argue from the distribution of earthenware to the conditions of industrial production in general.[4] A comparison with other primitive civilisations, he says, makes it clear that trade in earthenware can be carried on between the most distant places before the making of it has even become a distinct profession. Further, it is quite wrong to assume that each large centre in Greece had its native

[1] *E.g.* we talk of ' Corinthian ' columns and ' China ' ware.

[2] Ephorus tells us (Strabo, viii, 6, 16) that articles were called Æginetan because they were sold by merchants from Ægina.

[3] Oertel, *Anhang*, p. 534 ; Bolkestein, *op. cit.*, pp. 65, 75 ; Bücher, *Beiträge*, pp. 66 ff.

[4] *Op. cit.*, pp. 65 ff. Bücher's discussion of this question has been wholly ignored by archæologists ; but they will sooner or later have to face its implications. It may be wrong in some details, but it is based on extensive statistical researches, and on many points it is quite conclusive.

pottery industry and its own local style of decoration. De-
corated pottery was an article of luxury (like the other commodities mentioned above), and there is no evidence whatever
that it was in demand among the ordinary people, or that it
was produced and exported by any particular state in large
quantities. As for the Attic vases, Bücher argues with considerable plausibility [1] that they are most likely to have been
made where they are found in the largest quantities. To
account for the general similarity in the evolution of the designs,
and for the appearance of the same signature on vases found
far apart from one another, he suggests that the potters themselves may have travelled from place to place—and rightly
quotes as parallel such examples as the modern wandering
potters of the island of Siphnos.[2] He has nothing to say in
this connection about the metics, except in passing; [3] but
clearly our view as to the part played by them in Greek trade
and industry only serves to support his contentions.[4]

It seems clear, therefore, that though there was, no doubt,
a certain amount of traffic in earthenware between different
parts of the Greek world, yet this gives no support whatever
to the prevailing views as to the industrialisation of ancient
Greece.

We may pass on, then, to an examination of conditions, as
far as we know them, in those states which are supposed to
have been the centres of Greek industry. Let us start with
the two largest in Greece proper—Ægina and Corinth. Here,
as before, we shall find that an unprejudiced survey of the
evidence in no way bears out current interpretations.

The colligations of Blümner and Büchsenschütz show that
the word 'Æginetan' was applied to all sorts of fancy goods

[1] P. 90.
[2] P. 95. Bücher fails to mention, however, the one positive piece of
evidence—important because isolated—in favour of his hypothesis. In the
fourth century we hear of the Athenian Xenophantus travelling round
South Russia making and selling 'Attic' pottery. For the œnochoë of
Xenophantus see Springer-Michælis, *Kunstgesch.*, p. 506, and Reinach,
Rép., i, 23.
[3] Pp. 78, 90.
[4] See above, pp. 42 ff.

and small articles of everyday life.[1] We hear of Æginetan
ointment, paint, rouge, necklaces, chains, glass, and so on.
This does not mean, however, as we have just seen, that these
goods were produced in Ægina, but rather that they were sold
by Æginetan dealers.   Ægina was essentially a *trading* community.[2]   Itinerant hawkers of any and every article were
known as ' Ægina-merchants.' [3]   It was through trade that
the Æginetan Sostratus gained his enormous wealth; and
Ægina was the only state in Greece proper which had a depot
in the Egyptian port of Naucratis.[4]   Hesiod praises the Myr-
midons of Ægina as the first men to build ships and set sail
upon the sea.[5]   We may also recall here Herodotus' story of
how the Spartan helots sold to Æginetans the rich spoil they
had secured from the Persians at Platæa.[6]

Ephorus informs us that owing to the poverty of the soil the
proletarian citizens of Ægina were driven to trade and commerce.[7]   In other words, Ægina was not a typical Greek city.
Its merchants were probably the first in Greece to compete
with the Phœnicians: its standards of money and weights and
measures were in use far beyond its own territory: its trade
was essentially wholesale inter-district trade.[8]   It did, indeed,
produce good earthenware,[9] and no doubt its merchants often
took with them on their journeys vases bought in the home
market or from a local producer.   Its bronze, too, was well
known throughout the ancient world, and at the end of the

---

[1] See Blümner, *op. cit.*, pp. 88 ff. and Büchsenschütz (*Bes. u. Erw.*,
pp. 366 ff., 388, 398, 442 ff. ; *Die Hauptstätten*, pp. 19 ff.).

[2] Strabo, viii, 6, 16 ; Ar., *Pol.*, 1291*b* (above, p. 37).

[3] Αἰγινοπώλης· παντοπώλης. Schol. Pind., *Ol.*, xxviii.

[4] Hdt., ii, 178.

[5] Schol. Pind., *Nem.*, iii, 21.

[6] Hdt., ix, 80 ; Strabo, viii, 6, 16.

[7] *Ap.* Strabo, viii, 6, 16.

[8] Though, of course, it included hawking and peddling as well (Bücher,
Beiträge, p. 96).   For the importance of Ægina as a trading centre and
the vigorousness of its traffic, see also Pind. (*Ol.*, viii, 25 ff., *Nem.*, iii,
35 ff. ; iv, 36 ff.).   Meyer goes too far, however, when he talks of the
Æginetan ' mercantile marine ' (*Kl. Schr.*, i, 113).

[9] It was known as the ' seller of earthenware,' and we hear of the
phrase ' Æginetan pots,'

sixth century it had a famous school of bronze-founders.[1] But there is no evidence that its industry reached any very large scale. Beloch's supposition that it had a population of 70,000 slaves is pure conjecture [2]—in fact we are not entitled to assume that it contained any exceptionally large number of slaves in productive employments.[3]

About Corinth there is more to be said. It has been described as 'an important industrial town and the largest commercial centre in Greece',[4] as a place where politics was dominated by commerce, and which 'after the fall of the tyrants gave itself over whole-heartedly to trade and industry.' [5] We have seen that Thucydides knows nothing of this. He speaks, indeed, of the naval strength of the Corinthians, of their strong fleet, their numerous colonies, and the many communities which they were able to subjugate. They established themselves, he tells us, in Corcyra, Sicily, Acarnania, Ætolia, and Epirus; and their power extended over Ambracia, Leucas, Epidamnus, Apollonia, and Potidæa.[6] They thus made themselves the centre of a wide sea-empire and grew rich on the tribute which they received, and on the market dues and tolls which they levied.[7] They were said, moreover, to be the inventors of the trireme—the typical Greek warship—and to have taken part in the first naval battle ever fought by Greeks.[8] The reputation of their warships continued down to later times. At the beginning of the fifth century the Athenians 'borrowed' from them twenty ships for use in the war with Ægina,[9] and according to Moschion,[10] Hiero II of Syracuse sent for a Corinthian to direct the building of his fleet. Even

---

[1] According to Pliny (34, 11), Ægina made a speciality of candelabra. We have, however, no means of knowing at what date this started.

[2] It is an emendation of the fantastic figure of 470,000 given in Athenæus from Aristotle (Beloch, *Bevölkerung*, pp. 84 ff., 122).

[3] Theophrastus' praise of the quality of Æginetan ointments has, of course, no bearing whatever on the early period we are at present considering (Theophr., *de Odoribus*, vi, 37 ; Athen., xv, 689d).

[4] Busolt, *G.G.*, i, 631.   [5] Meyer, *Kl. Schr.*, i, 114.

[6] The source of the timber for its triremes.

[7] Even Homer speaks of ' Corinth the rich.'

[8] Thuc., i, 13.   [9] Hdt., vi, 89 ; Thuc., i, 41.

[10] *Ap.* Athen., v, 206.

in their myths they were connected with the sea; their king Amphidamas was said to have been killed while fighting on board his ship, and the Ephyræans (the original inhabitants of the Isthmus) were connected with the Argonauts.

But all this does not justify us in concluding that Corinth had 'trade connections from Sicily to Lydia and the Pontus.' [1] The view that the wars of Corinth were trade wars and its colonial empire an area of commercial exploitation depends upon the belief among modern scholars that the Corinthian nobles themselves took part in business, and that the whole spirit of the citizen body was essentially commercial.[2] The basis for this assumption is small. We know that cadets of the Cypselid house were set up as rulers in the conquered cities.[3] We also hear from Athenæus of a Corinthian who, during the reign of Hiero II of Syracuse, became rich (like Sostratus and Colæus) 'by devoting himself for long to trade.' [4] And Pausanias, writing at the time of the Roman Empire, declares that trade was already in existence between Corinth and Arcadia a hundred and eighty years after the Dorian invasion—the goods being conveyed on mules from Cyllene, under the care of Æginetans.[5] None of this is of any particular significance.[6] Thucydides tells us, further, that the Corinthians cleared the seas of pirates;[7] but the object of this was not to further their own commercial interests so much as to consolidate their empire and to enable foreign merchants to visit their port in greater

---

[1] Busolt, *G.G.*, i, 446, following Curtius (*Hermes*, 1876, pp. 216 ff.).

[2] This is the view of Curtius (*op. cit.*, p. 228) and Pöhlmann (*G.G.*, p. 50). The latter declares that Corinth made the attempt to found a complete colonial empire, and calls the war with Corcyra a colonial war. Similarly Meyer (*Kl. Schr.*, i, 119, 128) says that public life in Corinth was 'permeated with commercialism.'

[3] Nicol. Damasc., fr. 60 [*F. Gr. Hist.*, 59]. *Cf.* Thuc., i, 56, 2 (the college of Epidamiurgi).

[4] Athen., vi, 232*b* (from Theopompus).   [5] Paus., viii, 5, 5.

[6] Pausanias' statement, indeed, has been proved by Francotte (*L'Industrie*, i, 96) to be purely legendary. Curtius, however, writes on the strength of it (*op. cit.*, p. 229): 'The Æginetans established overland routes between Arcadia and the sea, in order to supply the Arcadians with industrial products from the outer world.'

[7] Thuc., i, 13.

numbers, thereby increasing their public revenues. Again, there is no justification whatever for saying, with Francotte, that the war of Corinth and Athens against Ægina, and the ultimate overthrow of the latter, really represented the ousting of Ægina from the economic control of the Peloponnese.[1] And finally, the fact that Corinth was the centre of a unified monetary system (the Euboic system) was a symbol of its political, not of its commercial, importance.

Similarly with Corinthian industry. It is said of Greek states in general that owing to the actual inadequacy of the land and the limited possibilities of agricultural production the inhabitants had to turn to manufacturing goods for export, in order to secure the means of subsistence from abroad;[2] and the leadership of Corinth in this respect is explained by the fact that, as we know, its soil was unusually barren. The truth is that the problem of over-population was solved, in Corinth as elsewhere, not by industrialisation but by emigration and foreign conquests. Let us examine the evidence.

Pindar[3] speaks of the 'many ancient inventions' which Corinth received from the Muses (among them, presumably, the invention of the trireme). Pliny tells us that a Sicyonian potter Butades, who lived in Corinth, was the first to mix ruddle with his clay,[4] and that the potter's wheel (already known in Homeric times) was the invention of a Corinthian, Hyperbius.[5] The famous 'Thericlean' vessels, further, are said to have been the invention of a fifth-century Corinthian potter Thericles.[6] Pliny says the Corinthians disputed with the Sicyonians the credit of having originated both painting and small terracotta work (though he gives the name of a

---

[1] *Op. cit.*, p. 98.   [2] Pöhlmann, *G.G.*, p. 46.   [3] *Ol.*, xiii, 24.

[4] Pliny, *N.H.*, 35, 152. Butades was also said to have been the first to decorate brick key-stones with carved heads (*ibid.*).

[5] Pliny, *N.H.*, 7, 198. Pliny agrees, however, with Theophrastus (Schol. Pind., *Ol.*, xiii, 24) that Hyperbius was the name of an Athenian, who was the first to use brick for buildings (and he adds that some people gave the name of the potter as Anacharsis). Thus the invention of the potter's wheel was connected with Athens. (*Cf.* Critias, fr. i, 12 ff.)

[6] But other explanations are also given of the origin of the name (Athen., xi, 470. See the references in Büchsenschütz, *Hauptstätten*, p. 17, n. 10).

Samian as the inventor of the latter).[1] The inventor of the
'pictura linearis' was said to have been either a Corinthian or
an Egyptian, and the first practical exponent of the art a
Corinthian or a Sicyonian.[2]

These legendary statements mean no more than that the
Corinthians had the reputation of being gifted 'in the useful
arts',[3] and of not 'looking down on' craftsmen, as Greeks
did elsewhere. This being the general opinion it was natural
that art products of all kinds, wherever they were made, should
tend to be called Corinthian. For example, two mixing bowls
'of Corinthian work' appeared (along with Delphic tripods
and Panathenian amphoras) in the triumphal procession of one
of the Ptolemies—so called, perhaps, because they were made
in Alexandria after a Corinthian pattern.[4] So, too, we hear of
Corinthian jars (κάδοι),[5] embossed terracottas,[6] rugs, clothing,
ointments, helmets and breastplates.[7] Herodotus mentions
that the Auseans in Libya used a Corinthian helmet as a crown
for the most beautiful of their maidens.[8] But he goes on to
ask himself—and this sheds an interesting light on the volume
of trade in such articles—how these people would have decor-
ated the girl before the time when there were Greeks resident
there. It never occurs to him that Auseans could get a helmet
except from a Greek settler. Possibly the one in question was
the only one which had ever found its way to Libya.

[1] Painting: Pliny, 35, 15 ; Strabo, 8, 6, 23.   Terracottas : Pliny,
35, 152.
[2] Pliny, *loc. cit.* ; Strabo, *loc. cit.* We may compare with all this the
painting contest between Corinth and Delphi (Pliny, 35, 58).
[3] Strabo, viii, 6, 23.   [4] Athen., xi, 488d.
[5] They are mentioned in the *Parasitus* of Diphilus (c. 300 B.C.) as standing
in a rich man's house (Athen., vi, 236b) [Kock, 61 ; Pickard-Cambridge, 9].
[6] Strabo, viii, 6, 23.
[7] Athen., xii, 525d ; xiii, 582d ; i, 27d. Pliny, 13, 5. Diosc., v, 103.
Helmets and breastplates : Cic., *Verr.*, iv, 44.   Aristophanes, *Ran.*,
l. 440, cannot be used as an example of Corinthian στρώματα, as Barth
has done (*Corinth. commercii et mercaturæ hist. part.*, Diss., Berlin, 1844,
p. 24). The passage must be read in its context. The only point is the
pun on Διὸς Κόρινθος and κόρεις ; the rugs exist only for the sake of the
bugs. (Kock thinks it highly probable that the Corinthians marked their
rugs with the trademark of the city hero, Corinthus !)
[8] Hdt., iv, 180 ; Bücher, *Beiträge*, p. 52.

The rest of the evidence need not detain us long. With the fact that 'Corinthian' vases are to be found all over the Greek world we have already dealt. Athenæus, vi, p. 128*d*, refers to the Hellenistic age, and is not relevant to our present discussion. So, too, with the famous Corinthian bronze. Bücher has properly pointed out [1] that art products made from 'Corinthian alloy' did not achieve any great popularity till the Roman period [2]—and that the Romans themselves traced its discovery (and its name) to the accidental melting and inter-mixture of the component metals during the burning of Corinth. Again there are the votive tablets of Corinthian origin, with inscriptions such as 'for good luck' upon them, which were dedicated in the temple of Poseidon as thank-offerings. These represent labourers in the mines or the vine-yards, or metal-workers at their furnaces, or sculptors, or—most frequently—potters at their wheels and ovens; but they merely serve to show (as Bücher has emphasised) how small were the enterprises for which they were dedicated: for no tablet shows more than two workers. [3]

This, then, is the kind of evidence on which scholars base their belief that Corinth was a large industrial state. Apart from its inherent weakness, we must insist that none of it is older than the fifth century. About the period at which Corinthian commerce and industry is supposed to have been at its prime it tells us nothing. We cannot but agree with Francotte that there are few traces of industry in Corinth; [4] that it was not an industrial state but remained essentially agricultural. Yet we hear of many Corinthian craftsmen. If Ægina was the home of the trader, Corinth was from the

---

[1] *Beiträge*, p. 51.

[2] 'Aes Corinthium' is never mentioned before the time of Cicero.

[3] One tablet—which shows a ship and a number of vases—is used by Bücher (*Beiträge*, p. 78) to support his theory of travelling potters—the ship representing the vessel which they have chartered for their journeys. This is most improbable. Bücher himself lays stress on Furtwängler's view that the vases at the upper edge of the tablet have nothing to do with the ship at all but are merely ornamental. At any rate, there is in this no adequate evidence for extensive foreign sales in Corinthian earthenware.

[4] *Op. cit.*, pp. 105 ff.

earliest times the city of the skilled worker. No doubt many of the technicians and producers who travelled round Greece, doing so much fruitful work of all kinds, were Corinthians—like Ameinocles, or Hiero's shipbuilder. Artists, too, abounded in Corinth: architects, sculptors, poets, inventors, all received the encouragement and support of the Cypselid house. The State was itself, one might say, the patron of the arts—as indeed, with its large revenues from port and market, it could afford to be. And if the merchants who came thither took away with them sometimes the products of Corinthian labour for sale abroad, that did not make Corinth a commercial state dominated by thoughts of industrial exports and the economic exploitation of foreign countries.

Let us turn, thirdly, to Miletus, the supposed centre of the Greek textile industry. The wool of Miletus was world famous (a particularly fine breed of wool-bearing sheep was reared in the surrounding country), and most of the articles which bear the name Milesian were woollen products—rugs, blankets, clothing, etc. There is, indeed, no ground for supposing that these articles were manufactured in Miletus for export in any large quantities. But Bücher goes too far when he says that nothing was exported except the raw wool and the sheep themselves.[1] On the one hand there is no evidence whatever of a regular exportation of either sheep or wool; we hear once or twice of Milesian sheep in other parts of Greece, but that is all.[2] And, on the other hand, his attempt to prove that no manufactured woollen products ever left Miletus is perfectly absurd. We need not doubt that itinerant merchants from time to time came and bought the products of Milesian work-shops (not factories) and sold them in other parts of the world.

Sappho speaks [3] of Lydian shoes, and Alcman mentions a Lydian 'mitra' in Sparta.[4] Again Alcæus sings the praises

---

[1] *Beiträge*, p. 40.

[2] Polycrates is said to have imported some into Samos (Athen., xii, 540d) ; and in a recently discovered papyrus there is mention of Milesian sheep in Egypt (*P. Cair.*, 24. See also Wilcken in *Schmollers Jahrbuch*, xlv, 2, pp. 107 ff.; Oertel, *Anhang*, p. 523, n. 2).

[3] Fr. 17 [Diehl 17].   [4] Fr. 5, l. 67 [Diehl 1].

of Chalcidian swords.[1]   No doubt in these places small work-shops might produce one or two articles of exceptional value and renown: but one has no right to speak on the strength of these passages of a 'flourishing textile and leather industry' in Lydia,[2] or of large metal factories in Chalcis.   The evidence is equally weak for industries in Argos and Sicyon in the early times.   And there is simply no ground whatever for attribut-ing, as has been done, dye works to Miletus,[3] or metal works to Chios[4] and Samos,[5] or textile mills to Megara[6]—or for believing that Cyrene, Thebes, and Sicily manufactured chariots for export, simply because they are called 'well-charioted' by Pindar and Sophocles.[7]

Finally we are told that Athens, too, exported large quantities not merely of oil and earthenware but also of metal goods.[8] Athens, it is said, was a latecomer in the world of industry and commerce,[9] but from the time of Peisistratus onwards it was an active competitor for world markets and sold its products in all parts of the Greek world.[10]   This picture is very much over-drawn.   The constitution of Solon shows that at the beginning of the sixth century Athens was a purely agricultural state: it was a community composed exclusively of shepherds and peasants, and political rights depended upon and varied with the ownership of land and the volume of 'dry and liquid' produce.   Solon, it is true, is said to have persuaded many foreign craftsmen to settle in Athens;[11] but, like Themistocles

---

[1] Fr. 56 [Diehl 5, 4].   [2] Beloch, *G.G.*, i, 1, 266 ff.

[3] Homer speaks of a Mæonian or Carian woman 'who stains a piece of ivory with purple, to be a cheek-piece for a horse' (*Il.*, iv, 141 ; Beloch, *loc. cit.*).

[4] According to Herodotus the Chians were said to have discovered how to weld iron (i, 25).

[5] Pliny says that bronze founding was introduced into Greece by two Samians (35, 152).

[6] The Megarians claimed to have invented the art of dry-cleaning. (On Megara's textile industries see below, p. 79.)

[7] See also Oertel, *Anhang*, p. 523.

[8] Beloch, *G.G.*, i, 268 ; Busolt, *G.G.*, ii, 198.

[9] Meyer, *G.G.*, i, 636 ff.; Beloch, *op. cit.*, p. 279 ; Büchsenschütz, *Bes. u. Erw.*, p. 390.

[10] Beloch, *op. cit.*, p. 387.   [11] See above, p. 24.

a century later, he did this not in order to develop large scale industries in Athens but to enable the demands of the citizens for manufactured goods to be satisfied at home—in other words, to make Attica self-supporting.   No doubt even in this early period Athens, like Ægina and Corinth, was a port of call for foreign merchants; and these merchants would carry away with them, when they left, a certain number of Athenian products for sale abroad.[1]   Beyond this we cannot with certainty go. It is likely, however, that the chief Athenian exports were not manufactured products, but wine and, more important, oil. These were perhaps the only commodities in which Attica produced beyond its own needs, and which could be sent abroad regularly and in fairly substantial quantities.[2]

The Athenian coast dwellers, we may add, were peasants, as were also those impoverished citizens to whom Peisistratus gave monetary assistance.[3]   The object of the Cleisthenic reforms was to make the local deme the political unit instead of the clan (the stronghold of the landed nobility), and so to raise the political status of the small peasants.[4]

It will be worth while to end our discussion of Greek industry in this period by examining the position of Naucratis.[5] Naucratis was the *entrepôt* of traffic between Greece and Egypt, and perhaps also the economic centre of the Eastern Mediterranean.   It is therefore supposed, in accordance with current views as to the nature of Greek economic life, to have been a flourishing commercial and industrial city.   It was founded, so we are told, by the Milesians for the sake of their export trade.[6]   All the commercial Greek states of the time took part in the building of its great market.[7]   It had warehouses

---

[1] Presumably, too, the Alcmæonids, like the Bacchiads, extracted what they could from the foreign merchants for the revenues of State.

[2] See further on sixth-century Athens below, p. 144.

[3] Ar., *Resp. Ath.*, 13 ; *ibid.*, 16, 2.

[4] Weber, *Wirtsch. u. Gesellsch.*, pp. 586 ff. ; see above, p. 31.

[5] [See the article by Hogarth and others in *J.H.S.*, 1903 ; and Price, *J.H.S.*, 1924 (pottery).]

[6] Prinz describes its foundation as a brilliant act of commercial policy (*Funde aus Naucratis*, p. 2).

[7] Meyer, *Kl. Schr.*, i, 204.

built by the Greeks on land provided by the King of Egypt,[1] and used as trade depots (like the trade depots of the Hansa towns).[2] First in importance was the Milesian pottery ware-house, to which were regularly brought large numbers of jars and bowls from Miletus to be sold in Egypt. After it came the establishments of the other Greek states—Samos, Lesbos, Clazomenæ, Cyrene, Melos, Corinth, Athens. These states, too, exported goods to Egypt, though they could not seriously compete in this respect with Miletus. After a time, moreover, Naucratis lost its character as a Milesian trade-depot and developed industries of its own—first and foremost an earthen-ware industry whose products competed seriously with those imported from Greece, and were themselves sold in Cyprus, Rhodes, Miletus, Pitane, Gordium, Olbia, Delos, Ægina, Athens, and Etruria; a flourishing faience industry which produced for the whole Greek world,[3] an iron industry also, and an alabaster industry.

The basis of this picture of Naucratis in the sixth century is to be found partly in the descriptions of Herodotus and Strabo, and partly in the results of the British excavations.[4] We shall find that here, as before, an unprejudiced examination of the evidence, both archæological and literary, will lead to con-clusions considerably more modest than those now current.[5]

In the first place, then, it is by now clear that Naucratis was founded during the seventh century, in the reign of Psamme-tichus I—perhaps about 650 B.C. But there is no evidence that it was meant as a trade colony or depot.[6] Strabo's report

---

[1] Beloch, *G.G.*, i, 1, 263 ; Prinz, p. 1.

[2] Pöhlmann, *G.G.*, p. 46 ; Otto, *Kulturgesch.*, p. 85.

[3] Faience : Prinz, pp. 104, 107 ff. Iron : Flinders Petrie, *Naucratis*, i, 39.

[4] Hdt., ii, 178 ff. ; Strabo, 17, 1, 18. A very large number of vases were brought to light, and it is largely on the strength of these that Prinz has built up his reconstruction of Naucratis' economic history—a recon-struction which, as he himself says (*op. cit.*, p. 146), accepts as given the general view-point of Beloch and Meyer.

[5] In a detailed treatment of the question E. W. Reichardt has recently given serious grounds for suspecting Prinz's conclusions. See his *Das Gewerbe im Alten Griechenland u. d. Kapitalistische Gewerbe*, pp. 260 ff. (*Jahrb. f. Nat. u. Stat.*, p. 126, 3rd series, vol. lxxi, 1927).

[6] Prinz, pp. 1, 119 ; Busolt, *G.G.*, i, 478.

makes it clear that the founders were not traders but soldiers and adventurers, attracted thither by prospects of plunder.[1] What Strabo says is that the Milesians came with thirty ships to the Bolbitic mouth of the Nile and built there the 'Milesian Fort'; that a little later they sailed to the Saitic nome and there defeated Inaros in a naval battle; and that thereafter they founded the city of Naucratis ('strong in ships') at a point on the Canobic arm of the Nile not very far above Schedia.[2] It has been rightly suggested that this victory over Inaros is connected with the struggles of Psammetichus I to establish himself as king over Egypt. It is known that Psammetichus owed his throne largely to Greek mercenaries,[3] and no doubt the Milesians with their thirty ships were among those who came to his assistance.

Now it is argued that the large number of seventh-century vases of Milesian origin which have been found in Naucratis enable us to see this expedition which Strabo describes in its true light: that its object must really have been commercial and not military. But all, or almost all, of these vases are votive offerings from the shrines of Apollo and Aphrodite, which the priests seem to have thrown away in a heap.[4] They are none of them meant for practical uses, and are scarcely good evidence for extensive commercial relations between Greece, Miletus, and Egypt. Moreover, it is still by no means certain—as Prinz himself admits [5]—that they really do come from Miletus. Originally they were supposed to be Rhodian, though Dümmler suggested that they were from Argos. Then Löschcke argued that they must have come from a large exporting centre, and pointed out further that the area over which similar vases have been discovered corresponds closely

---

[1] The Nile valley from the earliest times attracted the attentions of Greek pirates (Busolt has collected the Homeric references, *op. cit.*, p. 126, n. 1).

[2] Strabo, 17, 1, 18.

[3] Herodotus (ii, 154) tells us that Psammetichus gave to some Ionians and Carians 'who had helped him' pieces of land (called by Herodotus 'camps') to settle on. Moreover, it is known that at this time the fortresses in Egypt were manned with Ionian and Carian mercenaries (Busolt, *op. cit.*, i, 477).

[4] Prinz, p. 14.

[5] *Ibid.*, p. 30.

with the Milesian 'sphere of influence'; and it is also observed
that this same type of vase is also to be found in Miletus itself.
Clearly these contentions cannot be regarded as having settled
the matter.   But even if we admit that the Naucratite vases
are rightly called Milesian, that does not show that Naucratis
was founded as a trade colony or depot of Miletus.   The
soldiers who settled in Egypt required votive offerings, and
they may well have sent for them to their former home.   Or
it is possible that they made them themselves, after the style
and pattern with which they were familiar; or that if they had
not the requisite skill they summoned craftsmen, presumably
from Miletus itself, to come to Naucratis and work for them—
no unusual occurrence in ancient Greece, as we have already
seen.

But while there is no ground for believing that the original
intention in founding Naucratis was commercial, it did, as time
went on, develop into an important trading centre.   It was
not merely the best, it was the only port through which goods
could pass between the valley of the Nile and the Mediterranean.
The reason for this was partly geographical, partly, also,
political.   'Naucratis has been from the earliest times the only
port in Egypt.   If anybody entered one of the other mouths
of the Nile, he was made to declare on oath that he had come
thither unintentionally, and then to sail to the Canobic mouth.
If storms made this impossible he was obliged to convey his
goods in boats through the delta' (*i.e.* by canal) 'and so come
to Naucratis.' [1]   Here we see clearly a fundamental principle
of ancient law.   The State is essentially shut off from the
outer world, and foreigners who enter its territory are regarded
in general as enemies, but certain limits are set within which
they are allowed to do business.[2]   At the same time, however,
as the kings of Egypt limited Egypt's intercourse with the outer
world, by concentrating it in one port, they also, no doubt,
took advantage of this concentration (like the Bacchiad house

[1] Hdt., ii, 179, 168.
[2] The same sort of rules and conditions are laid down in the treaties
between Rome and Carthage.   See below, p. 119.

in Corinth) to secure revenues for themselves—for we must not forget that they, and not the inhabitants of Naucratis, were ultimately in control of Egyptian foreign trade.

At what period Naucratis was put in this exceptional position Herodotus does not tell us. To date it to the reign of Amasis (570–526 B.C.) seems somewhat arbitrary; [1] indeed, the context in Herodotus suggests rather that it was earlier, since the privileges which Amasis is reported as having conferred on Naucratis have nothing to do with trade monopolies.

Herodotus tells us a certain amount about Amasis and the Greeks. When he came to the throne, 'becoming a phil-hellene,' he gave to those Greeks who came to Egypt the city of Naucratis to live in. And to those who did not wish to live there but voyaged thither [2] he gave land for altars and sanc-tuaries.[3] The largest of these sanctuaries, the Hellenium, was founded jointly by Chios, Teos, Phocæa, Clazomenæ, Rhodes, Cnidus, Halicarnassus, Phaselis, and Mytilene. These states owned the sanctuary and also appointed the 'port authorities'; and no Greeks from other cities had any valid claims. In addition, the Æginetans built a separate sanctuary to Zeus, the Samians to Hera, and the Milesians to Apollo.

The philhellenism of Amasis, then, expressed itself in two ways. He allowed Greeks from all parts to come and settle along with the Milesians in Naucratis, thereby making it a Panhellenic instead of a Milesian city.[4] And he allowed those Greeks who came for temporary commercial purposes to build sanctuaries for themselves. These latter persons were kept very distinct from the full citizens of Naucratis; indeed, they were not really part of the city at all.[5] Thus even in Naucratis trade was in the hands of non-citizens and foreigners.

---

[1] Prinz, p. 109.

[2] αὐτοῦ ναυτιλλομένοισι. ναυτίλλομαι means 'to be a ναυτίλος, or ναύτης'—that is, 'to travel by sea'; αὐτοῦ is 'thither.' See Stein's note on the passage.

[3] τεμένεα. To translate by 'quarters' is to exaggerate.

[4] Herodotus seems to believe that Naucratis was first founded under Amasis. But Solon (fr. 25 [Diehl 6]) shows that it existed as early as about 600 B.C., and the finds of pottery carry it back to the middle seventh century. [5] As Prinz has rightly seen (p. 6).

We may observe from this passage, too, that in Naucratis as elsewhere, Greek traders were united with one another by religious ties only. Commercial gilds did not exist in classical Greece, and the cults of the merchants had no commercial aims.[1] And when Herodotus says that the several *states* founded these sanctuaries, that means merely that it was with the approval of these states that the national cults were conveyed by their citizens to Egypt. (So, too, when any colony went out it was allowed to carry with it the cults of the mother state. In this sense, therefore, cities always 'founded' the cults of their colonies.)

The 'port authorities', or overseers, must have been primarily police officers (such as we also find in the *emporium* of Athens).[2] When Herodotus says that this position belonged to the nine cities of Asia Minor, he presumably means that the national groups of these cities, as opposed to Greeks from elsewhere, had the right to appoint these officials from their own number. This was another example, then, of the philhellenism of Amasis. He was prepared to entrust the control of the port of Egypt to Greeks—though not, be it observed, to the citizens of Naucratis.[3]

The list of states given by Herodotus in this passage gives us some idea of the main lines of trade between Egypt and Greece. But this does not mean that the states mentioned were primarily commercial or industrial. On the contrary, goods would typically be conveyed to and from Egypt by producers and farmers, like the brother of Sappho;[4] we may presume that he, too, when he was in Naucratis, joined his fellow Lesbians in the Hellenium. Nor again can we say, with Otto, that the absence from Herodotus' list of all the cities of Greece proper (except Ægina) was due to the successful

---

[1] Poland, *Gr. Vereinswesen*, pp. 113, 116, 517 ; Hasebroek in *Hermes*, 1923, p. 419. Otto (*Kulturgesch.*, p. 85) compares the Hellenium to the Steelyard of the Hansa in London !

[2] Below, p. 174.

[3] Prinz (p. 6) assumes five distinct *emporia* in Naucratis ! This merely shows that he has not understood the facts of the case.

[4] Above, p. 13.

5

competition of the cities of Asia Minor.[1]   Finally, it is not to be concluded from the fact that 'Naucratite' vases are found in many places in the Greek world as well as in Naucratis, that it had a large earthenware industry and export business.   Here, as before, widespread distribution need not imply wholesale production.   The most that we can say is that the potters of Naucratis were famous over a wide area,[2] and that no doubt visiting merchants bought from them some of their specially good products to take with them for sale in other cities.   No doubt the faience and alabaster of Naucratis was similarly distributed through the Mediterranean world.

We may conclude, then, that the prevailing descriptions of Greek industry in the seventh and sixth centuries seriously exaggerate its volume and its importance.   This being so, it must follow that the picture of Greek commerce at this time is also considerably overdrawn.   The fact that these two centuries cover the period of great colonial expansion is no proof (as will be emphasised later) that they witnessed a great commercial and industrial revolution, even though they were also the centuries during which the Greeks first learnt to take an active part in trade.   And in any case, the part played by international trade in building up towns and town life has at no time in the world's history been as great as might be supposed.[3]   As a matter of fact we know little enough about the trade of this period.

(a) We have already seen that the voyages of Menelaus and Odysseus, of the Taphian chief Mentes and of the Phæacians, cannot have had commercial aims.[4]   In the *Odyssey* and the later epics, it is true, sea trade is frequently mentioned, and voyages to Egypt and Phœnicia for commercial purposes are regarded as normal and ordinary.[5]   But we cannot conclude from this, with Meyer,[6] that the Greeks were themselves beginning to travel as merchants and deal in foreign goods at the times when the poems were written.   There is no word

---

[1] *Op. cit.*, p. 85.
[2] Athen., xi, 480e.
[3] Sombart, *Moderne Kapitalismus*, i, 155.
[4] See above, p. 17.
[5] E.g., *Od.*, iv, 125, 351 ; xiv, 246 ff. ; xvii, 427.
[6] *Kl. Schr.*, i, 103.

whatever in the epic poets that the trade to which they refer was carried on by Greeks. On the contrary the merchant in Homer is always a Phœnician.[1] All Homeric references to trade are therefore irrelevant.

(b) Similarly when Hesiod tells about sailing in ships and commerce,[2] he is thinking of these activities not as whole-time occupations but as part of the normal work of the peasant who has produced more than he needs for his own use and wants to sell it abroad. There can be no question of his referring in this passage to the development in the purely agricultural Bœotia of professional commerce.[3] Nor was Hesiod's father a 'sailor' plying between Asia Minor and Greece proper. He himself says that he crossed the Ægean once and once only from Cyme to Bœotia where he settled down; and that he was driven to do this by 'accursed poverty.'[4] According to Hesiod one of the delights of peace is that 'no one needs to venture upon the sea, for the life-giving plough-land bears fruit enough.'[5]

(c) Herodotus' account of the foundation of Naucratis has already been dealt with, and it has been shown that it gives no support to the current views.

(d) We have already established that the Greek nobles were never merchants, and that the belief in a commercial aristocracy of the late mediæval type for the early period of Greek history is wholly without foundation.

(e) Finally, we may save ourselves from exaggerated conceptions of the commerce of this period by observing its nautical skill. In the earliest times no distinction was made between war vessels and commercial vessels. The only ships mentioned by Homer have twenty, one hundred, or a hundred and twenty oars. And all the many ships which are represented on the Dipylon vases are of this type.[6] Now according to

---

[1] E.g., *Od.*, viii, 161. See above, p. 18.   [2] *Erga*, 630 ff.

[3] One does not suppose that South Italy is becoming in this sense commercialised, because one sees boats belonging to Italian peasants lying in Dalmatian harbours.

[4] *Erga*, 633.   [5] *Ibid.*, 233 ff.

[6] *Il.*, ii, 510 ; xx, 247 ; ix, 322 ff.

Herodotus,[1] the Phocæans, when they sailed to Tartessus, chose to go on a penteconter (instead of a round boat) just because their object was rather piratical than commercial; and in a later passage Herodotus mentions a second penteconter which was used for piratical purposes.[2] Moreover, at the beginning of the seventh century the sea was regarded as being properly navigable only in late summer: one might perhaps put out in spring, but to do so was a foolhardy venture against which earnest warnings are given.[3]

Let us conclude by summing up our positive knowledge of the conditions of trade during the period preceding the Persian Wars. It was focussed in a number of ports and cities which by reason of their geographical situation were specially suitable as commercial centres. Chief among these were Corinth, Ægina, and Athens in Greece proper; Miletus in Asia Minor (the *entrepôt* of the trade between Asia Minor and the Mediterranean); Naucratis in Egypt (for trade between the Mediterranean and Egypt); and in the West, Carthage and Massilia. In addition there were fairs connected with the various national games. There were no commercial states as we know them to-day, nor were their populations commercial in any modern sense.

The traders were at first exclusively Phœnicians. Gradually they were joined by Greeks. These Greeks did a little trade in scarce articles, but they were primarily corsairs and adventurers (like, for example, the Phocæans described by Herodotus).[4] They sailed to the furthest limits of the then known world—to Tanais, to Asia, to Egypt, to Tyre.[5] Their explorations widened the Greek knowledge of other countries, and they were followed by colonists and emigrants; but they did not lead to an enormous development of world trade nor did they convert the whole of the Mediterranean Sea into an area of Greek commercial exploitation.[6] Apart from occasional wanderers such as these, Greek trade was carried on by the producers themselves. When a professional trading class first

---

[1] i, 163.   [2] iii, 39.   [3] Hesiod, *Erga*, 663 ff.
[4] i, 163.   [5] Ezekiel, xxvii, 13, 19.
[6] Busolt, *G.G.*, i, 491 ; Meyer, *Kl. Schr.*, i, 105.

emerged among the Greeks is not known.[1] Even in later times professional traders were mostly metics, and therefore to a large extent non-Greeks. Of the Greeks in Greece proper the Æginetans were probably the first to turn to commerce as a profession.

The commodities dealt in were mostly commodities of value;[2] they were never, so far as we know, articles of everyday need. Chief among them would be gold and silver and ivory, costly metal work (*e.g.* an inlaid sword), valuable vases, woven cloths, ornaments (such as were so dear to the warriors of Homeric times), above all, slaves, both men and women. For such commodities the demand was always considerable, and from the earliest times they would be exchanged against each other between nation and nation.[3] The trader bought them in this or that market and from this or that craftsman. If he sold them again at a profit he would return and secure further supplies; and perhaps he might secure for the craftsman valuable raw materials for his work—for besides trading in finished articles he must also have dealt in those natural products which though indispensable are in some places scarce—iron, for example (which the Taphian Mentes exchanged for copper), tin, purple, wood for shipbuilding, oil and wine. Articles of this sort corresponded in the trade of ancient Greece to the spices, wax, polish, and tar, the wine and the beer, which were imported into the towns of the Middle Ages.[4]

[1] The story in Herodotus of Colæus, the Samian ' merchant-shipowner', is of no assistance here, since it is clearly a fifth-century legend composed in order to give a historical explanation of the friendship between Samos and Cyrene (above, p. 12).

[2] This is borne out by the excavations of tombs both in the Mediterranean and in the Orient ; the articles, which evidently had been imported from other lands, are in all cases costly. In primitive times trade in such articles is always more extensive and important than in anything else (Goetze in *Festschr. fur Bastian*, 1896, pp. 339 ff. ; Montelius in *Prähist. Zeitschr.*, ii, 1910, pp. 249 ff.).

[3] These were the sort of goods which were displayed at the festival fairs in Delos and elsewhere. (*Hymn to Apollo*, 29 ff., 146 ff.)

[4] Trade of this sort—the articles dealt in being the excess produce of local agriculture and craftsmanship—can be clearly detected, even in the earliest time—*e.g.* Thucydides' reference to the ' surplus,' which is produced for sale. (See above, p. 45.)

We cannot tell the extent of this trade in surplus products, though we shall do well not to exaggerate it. Nor do we know how far at this early time it included corn.[1] States which found their population pressing upon the home food supplies may have been able to preserve their self-sufficiency by prohibiting export (as in Athens under Solon) or by colonisation. The theory that the colonies regularly provided their mother states with cheap food and raw materials in exchange for manufactured products is contrary alike to the evidence and to the inherent probabilities of the case—indeed, this whole idea of the division of labour between colony and home country is a product of the age of mercantilism. This conclusion is not affected by the discoveries of vases. Even if we do not accept Bücher's plausible theory [2] that in most cases the vases were made in the same place where they were found, they were not exported as articles of everyday need, but were merely the vessels in which the liquid exports of this period, oil and wine, were conveyed to the importing country, or were intended as decorations for tombs, and votive offerings (*e.g.* in Naucratis), or else were prizes taken home by the victor in some international contest.[3] Besides, a fairly extensive foreign trade in earthenware is to be found among people economically far less advanced than the Greeks.[4] Local needs were in general satisfied as far as can be seen by local production—and that in spite of great differences in the fertility of the soil as between different states.

In other words, then, by the beginning of the classical period Greece has passed beyond the stage (which we see in Homer) of separate household economies—especially in one or two states, in which industrial activities were beginning to manifest themselves. But it had not yet reached the stage of a single national economy overstepping the boundaries of separate states. We must altogether reject the picture of seventh-century Greece as a country with an elaborate inter-

[1] We hear from Herodotus (vii, 147) of the importation of Pontic corn into Ægina and the Peloponnese at the beginning of the fifth century.

[2] See above, p. 50.   [3] Like the (later) Athenian 'prize-amphoræ.'

[4] Bücher, *Beiträge*, p. 97.

city division of labour and specialisation of production, with an extensive foreign and sea trade and regular trade connections and alliances (resting on a basis of naval strength),[1] with commercial aristocrats and merchant princes. The political principle of self-sufficiency and the technical conditions of trade combined to put the development of a single national economy out of the question, at least before the fifth century, and the most progressive of the Greek states were not in this respect further advanced than the towns of the Middle Ages with their exclusive town-economies.[2] Even this stage was not universally reached. It was to be seen in its full maturity in such centres of culture as Athens, Corinth, Ægina, Chalcis, Eretria, Megara, Sicyon, and Miletus, at least as early as the sixth century. But in the most backward places we still find evidence of separate household economies long after the Persian Wars; and no doubt other places arrived at various compromises between household and state such as are not readily to be classified in cut and dried formulas.

Similarly we must hesitate to speak of Greece in this period as having a money economy. The precious metals were, indeed, practically everywhere the standards of value, but the coins into which they were made, starting from the seventh century, had at first a purely local currency, and it took a long time before they became the media of international payments. Even in the fourth century, as we shall see, commerce between different localities remained largely on a barter basis.[3]

II. *The Fifth and Fourth Centuries*

We have now to inquire into the evolution of Greek economic life during the fifth and fourth centuries. The years following upon the Persian Wars were years of unparalleled intellectual and spiritual advance. Were they also years of great industrial and commercial progress? Can we observe in them an enlargement of the circle of producers and consumers, an increased resort to foreign trade for the satisfaction

---

[1] Meyer, *G.A.* (1st ed.), i, 537.
[2] In spite of Otto, *Kulturgesch.*, p. 76.   [3] See below, p. 85.

of everyday needs,[1] a more complete division of labour between city and city?

The leading accounts of Greek history speak of this period as one during which industry and commerce reached an even higher level than that postulated for the two previous centuries. Production was undertaken on a larger scale and more universally. The area of the Isthmus and the Saronic Gulf, including as it did Corinth, Sicyon, Megara, the Argolid, Ægina, and above all Athens, became one large manufacturing area. After the Peloponnesian War the wave of industrialisation had spread so as to include Syracuse and Tarentum, Mytilene, Chios, Samos, and Miletus, even Sparta itself. All these states exchanged with one another the products of their factories, leather goods and metal goods, textiles, furniture, and ointments. And as they developed into commercial states, they grew wealthy, and their commercial classes, mine-owners and merchants, became politically powerful. Their raw materials and their corn they imported from abroad, selling in return manufactured goods, and also olive oil and wine.[2]

This, then, is the picture the basis for which we have to examine.

Let us start, as before, with the evidence for Greek industries. We have for this period several references (only in Athens, however) to individuals who owned workshops and employed in them slaves, or, less commonly, free labourers, in the production of goods at a profit. It will be worth while to list these references:

(a) Lysias speaks of a workshop which he and his brother Polemarchus owned in the year 404–403 B.C.;[3]

(b) Theodorus, the father of Isocrates, employed flute-makers and lived upon the proceeds of their work;[4]

(c) Leocrates employed bronze-smiths;[5]

---

[1] In Aristotelian terminology, ξενικώτερον γίγνεσθαι, (Pol., 1257a).

[2] See for all this, Meyer, Kl. Schr., i, 115, 116 ; G.A., iv, 53 ff. ; Beloch, G.G., ii, 1, 78, 84 ; iii, 1, 317, 318, 323 ff., 325 ff. ; Pöhlmann, G.G., p. 200 ; Soz. Frage, passim ; Otto, Kulturgesch., pp. 76, 83.

[3] Lys., xii, 8.   [4] Vit. x Orat., 836e ; Dion. Hal., Isocr., p. 1.

[5] Lyc., c. Leocr., § 58.

(*d*) Demosthenes' father produced knives (or swords) and bedsteads; [1]

(*e*) Timarchus owned slaves who were leather workers and also a woman who made 'Amorgines' and put fine garments on the market, and a male embroiderer; [2]

(*f*) Nausicydes owned a barley-flour mill; Cyrebus a bakery; and Demeas and Menon each a tailoring establishment; [3]

(*g*) Comon employed men in making sailcloth and preparing dyes; [4]

(*h*) Pasion produced shields; [5]

(*i*) Plato speaks, without any suggestion that he is referring to anything unusual or out of the way, of people who 'have many slaves producing for them.' [6]

Of the above references the first two belong to the fifth century, the remainder to the fourth. Three of them are of special interest in that they provide some idea of the number of persons employed. Let us examine these three more closely.

The first is the case of Lysias and Polemarchus. In the speech against Eratosthenes Lysias at one point says that the commissioners of the Thirty Tyrants 'broke into the workshop and commandeered the slaves'; and later on he mentions among his and his brother's possessions which were confiscated by the Thirty, 'seven hundred shields and a hundred and twenty slaves.' [7] From these two passages it is commonly argued that the workshop of Lysias and Polemarchus must have given employment to a hundred and twenty people.[8] But Bücher has rightly resisted this conclusion.[9] As he points out, we are nowhere told that the slaves who were confiscated were all employed in the workshop; and it is on the face of it far more likely that they included (for instance) the domestic

---

[1] Dem., xxvii, § 9 ff.   [2] Æschin., *c. Timarch.*, § 97.
[3] Xen., *Mem.*, ii, 7, 6.   [4] Dem., xlviii, § 12.
[5] Dem., xxxvi, § 4.   [6] *Laws*, 846e.   [7] Lys., xii, 8, 19.
[8] Büchsenschütz, *Bes. u. Erw.*, p. 338 ; Beloch, *G.G.*, iii, 1, 318 ; Pöhlmann, *Soz. Frage*, i, 217, n. 4. This is the principal piece of evidence for large 'factories.'
[9] *Beiträge*, p. 10 ff.

staff and the personal servants of Lysias himself, his brother, and his wife. Bücher, indeed, goes much further than this. He argues that very possibly the workshop of Lysias and Polemarchus was merely a temporary establishment for preparing the overthrow of the oligarchy,[1] that it was used not for producing shields (we are never explicitly told that Lysias ran a shield-making factory) but merely for storing them. But this argument shows more zeal than judgment. We hear of a workshop, of slaves in the service of the owners of the workshop, of seven hundred shields which were found in their house, and of two hundred shields which they had given to Thrasybulus. If we approach the matter without prejudice, we shall recognise here a genuine establishment for the production of shields. On the other hand, we must equally admit that we have no evidence of the number of workers employed therein.[2] And we can therefore deduce no conclusions from the workshop of Lysias and Polemarchus about the size of Greek industrial undertakings.

The other two factories about which we have information are those belonging to Timarchus and to the father of Demosthenes.[3] The figures given are:

(a) For Timarchus' leather factory, 9 or 10 men and a 'works manager';[4]

(b) for the bedstead factory, 20 men;

---

[1] We know from other sources that in 403 B.C. Lysias contributed 200 shields and 2000 dr. in cash to Thrasybulus, besides enlisting mercenaries for his army (*Vit. x Orat.*, 835 ff.).

[2] Meyer says that 'the larger part' of the 120 slaves must have been so employed (*Forsch.*, ii, 186). This is, of course, mere assertion.

[3] Beloch (*G.G.*, iii, 1, 318) has tried to estimate the number of workers in Pasion's shield factory by calculations based on the cost of its lease and its net yield, and in this way arrives at the conclusion that at least eighty men must have been employed. But the figures from which he starts are much too unreliable to be used so mathematically. And similarly with his attempt to deduce the number of slaves in Leocrates' smithy from the amount paid by Leocrates for slaves (35 minæ). There is no ground for supposing that this sum was spent exclusively on manufacturing labourers, and not in part on domestic servants. And in any case the value of slaves depended on all sorts of special and accidental factors. We must not think of them as having a 'normal' price (Boeckh, i, 85 ff. [67 ff.]).

[4] Æschin., *c. Timarch.*, § 97.

(c) for the sword (knife) factory, 32 or 33 men.[1]

Now in the first place it is to be noticed that Demosthenes speaks as though his father's two concerns were distinctly large. The ordinary manufacturing establishment, one might infer, contained not more than perhaps ten or fifteen workers (like the leather factory of Timarchus). If so, this would mean that anything like large scale industry was quite exceptional in fourth-century Athens.[2] This conclusion is borne out by a consideration of the general economic conditions of the period. As Oertel has shown, capitalistic methods could not become dominant in Greek manufacture—they could not increase the efficiency of the productive process—for three main reasons: the impossibility of forecasting demand; the difficulties of capital accumulation and investment; and the institution of slavery.[3] Moreover, the historical evidence shows that the production of commodities was and remained a craft and not an industry. Rich manufacturers like Pasion, Comon, or Lysias might take no personal part in the running of their establishments.[4] But we often hear of masters of workshops who worked alongside of their men. Plato in the Laws, for instance, puts forward as a hypothetical case the possibility of an owner being himself a woodworker but employing slaves as metal-workers.[5] A worker complains in one of the speeches of Lysias that he could secure no assistants in his craft, but had to work entirely by himself.[6] This was a reasonable ground for complaint, for as Xenophon says, 'those who can do so buy themselves slaves that they may have fellow-workers.'[7] The son of Anytus, we hear further, was taken into his father's workshop as an apprentice, and Anytus himself is called by Plato a workman.[8] To which of the two classes such people

---

[1] Dem., c. Aphob., i, §§ 9 ff., 33.

[2] Beloch, G.G., iii, 1, p. 318, n. 2 ; Oertel, Anhang, p. 533. For the parallel conditions in the Middle Ages see v. Below, Probleme, p. 419.

[3] Oertel, Anhang, pp. 523 ff.

[4] Thus the father of Demosthenes left his workshops under the control of a freedman (Dem., op. cit., § 19) ; and, as we have seen, Timarchus employed a slave as 'works-manager.'

[5] Laws, 846e.   [6] Lysias, xxiv, 6.

[7] Xen., Mem., ii, 3, 3.   [8] Xen., Apol., 29 ; Plato, Apol., 23e.

as Cleon and Hyperbolus belonged it is impossible to decide. Bücher 1olds that they were simply artisans, or, at most, the owners of tiny workshops, and that they themselves cut and tanned the leather, or shaped the lamps. But this is perhaps to take the jeers of the comedies too literally. An Aristophanes might easily have called the father of Demosthenes 'knife-maker' or 'bedstead man.'

These small manufacturing establishments, of course, produced for stock as well as to order. This was only to be expected; and it accounts for the presence in Lysias' workshop of the seven hundred shields which were commandeered by the Thirty.[1] Beloch thinks that as soon as the goods were made they may have been distributed among retailers on credit.[2] But we do not need to assume anything so complicated as this. It is true that the inventory which Demosthenes gives of his father's estate contains mention of raw materials but none of finished products, but no doubt that is because the products were being peddled round the neighbouring country by his own employees. The credit conditions of the period were too primitive to permit of an arrangement such as Beloch suggests. Incidentally we learn from Demosthenes that under certain circumstances the producer might be prepared to sell from stock not merely finished articles but also raw materials, such as ivory, iron, wood, nutgalls, and bronze.[3] This suggests the further inference that sometimes a workshop owner was in the first instance simply an importer of scarce materials for sale to independent craftsmen, and that he only manufactured himself when he could not find a buyer.[4] On the other hand, we have no right to describe these buyers as 'manufacturers.'[5]

---

[1] *Cf.* Dem., xxvii, § 21. [2] *G.G.*, iii, 1, 319, n. 2.
[3] Dem., *ibid.*, § 32.
[4] M. Weber in *Handw. d. Staatswiss.*[3], i, 55; *Wirtsch. u. Gesellsch.*, p. 214.
[5] Beloch, *op. cit.*, p. 320, n. 2. Laqueur holds (*Hellenismus ; Schriften d. Hess. Hochschule*, 1925, pp. 30 ff.) (*a*) that the slave-owner, so far from himself being actively concerned in the enterprises carried on in the work-shops, as a general rule left to his slaves even the selling of the products and merely collected from them a share of the proceeds (as in the ἀποφορά

The number of slaves in Athens who were trained in various forms of production was very considerable, even by the end of the fifth century; for Thucydides tells us that of the twenty thousand slaves who deserted to Sparta during the occupation of Decelea a large part were craftsmen.[1] Not all of these hand-workers, indeed, can have been employed directly in workshops. Many of them no doubt worked independently, merely paying their masters a certain proportion of their earnings.[2] Still we may reasonably conclude from the figure Thucydides gives that Athens was already well supplied in his time with small manufacturing establishments of the kind we have been examining. But here again, let us observe, we have no evidence of large factories employing anything up to a hundred and twenty men such as the current accounts of Greek history postulate. We hear of wealthy men owning several hundred slaves—Philemonides owned three hundred, Hipponicus six hundred, Nicias and Mnason of Phocis each a thousand [3]—but there is not the slightest suggestion in our sources that they were employed in the large scale production of manufactured goods. On the contrary, we know that Philemonides, Hipponicus and Nicias hired their slaves out to various private people for work in the silver mines, and lived as *rentiers* on the income thus yielded them; [4] and as for the slaves of Mnason, however many they may in actual fact have been, what we are told is that they worked 'in his estates'— which presumably means that they included domestic servants and agricultural labourers as well as industrial producers.[5]

system, see below, p. 77) ; (*b*) that citizen owners of workshops did not carry stocks of its output ; (*c*) that the only entrepreneurs in the whole system were the traders who adopted a kind of 'domestic system' similar to that which was common in the Middle Ages, and bought up the products as soon as the process of production was started. This account is un-supported by any evidence, and seems to me to be wholly erroneous.

[1] vii, 27, 5.

[2] This was known as the ἀποφορά system. Beloch gives examples of it in iii, 1, 323.

[3] Xen., *Vect.*, iv, 14 ; (Mnason) Timæus *ap.* Athen., vi, 264*d*.

[4] Whence the proposal in Xen., *Vect.* (*loc. cit.*), that the State should make use of publicly owned slaves in the same way, and so add to its revenues.

[5] Oertel, *Anhang*, p. 527, n. 4.

It seems certain that even in the fourth century manufacturing was primarily designed to meet local needs. There was no question of any extensive division of labour between state and state. This is well shown in Xenophon's discussion of the greater possibilities of specialisation in a large than in a small city. 'In small cities the same man makes beds, doors, tables and ploughs, and often he builds houses as well, and is happy if he can secure enough custom to earn his maintenance by his labours; but it is impossible, however, that a man who follows many occupations should be able to do them all well. In large cities, on the other hand, owing to the greater extent of the market, one single trade is enough to yield a livelihood— or not even a single trade but only a part of it, as when one shoemaker makes only for men, another only for women, or even sometimes one even lives exclusively by cutting out leather, another by stitching it, or one man lives by cutting cloth, another by sewing the pieces into coats. When a man has confined himself to a small part of a craft in this way, he is able to do that part most skilfully.' [1] The whole assumption here is that small and large cities alike must supply all their daily needs from the labours of their own inhabitants.

On the other hand, it is equally beyond question that some goods were produced with a view to sale abroad. Practical experience must have made the Greeks quite familiar with the idea of production for export, and the reasons which might make it necessary. As Plato says, 'And if the citizens are to get what they need from other people, their agent must take with him something that those others want. If he go empty-handed, he will return empty-handed. . . . Therefore, the workers of our city must not only make enough for home consumption; they must also produce goods of the number and kind required by other people. . . . Thus our city will need more farmers, and more of all the other craftsmen.' [2] In this passage, evidently, the articles to be produced in excess of local need include both agricultural produce and manufactured goods.

[1] Xen., *Cyrop.*, viii, 2, 5.   [2] *Rep.*, 370e–371a.

Production for export, then, was a perfectly ordinary phenomenon of Greek economic life during this period. The only
question is how extensively and regularly it was carried on.
In particular, did it or did it not include articles of common
everyday need? On this point the *Republic* does not help us.
We hear from Demosthenes, however, of a law proposed by
Timarchus imposing the death penalty on anyone who exported
weapons or naval supplies to Philip of Macedon.[1] Bücher tries
to dispose of this by the argument that the materials of war in
question need not have been new.[2] But this seems to be mere
special pleading. Plato himself in the *Laws* [3] justifies both the
import and the export of arms—the latter on the ground that
the ideal city ought to 'give as well as to receive.' And when
we remember the shield-making establishments of Lysias and
Pasion—and Pasion was a man of sufficient wealth to be the
owner of several ships—we shall not, perhaps, be inclined to
doubt the existence of a fairly active international traffic in
arms.

Commodities of this sort, however, are only in a rather
special sense articles of everyday need. We may find elsewhere references to trading in goods of a more peaceful nature.
Xenophon tells us, though we need not take him too literally,
that most of the inhabitants of Megara lived by making vests—
i.e. clothes *of a particular kind*.[4] Again the Athenian export
trade in pottery was sufficiently extensive for both the Argives
and the Æginetans, as a demonstration of hostility, to put a
ban upon the introduction of Attic products into their temples,
and upon drinking out of any except native earthenware.[5] We
may also quote here Antiphanes' reference, in the fourth
century, to 'ointment from Athens.' [6] And finally, it is
worth while pointing out that each city would provide the
manufactured articles required by the peasants in the surrounding country, and to that extent at least must have had an export
trade in manufactures.

---

[1] Dem., xix, § 286.   [2] *Beiträge*, p. 28.   [3] 847*d*.
[4] *Mem.*, ii, 7.   ἐξώμιδες were worn by poor men and slaves.
[5] Hdt., ỿ, 88.   [6] *Ap.* Athen., i, 27*e* [Kock, fr. 236].

Nor, on the other side, can we deny, with Bücher, that Athens *imported* industrial raw materials of various kinds. Demosthenes tells us of wood that was imported by Timotheus from Macedonia; and we know that his own workshop made use of iron and ivory from abroad.[1] Let us observe, too, that Plato (*Laws*, 847b, c) in drawing up the laws for his second-best state makes a specific regulation against the importation of 'incense and aromatics for the service of the gods, and all foreign articles which are required in the production of un-necessary articles.'[2] Plato would not have required to make this prohibition, if the import of raw materials for manufacture had not been frequent and normal in the actually existing cities of his time.

Still we have no right to draw from these evidences ex-aggerated ideas as to the extent of Greek export trade and the development of production for international markets. Beloch, following Boeckh, has boldly tried to arrive by purely arith-metical means at an estimate of the foreign trade of Athens, and the value of its imports and exports.[3] But his calculations ignore the two factors which must have been decisive in determining the character of Greek economic life and the evolution of Greek industry and commerce. Production on a large scale requires an extensive market and a demand com-mensurate with the supply; and it requires a well-developed commercial technique. In classical Greece neither of these

[1] Dem., xlix, § 34 ff. ; Oertel, *Anhang*, p. 519.

[2] *Cf.* the distinction in Isocrates (iv, 40) between crafts which are ' useful for providing necessities of life,' and those which are ' devised to give pleasure.'

[3] In *Jahrb. f. Nat. u. Stat.*, 3rd Series, xviii (1899), pp. 626 ff. Cf. *G.G.*, iii, 2, 424 ff. The reliability of Beloch's figures—he estimates the trading activity of the Piræus at 2000 talents in 399/8 B.C., and at least 4000 talents in the time of Alexander—has been disputed by Weber, *Handw. d. Staat-swiss.*[3], i, 54, and particularly by Bücher (pp. 17 ff.) and Oertel (pp. 521 ff.). The material available is not nearly adequate for a statistical approach, and nearly all the figures on which Beloch thinks himself able to reckon are uncertain. The papyri have given us further opportunity of recognising how complicated was the ancient system of tax-farming; and it is upon this farming of import and export duties in the Piræus and upon the sums paid by individuals for these rights that Beloch's whole calculation is based.

conditions was satisfied. Not merely was the market practically limited to the coastal areas, but the standard of living, even within these areas, was extremely low, and the needs of the ordinary people for manufactured goods could most naturally be satisfied by local handwork.[1] And, on the other hand, the methods of carrying on inter-district trade were so primitive as to put entirely out of question the possibility of an extended division of labour between state and state, at least as regards the cheap and easily produced articles of everyday need. We must conclude, therefore, that the areas of production and consumption remained in essence the same during the fifth and fourth centuries as they had been before the Persian Wars. The reason for this was, of course, political. The ideal of the city-state was always isolation and self-sufficiency; and so long as there was no international organisation uniting the whole Greek world, it was only to be expected that any tendencies towards economic internationalism should be stifled at their birth. Not until the Hellenistic period, with its large political empires, do we find Greek commerce and industry free from its shackles and able to expand beyond the narrow limits of the city-state. Before that time there is little trace of economic progress. If the general advance of civilisation had its material side, it was not sufficiently far-reaching or important for us to be able to define it clearly or mark its stages.

The form and extent of fourth-century trade has been fully dealt with elsewhere.[2] What strikes one most forcibly in it is its simplicity and exiguousness. The difficulties of sea traffic (and still more of land traffic) were too great to admit of the growth of transport and shipping companies such as are characteristic of modern times. Greek merchants were compelled themselves to convey and accompany their wares. We do, indeed, hear of individuals who owned more than one ship, and who, therefore, like the merchants of the Middle Ages, might have to leave the transporting of their wares to

[1] Oertel, *Anhang*, p. 523 ; Bolkestein, *Het economisch Leven*, p. 79.
[2] *Hermes*, 1923, pp. 393 ff.

6

representatives or supercargoes; just as we hear of ships which carried a captain and a helmsman as well as the owner himself and his merchant passengers. But the typical merchant ship-owner had to rely entirely upon himself. He had no foreign correspondents or central commodity exchange to supply him with news about market conditions abroad. For that he had to rely upon the chance information he might pick up from friends and acquaintances.[1] And he was his own captain, helmsman, and commercial traveller.

As we might expect, the costs of commerce were as great as its facilities were small.[2] The chief cause of this was the high rate of interest on commercial loans. Being a merchant was a hazardous occupation,[3] and investors had to be promised high premiums before they would lend money for enterprises which were likely to end in failure and disaster. The borrower might be trustworthy, but the sea (and still more the land) was not. Right through the classical period, and increasingly as time went on, ships were liable to be molested by warring powers, or seized as reprisals by hostile states, or captured by pirates.[4] And in any case the voyaging season never lasted more than six months.[5] From October to March no Greek ship ventured out to sea. During these months, therefore, the states were to all intents and purposes wholly cut off from one another. This being so, it is difficult to see how they would ever have become to any significant extent economically interdependent.

To the difficulties of the voyage one must add the still

---

[1] In this respect the powerful Cleomenes of Naucratis was an exception. He had agents in various ports to advise him of the movements of local prices, and thus was able to some extent to plan his voyages beforehand and avoid the risk of sending goods to places where there was no demand for them.

[2] Demosthenes tells us, for instance (xlix, § 29), that as much as 1750 drachmæ was paid for conveying wood from Macedonia to Athens.

[3] Dem., xxxiii, § 4.

[4] E.g. in Demosthenes : (1) the ship that was captured in the Gulf of Argos on its way to Libya, its cargo stolen, and its owner killed (lii, § 3 ff.) ; (2) the fate of Nicostratus when pursuing his runaway slaves (liii, § 6) ; (3) the activities of the citizens of Byzantium, Cyzicus, and Rhodes during a temporary dearth of corn (l, §§ 6, 17 ; Lyc., c. Leocr., § 18).

[5] Dem., xxxiii, § 23.

greater difficulties which attended the disposal of the cargo. Goods were never exported from abroad on order. When a merchant put out to sea he did not know in what port he would be able to make sales. Markets could only be found if he took his wares with him and could display them to potential buyers.[1] Moreover, he had no certainty of being able to secure an acceptable return cargo. This has always been an important problem for commerce, and it was especially so in ancient Greece, where, right down to the third century,[2] the money of various states had a purely local validity and was normally worth considerably more [3] in legal value than in metallic content.[4] Under these circumstances, to be compelled to carry away coin instead of goods as a return on his sales involved the merchant in considerable loss.

And as a result commercial specialisation was quite impossible in the Greek world. Traders bought and sold whatever articles seemed, in view of the demand in the various markets, and the prevailing prices, to promise the greatest profits. Xenophon says of the corn-dealers [5]: 'Wherever they hear that corn is most plentiful,' and therefore lowest in price, 'they sail thither, crossing the Ægean, the Euxine or the Sicilian Sea, and take of it as much as they can on their ships for cargo. And when they have need of converting it into money they do not part with it wherever they may chance

[1] In Euripides' *Cyclops* (l. 137), Odysseus calls upon Silenus to bring out his wares : 'goods are not to be bought in the dark.' The 'Deigma', where goods were displayed for sale, meant originally only a sample (Harpocr., *s.v.*). The trader only takes samples ashore with him. See Knorringa's *Emporos* (Utrecht, 1926), p. 29. [This dissertation is written in English.]

[2] As we see from Xen., *Vect.*, iii, 2.

[3] The only exceptions of which we know were the Attic drachmæ.

[4] See for a typical example of Greek monetary policy the (fourth century) law of Olbia (below, p. 156). According to the regulations there given, coins might be freely imported and exported ; but no money other than that minted by the city might be used in internal trade. In other words, the city reserved to itself the issue of legal tender coin, and presumably by charging more for it than it was intrinsically worth, secured a handsome seignorage. We need not doubt that most other Greek states supported their tottering finances in the same way—as did the lords of the Middle Ages.

[5] *Econ.*, xx, 27.

to be, but carry it to those places where they hear that it is most highly prized and most eagerly demanded, and there they dispose of it.' Their activities were hedged about with dangers and uncertainties.[1] They were at the mercy of pirates and warships, and of the chance demands of their customers. They could not protect themselves against disastrous falls in the value of their merchandise during the time of its transportation. We need not be surprised, then, that their creditors not merely exacted high rates of interest but also demanded as security cargo mortgages to amounts well in excess of the loan.

It seems clear, therefore, that the whole structure of Greek commerce was of an extreme simplicity. There were no large shipping companies as in the mediæval or modern world. The ordinary merchant, if he owned a ship at all, either owned it entirely himself or shared it with at most two or three partners, commonly members of his own family. Nor had he extensive trade relations with his fellows in other respects. The merchants' unions of which we hear (particularly in Athens) were not gilds or Trade Unions, but cult associations. There is scarcely a trace of any attempt among merchants at joint action for commercial ends, except of a most ephemeral kind.

And if commerce in ancient Greece was rudimentary and undeveloped, so also was finance. We have already seen that each state had its own currency, and that usually these currencies were more or less depreciated. The Greeks were accustomed to money which was constantly falling in value and which had a legal purchasing power considerably higher than its intrinsic worth. The Aristotelian *Economics* (1345*b*, 22) gives extreme examples of the use of substitutes for gold and silver in the coins issued by states and rulers; and Demosthenes speaks of this as something normal and natural.[2] Plato in the *Laws*

---

[1] *Cf.* the terms of the bottomry contract in Dem., *c. Lacr.*, § 10 ff.

[2] Dem., xxiv, § 214 : 'Many states openly use money which is mixed with copper and lead, and suffer no hurt or damage therefrom.' (*Cf.* for Athens, Aristoph., *Ran.*, 720 ff., *Eccles.*, 815 ff., and see below, p. 157.) The writer of the Aristotelian *Economics* appears to say—though the translation is not certain—that the central problem in monetary policy which kings (and presumably also cities) have to face is whether coins shall be worth their face value or not.

(742*a*) decides to allow the co-existence of a local currency
and a Panhellenic currency for inter-state dealings. And
Xenophon puts the matter beyond all doubt by saying that
'most cities' issued coins which, unlike the Athenian drachmæ,
could not be used outside their own territory.[1] Thus the effect-
ing of international payments was hampered and complicated
by the difficulty of finding money which could circulate from
one state to another.

Banking businesses seem to have been a regular part of
Greek economic life, though they were scarcely as well developed in ancient times as in the later Middle Ages.[2] In
Athens, for example, the banks fulfilled many different functions.
They undertook the business of money changing;[3] they acted
as intermediaries for the payment of debts (this must have
brought them into financial relations with one another—though
there is no evidence of their having established a clearing-house
for the cancellation of reciprocal obligations);[4] they acted as

---

[1] *Vect.*, iii, 2.

[2] See *Hermes*, 1920, pp. 113 ff., for a full discussion of the banking system
of classical Greece.

[3] This was the original business from which banking sprang in Greece
as in the Middle Ages. As the banks grew it became less and less important,
and the most developed of them—*e.g.* that of Pasion—seem to have abandoned
it altogether.

[4] Oertel agrees with me (*Anhang*, p. 530, n. 3) that we have undoubted
evidence for saying that in the fourth century (*a*) money was deposited with
banks not with a view to bearing interest, but to be paid to third parties—
i.e., the bank would pay out in cash on receipt of verbal instructions from
its depositors ; (*b*) banks used to act as cashiers for their customers on
receipt of such deposits, settlements being made periodically between them.
The question arises, however, whether we can go further than that, and
maintain the existence of a chequing system in the same period. Some
years ago I accepted this view (in *Hermes*, 1920, pp. 117 ff.) ; but I am
bound to admit that no concrete case is known to us in which two customers
of a bank settled their indebtedness to one another by means of transferences
in the bank's books. I believe, however, that one is entitled to argue from
the existence of paying out by cheque from deposit amounts to the existence
of the completer form of the chequing system (see *Klio*, xviii, pp. 375 ff.), both
because of the fourth-century use of διαγράφειν = διὰ τῆς τραπέζης ἀριθμεῖν and
also because the only way in which a banker could discharge a debt to one
customer on behalf of another would be by crediting the amount paid to
the account of the recipient. He would not be likely to have enough till-
money to be able to pay the sums involved in cash. Attic bankers of this

guarantors of their customers' liabilities; they accepted and paid interest on savings deposits;[1] they took objects and documents of value into safe-keeping; and finally, they made loans of all kinds—commercial loans, accommodation loans, security loans, mortgage loans, loans on private and public credit. The traces which we find, moreover, of the existence in them of 'sleeping' partners or shareholders shows that they had begun to develop some form of organisation. Yet when all is said we cannot speak of anything like a credit system in ancient Greece.[2]

The clearing of international debts by means of bills of exchange (such as we find in the later Middle Ages) was practically unknown. Nor had the Athenian banks branches

time used to enter sums in their books as (simply) ' deposited ' and ' withdrawn ' (τιθέναι, λαμβάνειν, Dem., lii, § 4, xlix, § 5) ; but as in his other book entries, so here, no cash transfers need have been involved (provided that both the payer and the payee were his customers).

Be that as it may, however, we are certainly entitled to call the Greek system a deposit banking system ; since in ordinary usage this expression is used to cover any arrangement whereby a bank disposes of a customer's deposits on his behalf and by his advice. What we are not justified in doing is to assert with Oertel that these advices took the form of written cheques. Even the big deposit banks of Hamburg and Amsterdam expected their customers' instructions to be given in person, as also did the Italian banks of the Middle Ages (see Nesse, *Handw. d. Staatsw.*[3], ii, 329). In both these cases the payer accompanied the recipient to the bank to authorise him to collect what was due to him. The advantage of the modern deposit bank, it is true, rests as much in the facilities it provides for payments by cheque as in its avoidance of cash transfers ; in more primitive times it rested rather in the fact that the banker would guard against debasements and manipulations on the part of the minting authorities in a way which was rarely possible to the private trader, and also that he could keep the rates of exchange between different coinage systems from unnecessary fluctuations, and secure to his customers the payment of their debts in standard coin. Not merely that : but, conditions being what they were, to carry one's money on deposit at a bank offered greater external security than keeping it in private houses or employing it on the open market. (*Hermes, loc. cit.*, pp. 116 ff.)

It is going too far, on the other hand, to suggest, as I once did (*ibid.*, p. 139), that the bankers may have developed a clearing-house system for the mutual cancellation of their debts.

[1] This was a recognised way in which *rentiers* invested their capital, and quite large sums were often so invested.

[2] See Oertel, *Anhang*, p. 530.

in other places, between which to transfer deposits.   In fact there were no international credit dealings.   Money could only be remitted from city to city by the costly and dangerous method of specie transfers.[1]   Again the lending business of the Greek banker seems to have been largely confined to the occasional accommodation of personal friends, and his deposit business was no doubt equally restricted, for most people in the fourth century preferred to keep their capital in their own homes.   And similarly with his other activities.   There is no evidence for the belief, which has sometimes been held, that he was a qualified broker or attorney or that his ledgers were admissible in evidence like those of Roman or mediæval banks. Unlike the Athenian bankers of the Roman Empire he did not undertake to collect debts or administer property for foreign clients, nor did he perform the functions of the Roman 'argentarius' at public auctions.   Moreover, banking was not at this time a matter of public concern, except in so far as the government reserved for itself the monopoly of business in the exchange of foreign currency.

The same sort of thing is true of credit conditions in general. Commercial life can only flourish on a basis of security and confidence between creditors and debtors, and this was wholly lacking in the Greek world.   Even in time of peace it was easy to avoid the payment of legal obligations,[2] for there was no international court in which they could be enforced, and the countless local city courts were prejudiced and unreliable. And peace might at any time give way to war, during which these courts suspended their activities.[3]   Or a revolution, like a war, might bring with it the renunciation of debts all round. Moreover, it is to be remembered that international credit dealings were commonly hedged about with statutory restrictions.   In Athens, for example, it was illegal to lend money

---

[1] For the actual transport of specie from Halicarnassus to Alexandria in Hellenistic times, see the Zeno Papyrus, 67, l. 6 (*Annales du Service des Antiquités de l'Egypte*, xxii).   Edgar rightly understands this as meaning an overseas shipment.

[2] Dem., xxxv, § 1 ff.

[3] Lys., xvii, 3.

to merchants not engaged upon the conveyance of goods to or from Athens itself. The State was determined that none of its capital resources should be used for the benefit of foreigners, and with this end in view did not hesitate to interfere with the free development of commerce and credit.

A still further illustration of the primitiveness of Greek economic life is to be seen in the attitude of the community to capital holdings and accumulations.[1] Not merely were property owners continually threatened with the danger of revolutions and wholesale confiscations, they were also subject even in normal times to large and reckless inroads and demands upon their wealth on the part of the State. Apart from the regular taxes about which we hear so many well-grounded complaints throughout the fifth and fourth centuries, they might be called upon at any time to submit to special exactions or to undertake heavy public responsibilities or 'liturgies'. Men naturally tried to avoid these unparalleled burdens by every means in their power. And therefore we find the concealment of wealth was a regular and ordinary practice in ancient Greece.

It was a dangerous thing to be known as a person of great riches (as the Attic orators show forcibly enough), and people were in general prepared to go to considerable lengths in order to hide the extent of their possessions and so protect them from the unwelcome attentions of the community. The economic consequence of this was twofold. In the first place, a large part of the capital of the community was kept in the form of gold or silver and was never used for productive purposes at all. And, secondly, in so far as it was not simply left idle, it was invested in such a way as to be as far as possible 'invisible',[2] that is to say, it was lent at interest. Used in this way it was out of sight and so was safe from popular greed. Here we have the explanation of the importance of the money-lending in ancient Greece, notwithstanding the grave risks

---

[1] See on this *Hermes*, 1920, pp. 145, 155 ff. *Cf.* Oertel, *Anhang*, p. 529.

[2] ἀφανὴς οὐσία = money out on loan ; *cf.* τὰς ἐργασίας ἀφανεῖς ποιεῖσθαι, to invest one's capital in someone else's plant.

involved. No limit was imposed on the rate of interest which a creditor might charge, and capital lent to finance commercial enterprises might in a short space of time yield profits of two or three hundred per cent. Hence the tendency of wealthy people to act as financiers rather than as merchants or industrialists and to leave to others less fortunately situated than themselves the carrying out of the operations from which they drew their revenue.[1] Greek trade and industry was not sufficiently well developed to attract the active interest of the well-to-do. It was a source of income to them, as it was to the State,[2] but apart from that they had no part nor share in it whatever.

Finally, as we have seen,[3] Greek merchants were for the most part illiterate and carried on their activities without the help of written documents. This is yet one more indication of the general level of Greek commerce. Until the Hellenistic period the granting of receipts for payments made was wholly unknown. Before then, no trader delivered goods, no banker contracted loans, except in the presence of witnesses.[4] When goods were deposited on trust no written acknowledgment was given, and charges of embezzlement of trust funds were common in the civil courts. Only in bottomry loans do we find evidence of the use of written contracts—and in view of the complexity of the terms on which these loans were made, we need not be surprised that they were an exception.

The lack of written documents added still further to the difficulties of enforcing commercial obligations at law. This is illustrated in many of the speeches of the Attic orators. The merchants whom we encounter there are people without culture or training. Like many of the ordinary citizens of this period, they could neither read nor write much less keep

---

[1] 'Commerce thrives on the lenders, not on the borrowers,' Dem., xxxiv, § 51. *Cf.* lvi, § 48, on the necessity of moneylenders for trade (above, p. 7).

[2] In the form of tolls and dues—*cf.* Xen., *Vect.*, iii, 5 (see above, p. 25).

[3] See above, p. 10.

[4] Dem., xxxviii, § 12 : 'Who would be so foolish as of his own free will to pay money on a written order ?' Cf. *ibid.*, § 14.

accounts.[1] The complicated arts of accounting and book-keeping must have been known only to a few exceptional financiers like Pasion.

We may conclude this chapter by saying something of the actual goods which were exchanged in international trade. Let us confine our attention to Athens and the Piræus.

A. Imports:

1. Pericles in a famous passage says: 'Owing to the greatness of our city we draw from the produce of the whole earth, and it falls to us to enjoy the goods of foreign lands as readily as those of Attica itself.'[2] Classen has pointed out that spiritual as well as material produce is included among the 'goods of foreign lands.' In support of this we may quote Plato's description of the 'needs of the soul' which are to be satisfied, like the needs of the body, by international exchange, and of the spiritual goods—music, painting, knowledge and the like—in which trade of this sort deals.[3]

2. The comic writer Hermippus, a contemporary of Pericles, gives the following list of goods which were imported into Athens:[4] silphium and hides from Cyrene; mackerel and salted fish from the Hellespont; spelt and beef from Italy; the itch from Sitalces of Thrace (a present for Sparta); ship-loads of lies from Perdiccas of Macedon; pigs and cheese from Syracuse; sails and papyrus from Egypt; incense from Syria; cypresses for the gods from Crete; ivory from Libya; raisins and dried figs (bringers of sweet dreams) from Rhodes; pears and fat sheep from Eubœa; slaves from Phrygia; mercenaries from Arcadia; slaves and branded rogues from Pagasæ; chestnuts and oily almonds from Paphlagonia; dates and fine wheaten flour from Phœnicia; carpets and coloured pillows from Carthage.

This list is not a mere jest of the poet.[5] Athenæus, it is

---

[1] The same thing was true in mediæval Italy till the thirteenth century and in the rest of Europe till the time of the Renaissance. See Sombart, *Moderne Kapitalismus*, i, 295 ff.

[2] Thuc., ii, 38.

[3] *Soph.*, 223*e*; note the bold use of words such as ψυχεμπορική, μαθηματοπωλική, τεχνοπωλικόν.

[4] *Ap.* Athen., i, 27*e* [Kock, fr. 63 ; Pickard-Cambridge, fr. 5].

[5] As Bücher holds (*Beiträge*, p. 26).

true, quotes it as showing the special products of the various places mentioned; he is not concerned in this or in his other citations with their commercial significance. But the words of Hermippus himself make it clear that all these articles were actually Athenian imports.[1]

3. The author of the Xenophontean *Athenian Constitution*, writing at about the same time as Hermippus, says: 'Blights upon crops, such as Zeus sends down from Heaven, bear hardly upon states that rule the land, but lightly upon those that rule the sea. For they do not descend on all countries at once, and so if a power controls the sea it can import from places where the harvest has prospered. Moreover, if one may mention less important matters, the Athenians by reason of their maritime greatness, and the journeyings and dealings of their citizens, have learnt to increase the comforts of their life. Whatever of the products of Sicily, Italy, Cyprus, Egypt, Lydia, Pontus, the Peloponnese, or anywhere else is pleasant ($\dot{\eta}\delta\dot{\upsilon}$), they have been enabled by this circumstance to gather together in one place.[2] . . . The wealth of the whole world, Greek and barbarian, is in the hands of the Athenians. If a country is rich in timber for ships, can it sell it anywhere without the permission of the ruler of the seas? If it is rich in iron or copper or hemp or wax can it sell these? These are precisely the materials from which ships are made—timber is bought from one place, iron from another, copper, hemp, and wax from others. Therefore we must either forbid such things to be exported to our rivals or else we must close the sea to them altogether.[3] By the help of the sea all these things come to me without effort on my part; since no country other than Athens is rich in more than one of them; but rather if it has flax in plenty then it is flat and lacks timber, and if it has iron then it has no copper, and so with other goods; no country

---

[1] ὅσσ' ἀγάθ' ἀνθρώποις δεῦρ' ἤγαγε [Διόνυσος] νηὶ μελαίνῃ—Dionysus being regarded as patron saint of ships.

[2] [Xen.], *Resp. Ath.*, ii, 6–12.

[3] This is the only possible translation of the corrupt passage. See Stail, *Die Pseudo-Xenophontische* Ἀθηναίων Πολιτεία, 1921, p. 50 ff.

abounds in several things, but this article is produced in one country, that in another.'[1]

4. Aristophanes speaks of the following articles as sold on the Athenian market by peasants from Bœotia—not from the country districts of Attica: marjoram, pennyroyal, mats, wicks, ducks, daws, godwits, coots, wrens, doves, geese, hares, foxes, moles, hedgehogs, cats, squirrels, weasels, otters, Copaic eels.[2]

5. The same writer also enumerates the following foreign goods which as soon as peace is declared can be offered once more for sale on the Athenian market: onions, early cucumbers, apples, pomegranates, slaves' tunics; and, in addition, the products of Bœotia: geese, ducks, pigeons, plovers, and baskets of Copaic eels.[3]

It is to be remarked that with the exception of the hides of Cyrene mentioned by Hermippus, none of the commodities listed in these passages are in any sense raw materials for industry. The writer of the *Athenian Constitution* explicitly states that the iron, copper, hemp, and wax of which he speaks are intended for the building of ships of war; and apart from these the only import to which he refers is corn. The same thing can be said of the imports of which we hear in the speeches of the Attic orators. They seem to have been exclusively articles of food (usually luxuries and dainties) or else manufactured goods,[4] rare articles of various kinds, and slaves.

B. Exports:

1. Olive oil, as is well known, was from the earliest times exported from Attica. It was the only form of agricultural produce the export of which was permitted by Solon.[5]

2. Attic wool was famous and no doubt was sold in many

---

[1] *Ibid.*, 11–13.
[2] *Ach.*, 870 ff. These articles are later (974 ff.) described by the chorus as 'articles of trade, some useful in the house, some good to eat when warmed.' The whole list is, of course, elaborated for comic effect.
[3] *Pax*, 999 ff.
[4] *Cf.* above, in the catalogues of Aristophanes, slaves' tunics, mats and wicks, and in that of Hermippus, carpets, pillows and sails.
[5] Plut., *Solon*, 24.

different parts of the world. We are told that Polycrates imported Attic as well as Milesian sheep into Samos.[1]

3. Attic wine must also have been produced for export.

4. The author of the *de Vectigalibus* urges that the state in order to increase its revenues should export:

(*a*) Such agricultural produce as can flourish in the soil of Attica but in most places never grows at all;

(*b*) marine products;

(*c*) and, above all, marble, 'for many people have need of it, both Greeks and foreigners.'[2]

It is most significant that it never occurs to this writer, in his search for articles which might bring wealth to the community, to mention industrial products or manufactured goods.

5. The Athenian in the *Acharnians* of Aristophanes asks the Bœotian whether he will accept Athenian goods, instead of money, to take back with him to Thebes. 'Yes,' the Bœotian replies, 'anything which is produced in Athens but not in Bœotia.' 'Sardines and pottery, for instance?' 'No, we have those already; but something which we do not possess but you have abundantly.'[3]

Now it is maintained by Beloch[4] and others that apart from olive oil practically no agricultural or mineral produce was exported from Attica, and therefore that the Athenians must have paid for their imports with manufactured goods. Francotte has shown the weakness of this argument.[5] Isocrates, in contrasting the economic development of Athens and Megara, explains that the Megarians became rich in spite of having a barren soil, no harbours, and no silver-mines. To Isocrates,[6] therefore, the source of Athenian wealth was the land of Attica, the trade of the Piræus (through the duties and tolls which were paid on it), and the mines of Laurium.[7] This evidence becomes conclusive when we remember that these are the three sources of revenue upon which the writer of the *de Vectigalibus* wished the state to draw in order to make

[1] Alexis, *ap*. Athen., xii, 540*d*.   [2] Xen., *Vect.*, i, 2–4.

[3] Ar., *Ach.*, 899 ff.   [4] *G.G.*, iii, 1, 326.   [5] *L'Industrie*, i, 117 ff.

[6] viii, § 117.   [7] *Cf*. Oertel, *Anhang*, p. 535.

up for the decline in the payments of tribute from the Empire.

Athens, then, was not a centre of Greek industry, it was not primarily an industrial state at all, but its position made it the focus of Mediterranean and Pontic commerce. It was a place of exchange, not of production.[1] This is the meaning of the words of Pericles, quoted above. As Isocrates says, 'no land is in every respect self-supporting, but each lacks some things and produces others in excess. Hence it is hard to determine whither to send the goods that are abundant and whence to secure those that are scarce. In this difficulty Athens provides assistance, for she has established a market at the central point of Greece, in the Piræus, which has so great a supply of goods that all things can be readily obtained there together, which are hard to bring severally from other places.'[2] And finally, we have the testimony of the *de Vectigalibus*, 'every wind brings her the goods which she lacks and carries away those which she will sell elsewhere. . . . And by land, too, she receives much through trade. . . .'[3] Traders can secure in Athens goods from any part of the world in exchange for those they wish to sell, 'for what is difficult to bring from other lands can more readily be obtained from Athens.'[4] We have no means of determining when the commercial importance of other Greek ports reached its highest point, or how nearly it approached that of the Piræus; but it is clear at least that Athens was the great central exchange of the whole Greek world of commerce.

That is to say, then, the trade of Greece in classical times was extensive enough to provide the State with an appreciable part of its revenue through tolls and dues, to yield a substantial income to private investors, and to require the whole-time services of a class of professional merchants. It is one of the most conspicuous gaps in our knowledge of Greek

[1] *Cf.* Wachsmuth, *Jahrb. f. Nat. u. Stat.*, New Series, xiii (1886), p. 90 ; Bücher, *Beiträge*, p. 30.

[2] Isoc., *Panegyr.*, § 42.   [3] Xen., *Vect.*, i, 7.

[4] We are expressly told that of the corn brought into Piræus as much as a third might be re-exported.

economic life that we cannot tell the average value of the goods which these merchants handled. But we must not under-estimate it, as Bücher does, at any rate for the fourth century. The evidence is as follows:—

(*a*) The amounts of the bottomry loans of which we hear in the Attic orators tend to be from 2000 to 5000 drachmæ. The value of the goods by which these loans were secured must have been considerably higher, and may have been anything from 3000 to 10,000 drachmæ.[1]

(*b*) Demosthenes' speech against Phormio (§ 7) contains a contract whereby a borrower agreed to buy in as security for his loan goods to the value of 15,000 drachmæ. This is not, however, a wholly genuine example, for in actual fact he spent only 3500 drachmæ on goods, and on the strength of them illegally raised a further sum of money.

(*c*) Lysias speaks in one place of a shipment of goods worth 12,000 drachmæ.[2]

(*d*) In the speech against Lacritus (Dem., xxxv, § 10) we are given information as to the amount of goods hypothecated: 3000 jars of the wine of Mende as security for a loan of 3000 drachmæ.

(*e*) The freight ship mentioned in the speech against Phormio (Dem., xxxiv, § 10) was large enough to have more than three hundred persons on board.[3]

(*f*) Thucydides (iv, 118.5) speaks of a ship with a load of 500 talents (about 13 tons) as small. In the fifth century a large ship might carry twenty times as much.[4]

---

[1] Possibly even more ; loans may have been limited to one-third of the value of the security (see Boeckh, i, 169, note a). See the author's remarks in *Hermes* (1923), p. 412.

[2] Lys., xxxii, 25, ὁλκάδα δυοῖν ταλάντοιν. The further context suggests that this may possibly represent the amount of the loan, not the value of the cargo—which, if so, would be still higher.

[3] Reading τριακόσια with S vulg. (see article in *Hermes*, lviii, p. 401). The Oxford text, and that of Dindorf-Blass wrongly read τριάκοντα with mg. ed. Paris a. 1570. We may compare with this passage Plut., *Dion*, 25, where it is stated that Dion transported some 800 soldiers in two cargo vessels.

[4] Thuc., vii, 25 ; Köster, *Das antike Seewesen*, pp. 161 ff. ; Knorringa, *Emporos*, p. 61 (Utrecht, 1926) ; see also my remarks in *Hermes* (1923),

Thus it appears that goods were exchanged between different parts of the Greek world in considerable quantities. But all the passages which we have cited are concerned exclusively with trade in corn, and it would be fatal to argue from the existence of a flourishing corn trade to the existence of trade in industrial products. For that, there is no evidence whatever. We know that in the fourth century commerce in general, in spite of high transport costs, heavy taxation and constant insecurity, yielded an astonishingly high revenue (though not to the merchant himself); and that in itself suggests that its volume was limited in comparison with the commerce of the Middle Ages, when profits were low.[1] We know that it was limited to half the year, that it was to a considerable extent left to non-professionals, that those who took part in it were aliens and poor. Under these conditions it seems clear that there could be no international division of labour or international competition. Trade was not able to bear the burden of conveying raw materials from all parts of the world for manufacture in one industrial centre and of distributing from that centre the completed products. The Greek economy of the classical period was neither commercial nor industrial, but agricultural. Even in Athens in the year 403/2 three-quarters of the citizens were peasants and were accustomed to live on the land.[2]

p. 401. Köster points out that the largest ship to put in at Hamburg in the year A.D. 1369 had a maximum capacity of 120 tons. Incidentally Herodotus mentions ships on the Nile able to carry many thousand talents (ii, 96), and on the Euphrates (i, 194) able to carry five thousand talents (=130 tons).

[1] Sombart, *Moderne Kapitalismus*, i, 608.

[2] 15,000 out of some 20,000 (Lysias, xxxiv, *Hypoth.*). The importance of agriculture throughout the history of this period is properly emphasised by Busolt (*Gr. St.*, i, 153, 178, 191) and Oertel (*Anhang*, p. 536). The audience to which Aristophanes' comedies are addressed is an audience of small farmers (Thuc., ii, 14, 16).

CHAPTER III

COMMERCE AND THE STATE

A. COMMERCIAL POLICY AND SUPPLIES

I. *Foreign Policy*

WE come now to the specific subject of this book, the relation of the State to commerce. We shall have to deal with all those manifestations of general policy which we ordinarily group under the head of commercial policy, with all the ways in which a state can deliberately promote or restrict trade, directly or indirectly, at home or abroad. But, in the first place, we shall consider commercial policy in the narrower sense to which the term is frequently restricted, namely, that department of policy which concerns itself with foreign trade.

Hitherto it has been comfortably assumed that the Greek city had a commercial policy with the same aims as that of a modern state; that the extension of trade and the acquisition of commercial pre-eminence were among the objects of its general policy and were closely bound up with its general development; and that the desire for commercial advantages was really a determinant factor in all its foreign policy, as it is in the modern national state which seeks to secure foreign markets and to maintain its own in order to benefit home production and home labour. Such modern notions of international commercial rivalry have been confidently transferred to the Greek world. We read of the commercial policy of Miletus, Ægina, Athens, Corinth—and this very notably in the earlier periods of Greek history. A few characteristic examples from the leading German historians will serve to illustrate the current view. The oldest trading cities, such as Ephesus, Colophon, Magnesia, Teos, Samos, Chios, appear as rivals of Miletus. The age-long enmity of Samos and

Priene is called a 'commercial feud.' Phocæa 'rapidly out-
stripped the majority of the Ionian merchant cities and opened
up new markets for her goods.' On the mainland Corinth is
said to have been the rival of Eretria, Chalcis, and Corcyra.
Argos 'was the commercial mistress of the smaller communities.' Athens and Chalcis go to war because of 'commercial jealousy.' In the seventh century Ægina 'dominated
Athenian trade.' Athens and Megara are succeeded by
Corinth and Ægina as commercial rivals.[1] The war between
Chalcis and Eretria for the Lelantine Plain is 'a war of rival
trading interests competing for supremacy,' in which Corinth
and Samos intervene upon the Chalcidian side, Miletus,
Megara, and Athens upon the Eretrian. We read of a 'trade
war' which split the Greek world into two camps.[2] After
the fall of the tyrants Corinth pursued, 'like the Netherlands,
a purely mercantile policy which aimed at the commercial
mastery of its hinterland.' 'Corinthian policy is now dominated by one main interest, the maintenance of commercial
communications with East and West.'[3]

In the same way historians have not hesitated to foist commercial policies upon the leaders and statesmen of these times.
Thus with the tyrants: 'For the first time,' says Beloch (*op.
cit.*, p. 357), 'the state recognised the duty of looking to the
material welfare of its citizens by promoting trade.' Under
Peisistratus 'commercial policy was dominant even in Athens';
'extension of Athenian influence in trade was part of his
foreign policy'; 'in every direction he laid down the lines of
Athenian colonial and commercial policy'—a policy 'which
came into collision with the older trading cities.'[4] Under

---

[1] See Meyer, *G.A.*, ii, 433 ff., 764 ff ; Pöhlmann, *G.G.*, p. 94.

[2] Meyer, *op. cit.*, p. 539 ; Pöhlmann, *op. cit.*, p. 50 ; Beloch, *G.G.*,
i, 1, 338. The notion that this was a trade war goes back to Dondorff's *de
Rebus Chalcid.* (Berlin, 1855). His further mythological fantasies in *Die
Ionier auf Euboia* were seen to be excessive as early as Büchsenschütz
(*Bes. u. Erw.*, pp. 370 ff.). [See A. R. Burn, *The so-called 'Trade-leagues'
in Early Greek History and the Lelantine War, J.H.S.*, 1929, pp. 14 ff.]

[3] Meyer, *op. cit.*, p. 627.

[4] Meyer, *op. cit.*, p. 774 ; Pöhlmann, *op. cit.*, p. 88 ; Busolt, *G.G.*,
ii, 331.

Cypselus and Periander Corinth became the first commercial city of the world. Thrasybulus of Miletus encouraged trade with Italy and a close connection with Sybaris. Under Polycrates the trade of Samos steadily advanced, and soon surpassed that of Miletus. Solon, especially by his attack on Megara and his conquest of Salamis, 'inaugurated a commercial policy,' and his legislation had 'markedly commercial aims.'[1] In short, modern historians invite us to accept a picture of the Greek world from the eighth century to the sixth—I have restricted my examples to this period—which is painted after the Europe of to-day: a picture of antagonisms between national states fighting each for its own economic advancement, of struggles for markets, of colonial and commercial wars.

Now if we are not to lose sight of what is really characteristic of ancient economics—and of ancient political life in general—we must be extremely cautious in applying to the past the ideas and conceptions of the present. Was there in fact anything in the Greek world before the conquests of Alexander which can fairly serve as the foundation and presupposition of such statements as these?

It is obvious enough that this doctrine of commercial policy in the Greek states rests on two assumptions: that the economic structure of those days was more or less national in character; and that export industry had reached an advanced stage of development. These assumptions must in any case be very considerably modified, now that it has become possible to see Greek industry and Greek trade in their true proportions; but quite apart from that, they are inadmissible in view of the very peculiar structure of the Greek State and of Greek society, a structure that permits of no comparison with the conditions either of the Middle Ages or of modern times.

To speak of the commercial policy of the Greek State in the sense indicated, and to ascribe to it the aims thus implied, is to assume that the State itself—not individual citizens, but the

---

[1] Meyer, op. cit., pp. 613 ff., 624, 663, 778 ; Wilamowitz, Staat u. Gesellsch. (2nd ed.), p. 82.

citizen community as a whole—was interested in trade and production. But there are no grounds for this assumption. The citizens of a Greek city must not be thought of as workers; they were essentially unproductive. We must not, therefore, speak of labour or production in such a city as *national*. Industrial production was only in part in the hands of citizens, only in part national. In the main it was carried on by resident aliens; and when citizens did engage in such occupations they were exposed, as the examples of Cleon and Hyperbolus show, to the contempt which attached to any 'banausic' means of livelihood. It is true that as democracy became more radical this class of citizens did win for itself some place in public life; and it would be natural to expect that it would then begin to champion a foreign policy which looked rather to commercial and industrial, than to agrarian considerations: Cleon, the leather-worker, might well be expected to have furthered interests of this kind when he came to power. But it was not so. The industrial interests which dominated the domestic policy of the mediæval city-state were entirely absent in Greece. Never in the whole history of Greek democracy was industrial policy a determinant factor either in domestic or in foreign policy. Neither workpeople nor business men had any controlling influence.[1]

There are reasonably full accounts in Thucydides, Xenophon, and Demosthenes of meetings of the Assembly, from which we can form a fair picture of democratic debates upon questions of war and peace; but there is no hint in these accounts of the importance of exports to national industry or of commercial interests of any kind. This cannot be mere accident; and it is highly significant that those independent craftsmen and employers of slave labour, who came to play a dominant part in the Assembly, never attempted to use their influence to improve their economic position. Moreover, such matters find no place among the topics discussed in comedy. And most

---

[1] As has been rightly pointed out by Max Weber (*Wirtsch. u. Gesellsch.*, pp. 586, 589) and Bücher (*Beiträge*, pp. 7, 29). See also Sieveking, *Handels- u. Wirtschaftsgesch.*, p. 3 (off-print from *Handw. d. Kaufmanns*, 1925).

important of all, the very notion of a protective tariff, which is implied in such a commercial policy as has been postulated, was utterly unknown to the classical Greek world. This proves at once that no Greek State had ever so much as thought of encouraging its own production against the competition of foreign rivals. Protective tariffs do not appear till Hellenistic times;[1] in the earlier Greek city, duties on exports and imports were imposed for revenue purposes only.

In classical Greece the class of regular traders, in so far as it was not foreign, was proletarian; and in fact it consisted almost entirely of resident foreigners. The Greek city was utterly different from the commercial State of the Middle Ages or of modern times: there commerce is represented by the dominant class, by a citizen aristocracy; in Greece, by a proletariat, mostly foreign, politically degraded, and standing outside the framework of the city. There was no exclusive class of merchants, no social stratum which can be called an aristocracy of commerce; there was scarcely a single merchant of citizen status. Greek commerce was in no sense national. Not only was it not based upon national labour, but it was divorced from national life. It was *cosmopolitan.* There was no such thing as 'Athenian commerce' or 'Bœotian commerce'; and there was no such thing as a national mercantile marine.[2] The commercial policy of the modern State has its roots in the old associations and unions of merchants. For it was from the most influential families that the great overseas merchants were drawn; and only so did the State take into its own hands the care of commercial organisation. There was nothing of the kind in Greece. Greek merchants had not yet come to feel the need for gilds and associations to safeguard their interests, to facilitate ventures in common, or to protect their rights abroad. Indeed, Greek merchants seldom worked with more than one or two partners; and such merchant associations as existed were of a purely religious character.

[1] Wilcken, *Grundzüge*, p. 172, and *Schmollers Jahrbuch*, xlv, 2 (1921), pp. 69, 101.
[2] The untenable doctrine of national merchant fleets is to be met with everywhere. See above, p. 52, n. 8.

Moreover, Greek trade abroad did not depend upon settlements such as we find in the Middle Ages, settlements varying from the so-called *fondachi* to whole quarters of a city in which the foreign traders lived under their own laws and under officers appointed by themselves or by their mother city. In the Middle Ages the State gradually identified itself with the merchant associations and took foreign commercial policy into its own hands, directed trading ventures, and saw to the establishment of settlements and *fondachi*. But in the Greek world we can find nothing even remotely comparable to the shipping monopolies of Venice or Florence or the Hansa towns, where the majority of the merchant vessels belonged to the State itself.

In Greece agricultural production was, of course, exclusively national, for foreigners were debarred from holding land. But it is surely unthinkable that a state which did not even protect its agriculture at home against foreign imports should ever have allowed its foreign policy to be determined by the export interests of its farmers and peasants, or by the desire to secure foreign markets for its wine and oil and other produce, or its marble, or the products of its seas (Xen., *Vect.*, i, 4). (The question of exporting corn, of course, would not arise in any case; for the yield was scarcely adequate to local needs.)

There is no room, then, in the Greek State for that self-centred preoccupation with its trade which we find in the mediæval city, where the supreme consideration was the interest of citizen commerce and industry. The citizens of the Greek city had no reason to promote the economic interests of producers or merchants.

The wars of rivalry in the Greek world, the fluctuations of military fortune, the rise and fall of states, which determine and characterise the history of these centuries, have a much simpler origin than the desire to obliterate a commercial rival in war, or to benefit a trading or industrial class by successful treaties of peace. Such rivalries belong to a higher stage of economic development. There must be a genuinely national trade and industry before a state will go to war in furtherance

of a commercial policy.   In the classical world wars were still
due to purely political causes; they arose from the primitive
desire to secure by force and political domination all those
advantages of national prosperity which in a higher stage of
development are secured by healthy national industry and
commerce.   This is the idea which lay at the bottom of all
ancient imperialism and gave it its characteristic stamp.   In
this striving for domination commercial aims counted for
nothing, except in so far as the control of 'cosmopolitan'
commerce gave an opportunity of enrichment through the dues
and taxes imposed upon it.   The fight for existence in those
days was a political, not a commercial struggle.   It was fought
in the interest of the consumer; it was a struggle for food-
supply.

There were, then, only two factors which determined the
attitude of the classical Greek city to foreign trade: (*a*) *the
exploitation of trade for revenue purposes* (by means of duties,
taxes, monopolies); and (*b*) *the utilisation of trade and traders
to secure the provision of food*—to which may be added the
provision of another indispensable commodity, timber for
shipbuilding.   All measures relating to trade—if we except
mere supervision and police regulation—depended upon these
considerations and these alone; and all the other motives which
historians have foisted upon the cities of these days are the
result of applying modern notions to the economy of the
ancient world.   It is not until the great Hellenistic kingdoms
had destroyed the framework of the city-state that we can
properly speak of commercial policy in a sense which permits
comparison in some degree with modern usage.

Where in our tradition is there the slightest indication that
the Greeks fought wars to capture markets?   Consider what
Herodotus (iii, 39) records of Polycrates of Samos, an island
in which the γεωμόροι, the landowners—not the merchants—
continued to be the dominant class until the Peloponnesian
War (Thuc., viii, 21), but which the moderns represent as one
of the foremost commercial and industrial states in Greece.   I
cannot forbear to quote Herodotus himself once more: 'Within

a short time Polycrates' power increased and was the talk of all
Ionia and the rest of Greece. For wherever he carried his
arms fortune followed him. He had one hundred fifty-oared
ships and one thousand bowmen. He plundered and robbed
all men without discrimination. . . . Thus he had subjugated
a large number of the islands and many cities of the mainland.
The Lesbians . . . he took prisoners in a victorious battle at
sea, and forced them to dig the fosse round the city wall of
Samos.' Nor was the sea-power of Corinth commercial; it
was political and imperial. Peisistratus of Athens had certain
imperialistic aims; apart from these he was solely concerned
with the material well-being of his people.[1] He endeavoured
to find new homes for the surplus population, and to safeguard
the city against starvation by securing, by force when necessary,
supplies of corn, timber, and precious metals from abroad, and
ensuring—by such measures as his seizure of the Dardanelles—
their safe delivery in Athens. There is no proof, again, after
Themistocles had created the naval power of Athens, that
Athenian policy was dominated by trading interests,[2] and not
by the interests of military aggrandisement and of supplies.
It has even been supposed—to keep to the more notable
examples—that the Peloponnesian War can be traced to motives
of commercial policy. We are asked to believe that Corinth,
under the pressure of the protectionist policy of Athens in the
West, sought to enlarge her commercial domain, and for that
reason involved herself in the civil war at Epidamnus, taking
the side opposed by Athens, while Corcyra allied herself with
Athens; that in Athens there were two parties, the landowners
and farmers who had no interest in overseas trade and therefore
opposed the war, and the others who could not have abandoned
Corcyra 'without most seriously imperilling the link with
Italy and Sicily and the whole mercantile and political position
of Athens in the West.'[3] Here, again, we look in vain for

---

[1] For further details see below, p. 144.
[2] As Meyer, *Kl. Schr.*, i, 115, assumes.
[3] Pöhlmann, *G.G.*, p. 146. *Cf.* Beloch, iii, 2, 817. [*Cf.* also Cornford, *Thucydides Mythistoricus*.]

confirmation in the ancient sources. Such views are the creatures of modern analogies.

II. *Colonisation*

Like the waging of wars, so the founding of colonies is ordinarily ascribed to a policy which aimed at furthering production and trade; and the vast extent of colonial activity, which carried the Greeks to every corner of the Mediterranean, is taken as evidence for the advanced development of Greek commerce and industry which is postulated by the current view.[1] Historians speak of colonial policy in the cities of classical Greece as though they were speaking of modern mercantile states. We are told that the needs of the colony opened up a rich market for the mother city, where it could sell its manufactured articles and purchase raw materials; that this necessarily led to the increase of manufacture; that its colonies were the surest strongholds of a city's trade and the best market for its products.[2] 'At an early date,' it is said, 'there grew up an overseas trade based upon a far-reaching colonial policy'; and the Greek cities, like the mediæval towns of the Mediterranean or the seaports of North Germany, established trading factories abroad.[3] Trade rivalry, too, is made to play its part in colonial history, as in the wars of Corinth and Corcyra in the seventh century.[4]

Colonisation is one of the regular features in the economic and cultural development of man, one of what Friedrich List calls the 'normal' activities of every civilised nation. And so the Greeks, like the Phœnicians and others before and after them, colonised. But Greek colonisation, in spite of many— mostly technical—points of similarity, is not really comparable to that of modern states. Even a superficial consideration of colonial history will make this clear. From the time of the

[1] Pöhlmann, *G.G.*, p. 46 ; Riezler, *Finanzen u. Monopole*, p. 76.
[2] Beloch, *G.G.*, i, 1, 230 ff. ; Pöhlmann, *op. cit.*, p. 47, n. 2.
[3] Lexis, *Handw. d. Staatswiss.*, vii, 255 ff. ; Goldschmidt, *Universalgesch. d. Handelsrechts* (*Handb. d. Handelsrechts*, 3rd ed., i, 1, 1891), p. 28.
[4] Pöhlmann, *op. cit.*, p. 48, n. 8.

great voyages of discovery the majority of colonies have owed their origin to commercial impulses. Portugal, Spain, Holland, and England founded their colonies for trade, and exploited them for three centuries on end by means of a rigorous system of restrictions. The colonies of the seventeenth and eighteenth centuries were (as the Greek colonies were not) markets for the disposal of home products and for the purchase of raw materials. It is to that end that the mercantilist state founds colonies and builds up colonial empires. Colonial wars have never been fought on such a scale as in the age of mercantilism.

But Greek colonisation of the pre-Hellenistic period had almost always one or other of two ends—empire, or the maintenance of supplies. The Greek colony was not a trading colony; it was either military—a colony of conquest—or agricultural. That the foundation of colonies was no part of public commercial policy is clear at once from the fact that the non-military colony always owed its origin to private initiative: that is what distinguishes it from the military colony. Moreover, it is well known that in the non-military colony settlers were drawn from various states.

The colonists of modern times are emigrants from powerful commercial nations, which keep a hold upon their colonies by means of a national trade. But Greek trade was not national; it was 'cosmopolitan.' Even the state-protected trading factory was unknown to the Greeks;[1] and yet it is from such factories that almost all the greater modern colonies have sprung. We find a colony called Emporium [2] on the coast of Hither Spain, and are told that it was founded by Massiliots and colonists of Massilia;[3] but it does not follow that the foundation was an act of Massiliot commercial policy, or even that the colonists were traders. It is true that Greek colonies often became centres of trade; but this is because they were not infrequently founded on sites which nature had marked

---

[1] Though some historians profess to find an example in Naucratis.

[2] The modern Ampurias. The earliest coins of Emporium belong to the fifth century (RE v. 2527).

[3] Scylax, *Peripl.*, 2 ; Scymnus, ll. 202 ff.

out as centres of exchange, or which had so been used long years before by Phœnician, Greek, or other private traders. In such places, no doubt, the agricultural settlers assumed control of the existing traffic as a source of revenue. Later, when there came an influx of foreigners who were debarred from holding land, it was these who took to trade. The Greek State, in fact, had no interest in founding colonies except in order to maintain its food-supply. It may be noted that in the days of Carthaginian domination the neighbourhood of the Lesser Syrtis was called Emporia. These *emporia* were the granaries of Carthage in the Punic War: their main business was to supply the city with food.[1]

This seems to be the only possible way to interpret the fragmentary Athenian decree, probably of the year 325 B.C. (*S.I.G.*, 305). The Assembly grants ships of war and the necessary equipment to a certain Miltiades 'in order that the decree of the people in respect of the colony in the Adriatic be carried out without delay' (l. 12). Later there comes (ll. 53 ff.) the following passage: 'In order that for all time the people may have a market and a source of corn-supply of their own, and may have an outpost against the Tyrrhenians by establishing an anchorage, and that Miltiades, the founder, and the colonists may have a fleet at their disposal, and that Greeks and foreigners, having an Athenian anchorage, may sail in safety into the Adriatic. . . .'[2]

This decree has clearly nothing to do with a commercial colony or the protection of Athenian commerce in the Adriatic. It is concerned with the dispatch of an agricultural colony under state protection, and, in the second place, with the safeguarding of the corn supply, by preventing piratical attacks on transports. The fleet is to protect the colonists and any other Greeks and foreigners who may be carrying corn to Athens. This last provision shows that the decree is not designed to further the interests of a class of traders and

---

[1] Polyb., i, 82, 6 ; Livy, xxix, 25, 11.
[2] Accepting the editor's probably correct restoration of the inscription. The principal clause of the sentence is missing on the stone.

producers in Athens. ἐμπορία οἰκεία means the direct supply of corn for the State by the State. 'A city must trade for itself, not for others,' says Aristotle, speaking of government supervision of supplies.[1]

The typical Greek colony, then, was agricultural; and Beloch is right in insisting against the current view that commercial motives counted for next to nothing.[2] It provided for surplus population, and was usually established in thinly populated territory and among less civilised peoples. As in all agricultural colonies the Greek colonists settled with their wives and children, and with the second and third generations a new and independent political organisation took shape.[3]

Early Greek colonisation was the result of the rapid expansion which followed the centuries of migration—it was wholly and solely due to surplus population, which the mother-country was forced to expel. The problem was the elementary one of food: the impossibility of feeding a continually growing population in a land whose soil was niggardly and little adapted to the growth of corn. Hunger, not commercial ambition, was the driving force. Herodotus says plainly of the foundation of Cyrene by the Theræans (iv, 151) that all the trees in Thera were parched by a seven years' drought, and the inhabitants emigrated to Africa and founded a new community. For thousands of years 'bonitas agrorum' has been the main ground for all migrations among the Indo-Germanic peoples.[4]

Like Sicily and Southern Italy, South Russia enjoyed a climate similar to that of Greece, and was among the most

---

[1] *Pol.*, 1327a. Just as Athens arranged by this decree for corn supplies from one of her colonies, so Corinth procured shipbuilding timber from Potidæa.

[2] Beloch, *loc. cit.* ; Gywnn, *The Character of Greek Colonisation (J.H.S.,* 1918, pp. 88 ff.). Büchsenschütz (*Bes. und Erw.*, pp. 356, 377, 381) had already recognised this. It may be noted that Beloch's reasons are different from those given above ; and that, while holding commerce to have been unimportant *at the time of foundation*, he assumes, in accordance with his general view, that the agricultural colony very quickly transformed itself into a trading stronghold of its mother city.

[3] Roscher and Jannasch, *Kolonien und Kolonialpolitik* (3rd ed.), pp. 10 ff.

[4] Political discontent and party strife may be added as causes of emigration.

important of Greek colonial areas. Modern scholars have taken these South Russian colonies to be commercial settlements, but only because they imagined their mother cities, notably Miletus, to have been great industrial centres. But even in Miletus there was no question of creating and organising a commercial or colonial empire in order to open up European Scythia to Greek trade,[1] or (in the case of Milesian settlements on the north coast of Asia Minor) to further trade with the Orient.[2] These fantasies are as baseless as the others we have mentioned—that Miletus allied herself with Sybaris in order to use it as a staple, or that Samos had a trading stronghold in Croton, or Rhodes in Tarentum.[3] Strabo (xiii, 3, 6) relates of Cyme, in Asia Minor, that the inhabitants were said to have taken three hundred years to discover that their city lay upon the sea!

It is a characteristic of the agricultural colony that the emigrants and their descendants settle permanently in the foreign country; and this is precisely what is characteristic of the Greek colony. A new, independent community came into being, politically emancipated from the mother city and bound to it only by loose ties of a moral and religious nature.[4] Objects of worship, in particular the sacred fire of the *prytaneum*, came directly from the mother city; its shrines were honoured by sacred embassies, sacrificial victims, and votive offerings. Citizens of the mother city received special honours when they visited the colony. For special and grave causes priests or arbitrators might be invited from the mother city (Thuc., i, 24). The coin types of the colony were influenced by the legendary history of its mother city. In a word, the tie was religious and moral, not political—nor commercial.

The Greeks distinguished, even in name, between their agricultural colonies (ἀποικίαι) and their military colonies, or *cleruchies*. These were founded at strategically important

---

[1] W. Otto, *Kulturgesch. d. Altert.*, p. 85.   [2] *Ibid.*, p. 78.

[3] *Ibid.*, p. 79. Against the supposed commercial relations of Miletus and Sybaris, see Bücher (*Beiträge*, p. 42).

[4] There were colonies which paid tribute to the mother city (Xen., *Anab.*, v, 5, 10), but this was exceptional.

points, and served to keep the subject peoples and allies in check and to provide land for surplus population—usually of the lower classes. As such they were regularly directed by the State. It was in Athens, so far as we can see, that the idea of the cleruchy was systematically worked out. Unlike the colony proper, the cleruchy remained politically dependent. But here, too, there is no trace of commercial motives: the sole aims were military domination and maintenance of supplies.

In the age of the tyrants both Corinth and Athens sent out colonies under the leadership of governors, usually members of the tyrant house, who kept the daughter cities in some degree of dependence upon the mother city.[1] Such was the relation of Corcyra, Leucas, Ambracia, Anactorium, Apollonia, Epidamnus, and Potidæa to Corinth. Peisistratus secured Sigeum, Rhæcelus on the Thermaic Gulf, and places on the Thracian coast; the Thracian Chersonese, Lemnos, and Imbros belonged to the Philaidæ, who were vassals of the Peisistratids.[2] Here, as in the system of cleruchies, we find colonisation as an instrument of thalassocracy: it served (with the support of powerful navies) as a means of controlling greater or smaller stretches of sea; of obtaining by force supplies of food and precious metals; and of securing the routes to other regions which might in turn be exploited for similar ends. The aim of colonisation was not *commercial*, but *imperial*.[3]

III. *Commercial Treaties*

All the agreements which historians have been accustomed to call 'commercial treaties' are concerned exclusively with the supply of necessities, and in particular with the supply of corn.

By commercial treaties we understand to-day such treaties

---

[1] Corinth : see above, p. 54. Athens : Peisistratus installed his son Hegesistratus as tyrant of Sigeum (Hdt., v, 94), and Hippias ruled there after his expulsion from Athens (*loc. cit.* ; Thuc., vi, 59).

[2] Hdt., vi, 39 ; Meyer, *Forsch.*, i, 17. On Athenian colonisation see below, pp. 144 ff.

[3] It may be noted that these colonies of conquest did ultimately achieve political independence like the normal agricultural settlements.

between state and state as are designed to facilitate and extend the commerce of the state concerned by providing the necessary protection for merchants abroad, whether the privileges secured are unilateral, enjoyed by only one of the contracting parties, or reciprocal, facilitating the commerce of both parties; as under the mercantilist system contracting powers secured favourable treatment for their own exports, and preference against foreign competitors in other countries.[1]

All the so-called commercial treaties which have come down to us from pre-Hellenistic times are concerned not with commercial advantages, but with the supply of corn and other indispensable commodities, including materials for defence and for shipbuilding. This fact has hitherto escaped notice; and yet in none of these treaties is there mention of any other commodities, and none of them subserves the interests of citizen traders or producers. They relate to those commodities the exchange of which Plato and Aristotle are forced to permit even in their ideal cities, where the principle of economic self-sufficiency is uncompromisingly applied. Aristotle speaks of 'the supply of necessaries' (εὐπορία τῶν ἀναγκαίων); and Plato contemplates the need of importing as munitions of war 'manufactured articles, metal-work, material for cordage, and certain plants and animals.'[2] The conditions which make true commercial treaties possible were absent in the Greek world of that time; for such treaties, even if concluded for short periods only, demand—as does trade itself—stability and peace.

Aristotle in his *Rhetoric* (i, 1359*b*) gives a list of five topics 'which are subjects of deliberation and on which an orator has to give advice':

1. State revenues.
2. War and peace.
3. Defence.
4. Imports and exports.
5. Legislation.

---

[1] Rathgen, in *Wörterb. d. Volkswirtsch.*, i, 1280.

[2] *Pol.*, 1327*a* ; *Laws*, 847*d*. The importance of shipbuilding materials is emphasised in *Laws*, 705*c*.

The fourth topic is dealt with more fully at 1360a, 13: 'In regard to supplies it must be considered how large the need of the city is, what can be produced in the country and what imported, and what imports and exports are necessary, in order that treaties and agreements may be concluded with those of whom the state must make use for this purpose.' The former are the so-called συνθῆκαι περὶ τῶν εἰσαγωγίμων, or import treaties, of which Aristotle (Pol., 1280a) says that they, among other kinds of treaty, are frequently concluded between states, as, for example, between the Carthaginians and the Etruscans. In view of the fact that they are concerned with food-supply, it is significant that Aristotle should call them 'import treaties.'

In the same way Socrates enumerates for Glaucon, who is ambitious to be a statesman, the subjects which a statesman must master (Xen., Mem., iii, 6, 3 ff.). These are:

1. State revenue and expenditure.
2. War.
3. Home defence.
4. The corn supply.
5. The silver-mines.

Thirdly, Aristotle, in the passage of the *Respublica Atheniensium* where he discusses the business transacted at the various meetings of the Assembly, names 'deliberation concerning corn supply and defence' among the matters handled at the stated meetings. Here again there is no mention of deliberation concerning commercial interests.[1]

The simplest means of securing adequate supplies is to prevent the flight of commodities abroad and to increase production at home. Hence the laws forbidding the exportation of goods, particularly of corn.[2] In Athens there was a permanent ban upon the export of corn, and shipbuilding materials, such as timber, pitch, wax, rope, might not leave the country.[3] Selymbria forbade the export of corn in time of

---

[1] *Resp. Ath.*, 43, 4.   [2] See below, p. 149.
[3] Ulpian on Dem., xxiv, § 136 ; Boeckh, i, 68 [p. 53].

shortage.[1] But as the city grew and its needs increased it was seldom that this simple plan sufficed. Economic self-sufficiency remained an unattainable ideal, as even the theorists were forced to admit. The city was driven to seek help abroad —and to that end concluded 'import treaties.'

The surviving treaties of this kind are few in number and exhibit some variety of content. But one thing is clear: they are concerned exclusively with those necessary commodities which we have named.

1. *Treaty between Athens and Leucon I of Bosporus* (middle fourth century). This may be reconstructed from the text of Demosthenes' *Leptines*, § 29 ff. We learn of a treaty (§ 37) concluded in accordance with a decree of the people (§ 35), the text of which was set up on three tables, in Piræus, in Bosporus, and at the temple of Zeus Urius. Leucon for his part engages 'to grant freedom from duty (*ateleia*) to those carrying goods to Athens, and to proclaim that merchants proceeding by sea to Athens should have priority in loading their ships." [2] That the agreement was based upon reciprocal concessions is clear from §§ 35 and 37; but of the Athenian side of the bargain we only know that *ateleia* was granted to Leucon. It has been assumed, but wrongly, that his *ateleia* also consisted in freedom from duty.[3] In actual fact it consisted in immunity from the great *liturgies*. The orator insists that Leucon is less moved by the munificence of the gift of *ateleia* than by the honour done him (§ 40 ff.): this honour must not, he urges, be taken back, as Leptines has proposed. These words alone suffice to show that this is no matter of exemption from duty; and throughout the speech there is mention of nothing except exemption from the *liturgies*—the choregia, gymnasiarchy, trierarchy, and so forth. Hence the insistence on the fact that Leucon is an Athenian citizen (§ 30) and 'has always money on deposit in Athens' (§ 40). Indeed Demosthenes

---

[1] Ps.-Arist., *Econ.*, 1348b, 33 ff.

[2] This proclamation was made by the herald at the *emporium* in Bosporus and Theodosia. For similar proclamations see Ar., *Ach.*, 623 ; Dem., xxxiv, § 36 ; and below, pp. 144, 122.

[3] Blass, *Att. Bereds.*, iii, 1, 269 ; B. Keil in *Gercke-Norden*, iii, 403.

says expressly that, should Leucon's *ateleia* be abrogated, it would be open to any Athenian to demand an 'exchange of properties,' whereby he would be compelled either to assume a *liturgy* or to lose his property. And with that any possible dubiety is removed.

It is clearly impossible to regard a covenant of this kind as a commercial treaty. Leucon made these concessions to any persons carrying corn from Bosporus to Athens. The service which he rendered, and for which he was called a benefactor of Athens, was to the Athenian corn-supply (§ 31), not to Athenian merchants.

A welcome addition to the treaty is the Athenian decree of honour (347–6 B.C.) for the sons of Leucon (*S.I.G.*, 206 [H.H. 140]). Its substance is as follows: The sons of Leucon, Spartocus and Pærisades, have sent an embassy to Athens to announce that the princes of Bosporus 'will charge themselves with the dispatch of corn to Athens as their father had done, and will at all times be ready to serve the needs of Athens.' The Athenians regard this service as a 'gift' (l. 20), and decree on their side 'that Spartocus and Pærisades shall receive the same "gifts" as Satyrus and Leucon.' This can only refer to the grant of citizenship and of *ateleia*. The envoys are honoured 'in that they care for those who pass from Bosporus to Athens' (l. 50). Finally, the Athenians determine to pay immediately to the sons of Leucon certain moneys which are owing—perhaps for purchase of corn (l. 54).

2. *Alliance between Amyntas of Macedon and the Chalcidian cities* (from the years 389–383 B.C. *S.I.G.*, 135 [H.H. 95]). The treaty is concluded for fifty years. After a promise of mutual aid in the field it proceeds (ll. 10 ff.) to lay down that each of the contracting powers may import from the other pitch and timber, that is to say, house timber of all kinds, and ship-building timber of all kinds except pine, unless the Chalcidian cities shall have no need of the latter; the Chalcidian cities, however, may import pine timber provided they inform Amyntas beforehand and pay the fixed tariff. Export and transit trade in other commodities may be carried on from Macedon to the

Chalcidians and from the Chalcidians to Macedon subject to the usual tariffs. It is further laid down (ll. 18 ff.) that neither Power may enter into alliance with Amphipolis, Bottiæa, Acanthus, or Mende unless both parties agree to the alliance.

This, it will be seen, is essentially a political treaty, although it includes permission to import commodities from the other state—bare permission, it should be noted; for no exemption from ordinary tariff charges is conceded.

3. *Treaty between Mytilene and Leucon I of Bosporus* (*S.I.G.*, 212). Leucon and his sons grant to the Mytileneans a reduction of 50% on the ordinary duty upon wheat.

This is a fragmentary inscription found in Mytilene. There is little doubt that we have here a treaty which substantially corresponds to that between Athens and Leucon. It is concerned once more with preferential treatment in regard to corn. No further details are known.

4. *Treaty between Pærisades of Bosporus and Athens.* This can be reconstructed from Demosthenes, xxxiv, § 36: 'Pærisades proclaims by herald in Bosporus that whoever desires to carry corn to the Athenian market may do so duty-free.'

Further information is wanting; but the analogy with the first treaty is obvious. This Pærisades is the son of Leucon.

5. *Treaty between the cities of Ceos and Histiæa* (before 363–2 B.C. *S.I.G.*, 172). The two states grant reciprocal rights of citizenship, and further agree that 'citizens of Histiæa may export goods from Ceos on the same terms as citizens of Ceos, and citizens of Ceos from Histiæa on the same terms as the Histiæans; and for import in like manner.'

It is clear that these five agreements [1] aim at securing either preferential terms in respect of tariffs or simple permission to purchase commodities in the market of the foreign state. These are advantages which any state concerned with its supply of necessities will naturally seek to secure.[2]

---

[1] For the treaty between Athens and Ceos in regard to the export of ruddle, see below, p. 140.

[2] In the treaty between Ceos and Histiæa the commodity is not named; but there is no reason to suppose that this treaty differs from the others. We may safely assume that corn and other necessaries are intended.

Such privileges could also be granted by a state to private individuals; and there are numerous inscriptions recording such grants. These are the decrees of *ateleia*, with their stereotyped formula: 'exemption from duty on all goods imported or exported.' The privilege granted is not always the same: besides complete exemption, we find reduction of the tariff to that normally applied to citizens.[1] These privileges were generally accorded in reward for some act of generosity to the State. But presumably the State looked also to its own interests; and just as the princes of Bosporus gained, or hoped to gain, political advantage by their grants of privilege to Athens, so it is reasonable to suppose that the private persons to whom *ateleia* was given were such as were likely to be useful to the public corn supply. How seriously the State regarded its duty to those who served it by importing corn is shown very clearly in *S.I.G.*, 304 (330 B.C.). The Salaminian (Cypriot) Heraclides, who is several times expressly described as an *emporos*, was captured by Heracleot privateers on his voyage to Athens, and his sails were stolen. The Athenians sent an envoy to the ruler of Heraclea, Dionysius, bidding him 'return the sails of Heraclides, and in future refrain from injury to vessels proceeding to Athens.' These grants of privilege to individuals are almost exclusively concerned with necessary commodities, as is shown by the fact that, whenever the commodity is named, it is without exception either corn or timber.[2]

It must not be supposed that these numerous grants of privilege to private persons were intended to further the interests of a class of regular and professional traders. Not

[1] Michel, 535, vii (Cyzicus); *S.I.G.*, 348 ; *Inschriften v. Magnesia*, 48, l. 26. The following are select examples of such grants to individuals : *S.I.G.*, 219 (Olbia to a man from Mesembria) ; 217 (Pærisades to a man from Piræus in Asia) ; 348 (Eretria to three men from Antigoneia); 126 [H.H. 89] (Erythræ to Conon); Theophr., *Char.*, 23 (the king of Macedon to an Athenian).

[2] Corn : *S.I.G.*, 136, l. 18 [H.H. 96] ; *B.C.H.*, 1889, p. 54 ; *Inscr. Jurid.*, p. 144, l. 9 ; *S.I.G.*, 75 [H.H. 60, Tod 61] ; *Or. Gr.*, 58 ; *S.I.G.*, 193 [H.H. 127] ; *S.I.G.*, 229 [H.H. 138]. Timber : Theophr., *Char.*, 23. A builder : *C.I.G.*, 2266 [Delos] ; *I.G.*, ii², 968 [2nd cent.].

once is the recipient described expressly as an *emporos*. Antigonus (*S.I.G.*, 278), Mausollus (168 [H.H. 134]), Conon (126 [H.H. 89]), and the mercenaries rewarded by Eumenes (*Or. Gr.*, 266) are certainly not traders. And most important of all, we have examples in which the privileged commodities are expressly described as being for the use of the recipient's household or as his private property [1]: they are not for sale, but for his own consumption (see above, p. 14). There must have been many private persons who wished to buy in the foreign market, and only sold because, owing to the backward conditions of currency, they were forced to trade by barter: as, for example, when Andocides relates that Archelaus of Macedon, his guest-friend, 'gave him permission to fell and export from Macedon as much timber for oars as he would' (ii, 11), or when the Boastful Man in Theophrastus (*Char.*, 23) brags that Antipater of Macedon had granted him duty-free export of timber—no doubt for building his own house, as in the case of Timotheus in Demosthenes, xlix, § 26.

As will be shown below, the use of foreign markets and harbours was closely restricted; so that—apart from any preferential treatment—the importance to cities of these 'commercial' agreements, and to individuals of *ateleia*, was that without them access to the foreign market would not have been possible at all.

IV. *National Self-sufficiency*

In principle the Greek state stood in sharp isolation over against a hostile outside world. It could only achieve self-sufficiency (αὐτάρκεια) by shielding itself rigorously from external contact. Even at the time of their highest development there was no idea of *solidarity* in the world of Greek city-states; and until the time of Alexander political evolution was determined by an exaggerated separatism. The most essential feature of the classical Greek states was this deliberate pursuit of independence, which was, of course, largely conditioned by the fact that they were city-states. But this very

[1] *S.I.G.*, 278, 941 ; Michel, 332 (*cf.* 321) ; *S.I.G.*, 332.

independence had the effect of limiting their formative political vigour. Outside his own state the citizen passed, as it were, into annihilation; his existence stood or fell with his city. The extreme distrust which prevailed among fellow-citizens, and which is very clearly revealed in the majority of Greek democratic institutions, prevailed in even greater degree among citizens of different cities. In that regard the world of Greek states is but any single state writ large.

The outlawry of the foreigner is common to all primitive law. It is found in early Greek law; and, in theory at least, it showed remarkable persistence both in Greek history and in antiquity in general. It is the necessary consequence of the principle of isolation. To the Greek mind the normal condition of things was war between state and state, not peaceable coexistence; and this view is reflected in the peculiarities of Greek law. It was not until the fourth century that εἰρήνη came to mean 'peace'; till then—and occasionally later—it meant 'armistice.'[1] Treaties of 'peace' for periods of five or ten years were regarded merely as interruptions of a state of war. The law of force prevailed until the days of Alexander —and even then was never abrogated. In accordance with it the foreigner even in times of 'peace' enjoyed no security of life or property. Piracy and privateering were practised with the protection and authority of the State, and in all periods of Greek history were recognised professions and lawful institutions. Even Aristotle treats brigandage as a kind of hunting, a direct and natural means of livelihood and therefore one becoming to any head of a household;[2] and it is noteworthy that in Athenian law companies of privateers are treated like any other form of association.[3]

To these uneasy conditions are due certain formulæ which constantly recur in Greek treaties. These were designed to secure, in part and for a time at least, escape from the danger which perpetually threatened any regular and adequate supply of necessities from abroad. In the armistice agreement be-

---

[1] Weiss, *Gr. Privatrecht*, i, 171 ff.   [2] *Pol.*, 1256a.
[3] Glotz, *La Solidarité de la Famille* (1904), p. 200.

tween Athens and Sparta of the year 423 (Thuc., iv, 118), it is provided that the Lacedæmonians may sail their own waters and those of their allies, not indeed with ships of war, but with other vessels up to 500 talents burthen. That is, the Athenians simply bind themselves to refrain from privateering against peaceable shipping in Lacedæmonian waters. In the treaty of Alexander with the Corinthian League in 336 B.C. (Dem., xvii, § 19), the contracting parties are free to 'sail the seas without hindrance or risk of seizure,' 'to sail the sea without fear,' as Isocrates puts it (viii, 20; cf. iv, 115). The guarantee of free use of the sea was to have been one of the points of discussion at the Hellenic congress proposed by Pericles after the Persian defeat (Plut., *Pericles*, 17).

All of which goes to show that a Greek city did not normally permit a foreigner to set foot upon its territory or to sail its seas—unless it urgently needed his services. The doctrine of the *mare liberum* is a product of modern times, elaborated after weary battles of politicians and theorists; and it is only in our own day that territorial waters are almost universally free, and that the harbours of states which recognise the common law of nations are open to the shipping of every other state. Free access to territorial waters is no longer, at least among European nations, dependent upon special treaties.[1]

The treaties of Rome with Carthage, which Polybius has preserved (iii, 22 ff.), belong to the fourth century. But even these are not 'commercial' or 'shipping' treaties, as Mommsen calls them. The Romans knew of no kind of treaty other than political;[2] and these treaties simply regulate the general relations of intercourse between Rome and Carthage. The two spheres of influence are delimited; and if mention is made of trade at all, it is only because trading is a part of inter-

---

[1] The closing of the sea to foreigners is not, of course, wholly unknown in more recent times—Portugal and Spain, for example, claimed certain seas as their own and excluded foreigners. But in modern times it is only an inland sea which is closed, or a strait commanded by the coast on either side ; whereas in ancient—even in Roman—times, the open sea, which to-day is subject to no sovereign power, might be closed. See Täubler (*Imperium Romanum*, i, 78, n. 3) on the treaties between Rome and Carthage.

[2] Täubler, *op. cit.*, p. 205.

course in general. Carthage set a limit beyond which no Roman ship—that is, in point of fact, no Roman—might show itself.[1] Should a Roman vessel be compelled by forces beyond its control to cross the boundary, there were special regulations, as in Naucratis, to deal with the emergency:[2] the shipwrecked sailor shall 'neither buy nor take any commodity'; he may have no dealings with the inhabitants. Outside the forbidden zone, a distinction is made between the Libyan and Sardinian territory on the one hand, and the Sicilian and city territory on the other. For the latter: 'In every respect Romans and Carthaginians shall be on an equal footing' (first treaty); 'Any transaction or sale which is lawful to a citizen may be carried out by a Roman; and so for a Carthaginian in Rome' (second treaty).[3] For this area, that is, there are no restrictions; but for the Libyan and Sardinian area the second treaty forbids any kind of traffic whatever, and the first lays down certain formalities in buying and selling (see below, p. 128).

In the terms of these treaties there is no thought whatsoever either of avoiding or of encouraging commercial competition. The clause which refers to formalities in regard to sales must not mislead us into any such assumption. The aim of the Carthaginians was not to reserve for their own use the markets in the areas closed to Rome, but to prevent the Romans from 'practising piracy' or 'founding cities' in these areas. In the same way the Carthaginians are forbidden to 'act injuriously' on the Latin coast; they are to 'keep their hands off' Ardea, Antium, Circeii, and Terracina (22, 11); they must seize no city, establish no garrison, take no prisoners. Polybius himself, in his discussion of the treaties, says that in excluding the Romans the Carthaginians 'had been unwilling that they should come to know these regions *because of the excellence of the soil*' (23, 2). It is wholly mistaken to speak of a Carthaginian commercial policy, and to compare it, as

---

[1] The geographical determination of the boundary need not be discussed here.

[2] See above, p. 63.　　　　　　　　　　[3] iii, 24, 12

Täubler does, to the monopoly policy of the Hansa.[1] Intercourse between the two states was regulated; but the end in
view was political, not commercial. This regulation can only
be properly understood if the peculiar features of ancient alien
law are duly taken into account: it is not traders and trading
intercourse which are debarred, but foreigners and foreign
intercourse of any kind. But if the foreigner is admitted at
all, so also is the foreign trader; and if any intercourse is
permitted, then trading intercourse naturally benefits by the
permission.[2] Trading is only one of many aspects of intercourse; this is clear from the very wording of the treaty:
'not to commit acts of piracy, nor to ply trade, nor to found
cities.'

Even Carthage in the fourth century was dominated, as we
see, by the principle of at least partial isolation from the outside
world. At the same time it aimed at concentrating at definite
points such external intercourse as it permitted: as Naucratis
was for Egypt, so was the city of Carthage and the Semitic
coast towns of Sicily for the whole Carthaginian empire.

The treaty of Rome and Tarentum tells the same story. (It
is described as already old in the year 282, and therefore belongs
to the period under discussion.) 'The Romans may not sail
beyond the Lacinian promontory.'[3] This, as the text clearly
shows, is an embargo upon all intercourse, not upon trade
alone, as has been held.[4] Such a view mistakes the degree of
development then attained by commercial organisation, and
misconceives the attitude of the ancient state to commerce.

We have seen that the foreigner, unless protected by special
treaties between cities or by personal privilege, was exposed to
seizure upon the high seas or in the coastal waters of another
state. He was also debarred from entering the harbour and
the market of another state. The Ozolian cities of Œanthea
and Chaleium (*I.G.A.*, 322 [H.H. 44, Tod 34; Schwyzer 363])

---

[1] *Op. cit.*, p. 429.
[2] Of course the formalities of sale mentioned above imply this permission.
[3] Appian, *Samn.*, vii, 1.
[4] See Täubler, *op. cit.*, p. 79. He speaks (p. 429) of the need of 'commercial protection.'

concluded a treaty in the fifth century by which they bound themselves to seize no stranger by violence in the harbour or on land, the ordinary privateering rights being preserved upon the open sea. The closure of harbour and market to the foreigner is normal; to throw them open is abnormal. The Athenians, for example, always regarded the open market as something unusual. Isocrates (*Paneg.*, 42 ff.) boasts that they had conferred a notable service upon the other Greeks by aiding them in the important task of balancing surplus and shortage: 'for Athens has set up the Piræus as a central *emporium* in the midst of Greece.' This he calls an act of friendship to foreigners. Foreign merchants come to Athens 'as to friends,' says the author of *de Vectigalibus* (iii, 4); and he describes the decrees designed to encourage foreigners to come to Athens as benevolent or 'philanthropic.' Pericles extols this practice as a notable merit of the Athenians and one which singles them out among their neighbours: 'Our city gates are open to all men's coming and going; we expel no stranger.' That is what the Greeks meant by an open market.[1] Aristotle, from his own hostile point of view, speaks of cities 'which make themselves markets for all comers,' and maintains that their motive is always gain and greed.[2] Corresponding to the open market is the closed market;[3] and nothing could be more significant than the way in which Lysias sets such a closure in the same class of accidents as shipwreck and piracy: it was a misfortune which might befall the trader at any time, and with which he is bound to reckon. When Lamachus is proclaiming war upon all the Peloponnesians (Ar., *Acharn.*, 623 ff.), Dicæopolis cries: 'And I proclaim to all Peloponnesians and Megarians and Bœotians that they may come to me and buy and sell.' He is 'opening his market': the foreigner may now enter it and do business.

It is only when this attitude is understood that the Megarian Decree becomes intelligible. It is commonly supposed to be a trade embargo, by which Athens annihilated Megarian trade

---

[1] Ar., *Av.*, 1523.   [2] *Pol.*, 1327a.
[3] Lysias, xxii, 14 ; Dem., ii, § 16.

in the whole Athenian Empire. According to many scholars this was preceded by a ban upon imports which closed the Athenian market to Megarian wares.[1] Kershaw [2] and Steup [3] have already pointed out that our authorities offer no evidence for this whatever. The passage in the *Acharnians* (515 ff.) refers only to ordinary evasions of the customs by the Megarian peasants; [4] and in any case the very idea of such a ban upon imports is quite out of place in the kind of economic organisation with which we are concerned. Moreover, the so-called trade embargo was no such thing: it was a general exclusion of the Megarians from any kind of intercourse whatever with any part of the Athenian empire, and is comparable to the total exclusion of the Romans from parts of the Tarentine or the Carthaginian territories. Aristophanes (*Acharn.*, 533) says the decree forbade 'the Megarians to exist on land, in the market, on sea or in heaven.' The decree of Charinus (Plut., *Per.*, 30), which I believe to be the Megarian Decree and not a further enactment,[5] lays it down that 'any Megarian who sets foot in Attica shall be punished by death'; and Pericles insists (Thuc., i, 144) that the Megarian Decree is no more contrary to the terms of the Peace of 446 B.C. than the Lacedæmonian practice of expelling foreigners. 'We will admit the Megarians again to our market and our harbours if the Lacedæmonians will cease to expel us and our allies from their territories.' Substantially the decree and the Spartan expulsion of foreigners are the same thing; and they are both normal manifestations of Greek alien law. It has been assumed [6] on the strength of Pericles' words that the treaty of 446 B.C. contained the stipulation of free intercourse or

---

[1] Duncker, Klett, Busolt. The problem is fully discussed by Busolt (*G.G.*, iii, 2, 811).

[2] *Comment. Philol. Monac.* (Munich, 1891), pp. 22 ff.

[3] *Thukydideische Studien*, ii, 21 ff.

[4] 'Smelling out cucumbers and hares and young pigs and garlic and salt in the Megarians' coats '—see Meyer (*G.A.*, iv, 290).

[5] So also Holzapfel, Duncker, and Klett. Busolt finds no fewer than three distinct decrees !

[6] See Classen on Thuc., i, 67 ; Meyer, *G.A.*, iii, 624 ; *Forsch.*, ii, 303 ; Busolt, *G.G.*, iii, 1, 437.

trade on either side; but this is to ignore the underlying facts of the case. Pericles takes his stand on the purely formal ground of law: Each state in virtue of its sovereignty has the legal right to close its territories against foreigners.[1] (Lysias' words make this abundantly clear.) If the Megarians none the less complain (67, 4) that the decree violates the Peace, they cannot be taking the legal point, as Plutarch wrongly thinks; their complaint can only be that Athens has singled them out for exclusion, and in so doing has belied its principle of friendship to foreigners (which was implicitly, not formally, contained in the Peace), and has thus outraged the ideal principles of justice in foreign relations. The Peace cannot have contained a clause governing the treatment of citizens of the one state in the territory of the other; at the most there may have been a clause, like that in the treaty of 423 B.C., by which the Athenians bound themselves to refrain from piracy in the territorial waters of the other party.

It is true that in the two places where he gives the substance of the decree Thucydides speaks only of exclusion from the harbours of the Athenian Empire and from the market of Attica (i, 139, 1, and 67, 4; cf. 144, 2); but he does so simply because this was the most painful feature of the general exclusion: it made it impossible for the Megarians to obtain the necessities of life. Not only the market of Athens, but Byzantium, for example, and with it the corn-lands of the north, was closed to Megara. The city which rules the sea controls the supplies of weaker cities as it will;[2] and the Megarians 'begin to starve' (Ar., *Acharn.*, 535).

The policy of isolation and exclusion, then, was not directed against commercial competition; nor was the opening of a market to the outside world designed to further the interests of citizen traders or to benefit national production. When a city abandoned its policy of isolation and involved itself in inter-city commerce, it had only two motives—the motives

---

[1] *Cf.* Plato, *Laws*, 950b, which shows that the practice of expelling foreigners was regarded as normal and usual.

[2] See below, pp. 142 ff.

which governed its whole outlook upon commerce: the maintenance of necessary supplies, and the fiscal exploitation of
such traffic as touched its shores. In this way, in spite of the
Greek attitude to foreigners and of other obstacles, commercial
intercourse between city and city was able to develop to the
limited extent which we have indicated. Moreover, a city did
open its gates to foreigners when their services were indispensable: handicraftsmen, artists, physicians, slaves; and
especially foreign merchants 'who move from city to city
bringing to one city from another that which it lacks; the
auxiliaries who deal with exports and imports,' and without
whom even the ideal city cannot exist.[1] Hence arose the class
of metics with its special privileges and exemptions. Indeed,
owing to the peculiar Greek attitude to technical occupations,
foreigners were more readily welcomed in Greece than in the
German and Italian cities of the Middle Ages. This is especially
remarkable in Athens, where Pericles was able to boast that
his city was open to all and that no foreigners were excluded.

But it must not be overlooked—and it is fundamentally
important to the appreciation of the Greek economy—that as
in the political life of the Greeks there was no trace of
solidarity, so in their economic life the principle of isolation
persisted in spite of everything, and everywhere determined
the whole organisation of exchange. This is shown by the
arbitrary opening and closing of markets and harbours, and
by the existence of piracy as a respectable means of livelihood.
Conditions were uncertain and uneasy; there was no compulsion upon a state to keep its market open except the bidding
of 'justice.' The Methonæans appealed to 'justice' in
seeking protection against Perdiccas: it appears 'just' that
they be allowed to sail the seas without restrictions and to
trade by land as heretofore, neither suffering nor committing
'injustice';[2] and an Athenian embassy was sent to Heraclea

---

[1] Plato, *Rep.*, 370e, 371d. In the *Laws* (952e), Plato speaks of foreigners
who come regularly to other cities for the sake of trade, crossing the seas
in summer like flights of migrant birds.

[2] *S.I.G.*, 75 [H.H. 60, Tod 61] : an Athenian decree of 428 B.C.

to demand that its tyrant, who was forcibly detaining corn-ships bound for Athens, should 'do no injustice.'[1]

Bare permission to purchase and export timber from their territory was in the eyes of the Macedonian kings a privilege which had to be specially granted even when the full export duty was paid (above, p. 114). Much the same significance attaches to the grant of *asulia*, whereby the State which grants it guarantees safe-conduct within its territory. This is, as it were, the germ-cell of Greek alien law.[2] Many of these grants, of which large numbers are preserved in inscriptions (usually in conjunction with grants of *ateleia*), may have amounted to little more than empty form: the idea of the right of forcible seizure always retained its vitality.

The stereotyped formula runs thus: 'To enter or leave the country by sea without being subject to seizure by privateers and without special treaty-agreement, in peace or in war'; or, in combination with *ateleia*, 'Exemption from duty on wares imported or exported; the right to enter or leave the country, etc.' So too by land, *e.g.* from Sardis to Miletus (*S.I.G.*, 273, fourth century). How large a part is played by corn transport in these grants, as in the grants of *ateleia*, is shown by the Athenian honorific decree for the Clazomenians (*S.I.G.*, 136 [H.H. 96]) which is valid 'for the harbours and cities of the Athenian League and Smyrna whence they buy corn' (l. 18).[3]

The supply of its elementary necessities was the gravest problem which faced the Greek city. Trade by itself was not in a position to solve it. Everything depended upon chance and upon incalculable risks. The city did what it could to master the situation by concluding import treaties with foreign states. By these treaties it secured (*a*) the right to buy neces-sary goods in the foreign market, and (*b*) advantages in trans-port. These latter were of three kinds: cheaper transport

---

[1] *S.I.G.*, 304 ; see above, p. 116.

[2] E. Weiss, *Griech. Privatrecht*, i, 172 ff.

[3] Further typical examples—not combined with *ateleia*: *S.I.G.*, 168 [H.H. 134] (Erythræ to Mausollus of Caria), 110 (Rhodes to a Naucratite), 92 (Athens to an Achæan), 187 (Cnidus to an Abydene).

(exemption, or partial exemption, from duties), safer transport (*asulia*), and swifter transport (priority in loading).

The Greek cities passed on to further and more complicated international relations—in other words, to further sacrifices of the principle of isolation; but these relations, except in so far as they affect the exchange of goods, lie outside our range. The σύμβολα, συμβολαί—treaties dealing with legal redress—must, however, be discussed here, since they do have a bearing upon trade. By these treaties a community assured to those of its members who lived or had dealings abroad a more or less effective legal protection. In the first place it guaranteed the safety of person and property; but beyond that, it agreed with the foreign state concerned as to the legal course to be pursued in the event of litigation between individuals of the two states, or between an individual and the other state.[1] The members of the contracting states were assured in this way of a regular common procedure in their private suits: otherwise a foreigner had no legal standing.

It is obvious that such treaties primarily benefited such persons as were engaged in the exchange of commodities between the contracting states. Their great importance to those who use *emporia* is most clearly brought out in the speech, *On the Halonnesus* (Dem., vii, §§ 9, 11, 12). Philip of Macedon wished to conclude such treaties with Athens; the orator opposes this, and argues as follows: History has shown that there is no need for treaties between Athens and Macedon. Neither Amyntas nor any other king of Macedon made such a treaty with us, although contact between the two states was more frequent in their time, and although we then made more use of their *emporium* and they of ours. He further argues, § 12, that 'emporial suits' (see below, p. 169) render these treaties of legal redress unnecessary.

It is in the traffic of the market that the first beginnings of international usage are to be found: the further ties of nation to nation do not come into being until later. Even in times when war is normal and the foreigner has no rights, a kind of

---

[1] The two states are then ἀπὸ συμβόλων κοινωνοῦντες.—Ar., *Pol.*, 1275a.

'trade peace' is, at first tacitly, agreed to while necessary goods are being exchanged; from this is developed the regular market, where traders, producers, and consumers can meet at fixed times. Originally it was almost everywhere a sacred place which was under religious protection. Hence the Greek 'gods of the market-place,' and 'sacred market.' Owing to its connection with regular racial festivals the institution of the market tends to be associated with the sites of ancient cults or with the rise of new.[1] It was from the market, then, that treaties of this nature developed — 'agreements to do no injustice to one another,' as Aristotle calls them (*Pol.*, 1280a).

But these treaties are not due to any concern of the State for its traders and producers. Aristotle is perfectly clear on the point (*Rhet.*, 1360a, 13): they are concerned with the maintenance of supplies (see above, pp. 111 ff.). They are designed to protect those who are engaged in the exchange of necessary goods. These may be men who are buying for their own household, or other private persons—such as those we meet in grants of *asulia* and *ateleia*—or they may be regular traders. All these persons were necessarily involved in some kind of legal business with citizens of other states (though the importance of such business must not be overrated; probably it was extremely simple);[2] but apart from that, a foreigner without legal protection was exposed to a multiplicity of dangers; and these treaties secured him the personal protection which he needed.

The clause concerning Sardinia and Libya in the Carthaginian treaty deals with protection of this kind: 'Those who come to trade may not conclude their business except in the presence of the herald or the scribe. Everything which is sold in their presence shall be credited under public guarantee to the seller.'[3] Polybius remarks, 'the Carthaginians engage here to give public guarantee of justice.'[4] In this connection

---

[1] Goldschmidt, *Universalgesch. d. Handelsrechts*, i, 24.
[2] *Hermes*, 1923, pp. 393 ff.
[3] Polyb., iii, 22, 9.　　　　　　　　　　　　[4] *Ibid.*, 23, 4.

we must not forget the many difficulties in which the foreigner might find himself through ignorance of the local speech, not least in Greece with its great variety of dialects.

Another protection for the foreigner is the institution of *proxenia*, which derives from the primitive 'guest-friendship.' In order to protect its interests and the private interests of its citizens, the Greek State appointed representatives in foreign cities. These were always appointed by a special decree in which special privileges were granted in return for their expected services. The institution is found in all Greek states. The *proxenus* had to be a citizen of the foreign city concerned, and had to reside there, so that he could be at hand to serve the city which had appointed him. His duty was to protect and help in every way the persons and property of citizens of that city. But he was only a private representative; unlike the modern consul he was not officially recognised by the city in which he resided. The appointment of a *proxenus* did not involve any official relation or any agreement between the two cities.[1] He acted as a middleman between the foreigner and the local officials—that is, primarily, the legal officials; in other words, he had to watch over all buying and selling and exchange of commodities between individuals from the one city and members of the other. Something of the same sort is found in the Middle Ages, and indeed elsewhere: the foreign trader carrying on his business under the control of a local personage—the *turcimanus*, or dragoman, of mediæval and later times. This control was not meant to be a restriction, but a privilege: it marks an advance upon the primitive 'silent trading,' which owed its origin partly to mistrust and partly to ignorance of language.[2]

The *proxenia* is clearly an older institution than the συμβολαί. It had very obvious limitations, whereas the latter provided for a regular legal procedure; and it is not surprising

---

[1] B. Keil in Gercke-Norden, *Einleitung*, iii, 402.

[2] Herodotus has a vivid account of ' silent trade ' between the Carthaginians and the Libyans (iv, 196). He remarks that neither party acts ' unjustly.'

that it gradually dwindled in importance and became a mere title.[1]

V. *Thalassocracy*

These treaties concerning imports, *asulia* and legal redress, together with the *proxenia* and the protection accorded to metics, make up the rudiments of a common international usage, which no doubt incidentally benefited trade. But it must not be forgotten that all such sacrifices of the principle of isolation were made in the first place to ensure sufficient supplies of corn and other necessaries. Complete economic self-sufficiency was impossible. The history of colonisation has shown that even in early times Greece could not support its population. Solon was forced to forbid the export of grain from Attica. Even Plato, an uncompromising advocate of isolation, was driven to admit that 'it is almost impossible to find such a site for the ideal city that it will not need imports.'[2] 'The city must be able to import agricultural produce, timber and other fruits of the soil.'[3] 'There is no city which is independent of imports and exports.'[4] 'No country is self-sufficient in all things; in one commodity it is deficient, in another it has a surplus.'[5] This is ample testimony; and

---

[1] προξενος never meant 'middleman' or 'agent,' as has been supposed. The fact that προξενεῖν (literally, to be someone's προξενος) early acquired the meaning 'to be a middleman' proves nothing ; for the *proxenus* was after all a *middle man*, a go-between in respect of legal protection. And even if the Latin *proxeneta* means 'middleman,' that is no evidence for Greek usage (Marquardt, *Privatleben der Römer*, p. 413). Nor is it certain that middlemen are intended in Philostratus (*Apoll.*, iv, 32, 2): 'the traders seek a market, mingle with *proxeni* and hucksters, buy and sell.' It was supposed as early as Pollux (vii, 11) that the meaning 'middleman' was to be attached to the words προπράτωρ or προπράτης (Dinarchus, Isæus, Lysias), and to προπωλῶν (Plato, *Laws*, 954a) or προπώλης (Aristophanes). (See Büchsenschütz., *Bes. u. Erw.*, p. 463, and Goldschmidt, *Zeitschr. f. d. ges. Handelsrecht*, xxiii, 129.) But Lipsius has shown (*Att. Recht*, p. 749) that these words can only refer to the guarantor—known as βεβαιωτής outside of Attica (Mitteis, *Grundzüge*, pp. 188 ff.)—against whom a purchaser could proceed if his rights were contested. In point of fact, Greek commerce found no use for the functions of the middleman in sale and purchase.

[2] *Rep.*, 370e.
[3] Arist., *Pol.*, 1327a.
[4] [Xen.], *Resp. Ath.*, 2, 3.
[5] Isoc., iv, 42.

for the rest, the peculiar attitude of the Greeks to handicrafts
left them no choice but to open their doors to foreign traders
and labourers.

Such a system of alliances and treaties between cities which
thus supplemented each other's needs might—in spite of its
partial sacrifice of the strict principle of isolation—have brought
about a kind of economic equipoise, a sharing of the burden of
production, without destroying the political independence of
the several cities.[1] But this was not to be. The unaccommo-
dating spirit of the Greek city-state proved unable to adapt
itself to the general movement of economic development. The
paramount aim was political independence; and this was
believed impossible without economic independence. Such
efforts as were made were feeble and rudimentary. Ties between city and city were weak and insecure, liable to rupture
at the slightest strain. International treaties had not the
solemnity and binding force which they have now acquired.
And the reason for this is to be sought not only in the absence
of the security which law affords or in the Greek habit of
regarding war, not peace, as the normal international relation,
but rather in the spirit of the Greek city itself: a city must
satisfy its needs, if it can, not by alliances and treaties or
peaceful trading with its neighbours, but by force and exploitation. 'Pigrum et iners videtur sudore adquirere quod
possis sanguine parare': Tacitus's words sum up the central
doctrine of Hellenic politics.[2] In his advice to Glaucon,
Socrates lays it down that one of the normal duties of a statesman is to give sound advice on questions of peace and war,
and 'to enrich his city at the expense of the enemy if it is the
stronger.'[3] 'It is the accepted opinion,' says Plato (*Laws*,
742*d*), 'that a good statesman must labour to make his city
as great and rich as possible, so that it may have gold and silver
in plenty and rule far and wide over land and sea'; and according to Aristotle a city must be of such size and strength that
its citizens may live at ease on others' labours.[4] The directing

[1] Riezler, *Finanzen und Monopole*, pp. 78 ff.   [2] Riezler, *op. cit.*, 73.
[3] Xen., *Mem.*, iii, 6, 7.   See above, p. 112.   [4] *Pol.*, 1326*b*.

principle of the Greek city was not self-preservation but the oppression and exploitation of others;[1] and it was this spirit which gave ancient imperialism its characteristic stamp.[2]

All modern thinking about international relations is governed by the lofty ideal of a fellowship of states, of a common law which binds nations together, of a family of peoples obedient to the dictates of civilisation and humanity. But this conception is a product of the modern mind. The idea of restricting the operation of force by law has found its expression in the principle of balance, that adjustment of power within an organised system, in virtue of which a number of independent states can co-exist without threat from a stronger power. This principle was first proclaimed in the seventeenth century, in the infancy of international law; and it took the place of the mediæval ideal of a Christian fellowship of nations at a time when the growth of nationalism, the rise of dynastic states, and the divisions of the Church combined to discredit the *pax Christiana*. In it the modern world has found the reconciliation of the age-long and inevitable conflict between the ambition of the single state and the ideal demands of the community of nations. In our own days it has widened into the magnificent conception of an organised League of Nations, which, although there never has been and never will be complete and stable balance of power, stands, in spite of all abuses, as a lasting achievement in international politics.

To the ancients such ideas were wholly alien. They came, indeed, to be aware of a cultural community of peoples, which embraced at first the Greeks, and later the *œcumene* of mankind; but they never attained the conception of common political organisation. Our ideas of an organised system of states must therefore be applied to antiquity with the utmost caution and reserve. Greek political theorists were fully aware of the distinction between force and justice in international relations, and discussed the rival principles of the Useful and the Just

[1] See Riezler, *op. cit.*, p. 73.

[2] The rest of this section is substantially a repetition of my Engelberg lecture, *Der imperialistische Gedanke im Altertum* (Stuttgart, 1926).

from every point of view. In fact, the relation of politics and morals was familiar enough long before the development of a Christian ethic. But to the Greek mind political justice was never understood as justice within a community of states; it was always the justice which a stronger state should observe in its dealings with a weaker. Accordingly, the 'unjust' was the misuse of force, not force itself. Even the word 'peace' connoted nothing of what we associate with the 'comity of nations.' The Greeks were the creators of political ethics; but it must never be forgotten that the object of their ethical thinking in this regard was always the structure of the single city. When the philosopher sought to find the counterpart of cosmic law and justice in the ordering of earthly states, he found it in the principle of the independent city. Neither Plato nor Aristotle attempted to apply ethical principles to the relations of one state to another; and when the philosopher sought to withdraw himself from the wickedness of city politics, he had to seek consolation in the gospel of a cosmopolis, where all men are citizens of one city.

From time to time something akin to a temporary balance of power appears in Greek history. But examination of the facts will almost always show that this is the result of no political principle, but represents a mere stalemate of rival powers. This is most obvious, perhaps, in the relations of the three great Hellenistic kingdoms: they did not come together until it became clear, after years of apparently interminable fighting, that no one of the three was strong enough to conquer the others. The Ætolian and Achæan Leagues may look like unions of equal and independent states; but, in fact, they were the outcome of sheer despair, a last instinctive effort at self-preservation in a moment of hopeless impotence.

The ancient city never attempted to make a place for itself as an independent member of a group of equal cities. It found the fulfilment of its purpose in the exercise of power, unhampered by any moral tie or any maxim of international law. No theories of justice were allowed to combat the principles of downright egoism and brute force. On the contrary, political philosophy came to the aid of *realpolitik* and provided it with a theoretical basis. The principle of justice was to be regarded as a mere form of words devised to cloak force with the appearance of righteousness: the 'useful' was not justice, but the appearance of justice; and that city or that man was the most fortunate who had learned to give a show of justice to the most unscrupulous injustice. Modern democracy repudiates the tactics of Machiavelli and preaches integrity in foreign relations; ancient democracy proclaimed—more insistently the more radical it became—the fundamental principle that the relentless use of superior power is not wrong, but right, and that the oppression of the weaker by the stronger is an eternal law of nature.

This kind of view is nowhere revealed more clearly than in Thucydides' treatment of imperialism.[1] In foreign policy, according to him, the proof that a cause is just is of no importance except as a lure and an adornment. Only the appearance of justice, not the endeavour to act justly, is politically useful. Under cover of moral justifications foreign policy is, in fact, a relentless struggle for power, in which the decisive factor is not ideal justice but the right of the stronger. No limit is set to this lust for domination except the strength of rival powers. Within this limit it is the task of the statesman to win whatever may be won. The same ideas are to be found in Xenophon, whose *Cyropædia* is based upon them, and in Isocrates; and if ever the right of the stronger is disputed, it is by the weaker side, and only on the ground of some specific misuse or excessive exercise of power. Aristotle denies that the State ought to aim at acquiring power over others—for it can achieve happiness without it—but he is forced to admit in so many words that it cannot maintain its sovereignty without military strength, and that imperialism may be justified if it benefits its subjects. Even Plato condemns only such selfishness on the part of the stronger as aims at the annihilation or enslavement

[1] See v. Arnim's *Gerechtigkeit u. Nutzen in d. griech. Aufklärungsphilosophie* (Frankf. Universitätsreden, 1916). On the views of Xenophon, Isocrates, Plato, and Aristotle, see Pohlenz, *Staatsgedanke u. Staatslehre d. Griechen*, 1923, pp. 131 ff.

of the weaker, or the total destruction of his land.   In short,
the whole of Greek political thought is dominated by this kind
of view.   The doctrines of Thucydides appear again in Car-
neades in practically identical form.

Greek imperialism, like Greek civilisation, was naval: it
took the form of thalassocracy.   From the very beginning the
existence of a Greek city was bound up in the endeavour to
secure control of neighbouring seas.   The Greeks themselves
recognised this fact, and worked out a schematic reconstruction
of history in the form of a list of successive thalassocracies; [1]
and Thucydides regarded the rise of great sea kingdoms as a
symptom of advance from a primitive to a more developed
civilisation: [2] Minos built a fleet, conquered the Cyclades, and
established a maritime kingdom which he governed with the
help of his sons; Agamemnon was able to compel the other
Greeks to follow him to Troy 'by reason of their fear alone';
the Ionians held the seas against Persia; Polycrates' fleet
subdued the eastern Ægean; and Corinth, the inventor of the
trireme, and the greatest of all the early naval powers, built up
a vast colonial empire and governed it through cadets of its
royal house.[3] With the conquests of Alexander there came a
change: the eastern conception of universal monarchy succeeded
the earlier idea of Ægean thalassocracy.   Finally, Rome conquered the whole world and made it one state; and the
ultimate realisation of the principle of force was the *pax
Romana*, the annihilation of independence.

Modern imperialism may have a variety of aims, economic,
national, or political.   But the aims of ancient imperialism
were never economic in the sense of seeking advantage for
citizen merchants or producers; and they were never, it need
hardly be said, national.   They were exclusively political.
Max Weber [4] has pointed out that the lines of political
expansion are not necessarily determined by export trade and

[1] The Eusebian list [Diod., vii, 11]. See R. Helm, *Hermes*, 1926, pp. 241 ff.
[See also Myres, *J.H.S.*, 1906, pp. 84 ff. ; and A. R. Burn, *ibid.*, 1927,
pp. 165 ff.]
[2] See above, p. 45.   [3] See above, p. 54.
[4] *Wirtsch. u. Gesellsch.*, pp. 621 ff.

capitalist interests (though he assumes that the growth of the Athenian empire was so determined), but that other economic factors may be equally or more important. Ancient political theory justified self-seeking by the principle of the 'useful'; and Thucydides explained imperialistic policy as the anxiety to secure independence and the necessities of existence. But we have to ask what these terms really meant. The Greek city was not concerned merely to ensure the free exercise of all the peaceable activities of its people, nor even to safeguard the development of national industry. Its duty, as the Greek mind conceived it, was to provide maintenance for its citizens. It was part of the privilege of full citizenship to live at the charges of the State. This somewhat primitive conception of the relation between the individual and the State continued to be the working ideal of the Greek city in spite of all the obstacles which hindered its complete realisation.[1] Something of the sort might have been achieved by peaceful labour, protected from foreign interference, and by friendly trading with neighbouring cities; but the Greeks preferred to rely on force. The whole structure of civilisation was built upon a permanent state of war, not upon international agreements. Economic independence was regarded as a necessary condition of political independence. The Greek city was thus unable to pursue its economic ideal by economic means, and was driven to solve its problems by conquering and living on its neighbours. Greek imperialism was the handmaid of supplies.

This attitude is nowhere more clearly revealed than in the *de Vectigalibus*, a work written in the days of the second Athenian League. The author introduces his programme of reform by insisting that Athens must develop her own resources more thoroughly than heretofore, in order that she may be less dependent upon her subjects. 'I have always been of the opinion,' he writes, 'that the character of a city is determined by that of its rulers. Now some of our rulers have been saying that they are as well instructed in justice as anyone

---

[1] See above, p. 33.

else, but that the poverty of the people has driven them to act unjustly to the subject cities. I have therefore undertaken to discover whether our citizens can be maintained from the resources of our own country, which would be the juster course. For it seemed to me that if this could be secured we should both relieve our poverty and render ourselves less suspect to the other Greeks.'[1]

The writer assumes in his readers the unquestioning belief that the well-being of the city is normally conditioned by the measure of its exercise of power over its subjects, and depends not upon the development of its own economic resources by native labour and industry and trade, but upon the contributions to its maintenance which its subjects supply. It is thus that the citizen ensures his income (μισθός, ii, 1) from the city. 'To be maintained by the subject cities' is contrasted with 'to be maintained out of our native resources.' The notion of maintenance (τροφή) is always recurring (iv, 13 and 19; vi, 1); and the aim of the writer is 'to secure adequate supplies for the Athenians' (iv, 33).

'It appears to be of great advantage to the *demos* that all Athenians should possess the money of the allies, and that the allies should have only enough to keep them alive and at work without being able to rise against us' ([Xen.] *Resp. Ath.*, i, 15). 'The demagogues give you Eubœa and promise you fifty medimni of corn a man' (Arist., *Vesp.*, 715 ff.). 'Eubœa yielded more to Athens than did Attica itself' (Thuc., viii, 96). Aristotle (*Resp. Ath.*, 24) expressly says that the aim of the Athenian hegemony was 'to provide maintenance for all, as Aristides had proposed. For by tribute, taxes, and other contributions of the allies it was possible to maintain more than 20,000 men. These were the 6000 members of the popular courts, 1600 archers and 1200 cavalrymen, 500 councillors, a garrison of 500 in the dockyards, 50 warders in the citadel, 700 officials in Attica and about as many abroad. Further, a normal strength of 2500 heavy infantry and a naval force of 2000; and finally, the Prytaneum with its pensioners, the

[1] i, 1.

orphans educated by the State, and the prison warders. The maintenance of all these was at the charges of the State.'

A Greek imperial city used two methods. Sometimes it annexed foreign countries and exploited them directly, driving out the original inhabitants and settling the surplus of its own population. This method appealed primarily to the peasantry. Thousands of Athenians found a permanent source of income as settlers in the overseas cleruchies. An ancient oath of the Athenian ephebi has been preserved: 'I shall consider the frontiers of Attica to be wheat and barley, vines and olives'; on which Plutarch comments that in this way the young Athenian was taught his duty to acquire all fertile land for his own city.[1] The other method, which rather benefited the town-dwellers, was to compel the conquered countries to pay tribute in money and in kind. The inhabitants were spared to become a source of revenue.[2]

The citizens of a Greek city—ideally, at least—belonged to a class which did not work: at home there were serfs and slaves and metics; abroad there were subject cities. This ideal was most nearly realised in imperial cities; but even where it was less fully realised it was extremely important. The body of full citizens became a 'military caste,' the city itself a 'military unit' (Max Weber). This was all the more inevitable since, as Thucydides pointed out, a city cannot rest content in the possession of independence and the means of existence: it has always to fear danger from a neighbouring city which is, or may become, more powerful. The legitimate

[1] Plut., *Alcib.*, 15.

[2] Rome also depended for its revenues on conquest. When Macedonia was made a province the Roman people ceased to pay *tributum*. (It may be remarked that at this period property tax was exceptional and income tax unknown.) State maintenance in Greece is paralleled by the corn doles of Rome. More than two-thirds of the inhabitants of Rome received public corn ; by the time of Cæsar the number was 320,000 males, which, with women and children, amounts to about 600,000 persons in all (Bücher, *Entstehung*, p. 378). Note that in Rome, too, imperial expansion was due not to the interests of trade and industry, but to the capitalistic interests of land speculators, office-hunters and tax-farmers (Max Weber, *op. cit.*, pp. 621 ff.).

desire for self-preservation and independence led naturally and inevitably to imperialism and conquest. In later periods of history war has been the means of fostering trade; in ancient Greece it served to bring in tribute for distribution among the citizens, who were thus enabled to approach their ideal of economic independence. They lived by war. They had no time for peaceful work or trade. Political responsibilities and unremitting military duties [1] absorbed their interest and energy. Moreover, the Greek world lacked the security and stability which is indispensable to a commercial civilisation. Force was the ruling principle at home and abroad. At home, private property was at the mercy of the State or of the irresponsible conduct of the popular law courts; and every revolution was followed by abrupt reversals of fortune. Abroad, conditions were no less precarious, and any profits earned in commerce were promptly withdrawn and used to purchase land—then the safest form of investment. In such a world there was no place for solidarity; everything made for the strictest isolation. The exclusiveness of the ruling class implied the exclusiveness of the State; for the State meant its citizens, not its territory. Each city stood in isolation against the rest—an isolation which is only partly explained by reference to the 'individualism' of the Greeks. It was impossible to pass beyond the city-state and to form a united nation—a political conception which was wholly alien to the ancient world. Apart from other overwhelming arguments, consideration of these conditions should have served as a warning against exaggerated conceptions of the Greek economy. The directing principle of the ancient State was utterly incompatible with the development of international commerce.

The life and independence of the State was, in the ancient view, conditioned by its food supply and the provision of other necessaries; and the fear of which Thucydides speaks was in the last analysis the simple fear that a more powerful neighbour might threaten these supplies. The Greek city was not concerned to achieve commercial supremacy and to capture

---

[1] Athens, for example, was almost continuously at war.

markets by peaceful means, but to ensure its own supplies and control those of other cities by the exercise of force.

Commercial, as distinct from political, supremacy was unknown in Greece. Even in classical Athens, where thalassocracy attained a fuller development than in any other state before the Hellenistic age, all those features of its foreign policy which are commonly described as commercial were in fact purely political and 'thalassocratic.' It is well known how rapidly the first Athenian maritime league lost its original character. The predominant position of Athens led inevitably to a change in the status of the allies. They became subjects, not allies; the confederacy became a centralised state: the συμμαχία passed into an ἀρχή. Contributions became tribute, and the revenues of the league became Athenian revenues. More and more, Athens took into her own hands the military duties of the league. In the end, only the three great islands, Samos, Chios and Lesbos were non-tributary. This was a manifestation of the principle of thalassocracy on such a scale as the Greek world had never known.

It has been customary to call this Athenian empire a commercial empire;[1] the treaties which Athens concluded with the dependent allies are called commercial treaties; and the imposition of the Athenian monetary system is taken to be part of a deliberate policy of consolidation and unification within the range of this commercial supremacy. But this is as unsubstantial as the shadowy 'commercial and colonial empire' of Corinth in the sixth century.[2] Athens, like Corinth, was not engaged in the peaceful activities of commerce and exchange but in plain robbery and exploitation.[3]

Import treaties inevitably took on a very different character when they were made between ruler and subject, and not between equal powers: they became mere arrangements for forced contributions. An example of this kind is preserved in the fragmentary treaty between Athens and Ceos regarding

---

[1] *Cf.* Meyer, *G.A.*, iii, 494.
[2] See above, p. 54.
[3] See the passage from [Xen.] *Resp. Ath.*, ii., 11 ff. quoted above, p. 91.

the export of ruddle.[1] In accordance with this treaty ruddle might only be exported to Athens, and that only in vessels specified by the Athenians. No export duty might be levied in Ceos, but an import duty had to be paid in Athens. The decisive point here again is the nature of the commodity. Cean ruddle was the best in Greece (Theophr., de Lapidibus, 52). Boeckh (ii. 315 ff.) believed that it was an article of trade used in mixing colours, and that the treaty was intended to benefit the Athenian emporium. He therefore described the treaty as a 'commercial treaty,' and all the moderns, including Riezler (Finanzen u. Monopole, p. 82), have followed him. But ruddle belongs precisely to the class of shipbuilding materials mentioned by the Pseudo-Xenophon.[2] It is indispensable in the painting of triremes, and for that reason alone were the Athenians interested in it. It would be a grave mistake to conclude from this treaty that there were similar treaties dealing with ordinary articles of trade, or to take it as a typical example of trading relations within the area of Athenian power. We must not argue from it to any general compulsion to use Athens as a staple.

Further evidence is provided by the treaty between Athens and Perdiccas of Macedon (I.G., i², 71 : 423/2 B.C.): 'I shall help the Athenians to the best of my power; I shall permit no one, not even the Athenian allies, to export timber for oars except to the Athenians.'[3] The whole Macedonian export of oars went to Athens, like the Cean ruddle. Macedon did not belong to the Athenian League; but the predominance of the Athenian power was such that the northern kingdom could not escape it. There is even a tradition of tribute paid to Athens by Perdiccas.[4] Macedon, too, was among the states which the Pseudo-Xenophon had in mind; which shows that others besides the allies of Athens were affected.

Like the import treaties, so the treaties concerning legal

---

[1] I.G., ii², 1128 [H.H. 137]. It dates from the fourth century, but is a renewal of an earlier agreement.

[2] Above, p. 91.   [3] Cf. the sons of Leucon (above, p. 114).

[4] Dem., vii, § 12 ; xi, § 16. See Meyer, G.A., iv, 76.

relations change their character in an imperial context. Athens did not regulate these relations with the allies on any general plan, but by separate treaties. Whereas the general principle in regard to states outside the alliance was that of the *forum rei* (Dem., vii, §§ 12 ff.), it was now laid down that all cases arising out of contracts made in Athens should be dealt with by Athenian law and in Athenian courts. This was done as early as 466 B.C. for Chios, one of the least dependent of the allies. The general tendency was to bring as far as possible all judicial proceedings, both civil and criminal, before Athenian courts. The law of Solon and the Athenian courts were never imposed outright upon the empire; the extent of compulsion varied from city to city according to the terms of the treaties.[1] This must not be described as a measure of commercial policy on the part of Athens; nor must the treaties be called 'commercial.'[2] It was a purely political measure — though, in the nature of the case, trading relations were also affected by it.

But the state which rules the sea is not only in a position to secure its own supply of food and other necessaries at the expense of weaker powers; it can control the entire supplies of these weaker powers, and use this control unscrupulously to enforce its imperial supremacy. The author of the Pseudo-Xenophontean *Respublica Atheniensium* writes: 'Of the mainland states which are ruled by Athens, the small are ruled because of fear, the great because . . . (*lacuna*); but all because of need: for every state must import and export; and this it can only do if it is obedient to the ruling sea-power' (2, 3). And again (2, 13): 'Moreover, every mainland has its promontories, or islands off the coast, or straits, which the ruling sea-power can occupy and so inflict damage on the country.'

The ruling state, then, has all the food supply in its hands

---

[1] See Lipsius, *Att. Recht. u. Rechtsverf.*, pp. 969 ff.; Meyer, *G.A.*, iii, 496 ff.

[2] As is done by B. M. Romstedt, *Die Wirtschaftliche Organisation d. athenischen Reiches* (Leipz. Dissertation, 1914), pp. 47 ff. The idea of this dissertation, which was suggested by Wilcken, is brilliant; but the writer has shown himself wholly incompetent to carry it out.

(σιτοπομπίας κύριος, Dem., xviii, § 87), and thus has weaker cities entirely at its mercy. It can apply the grimmest kind of compulsion. 'See that the Athenians do not become too powerful at sea,' said the Corinthians at Sparta (Thuc., i, 120), 'for then it will be harder for your inland people to bring down their produce to the coast and receive in exchange what the sea brings to the land.' In the fifteenth year of the Peloponnesian War the Athenians proclaimed a blockade of Macedon (Thuc., v, 83), on which the ancient commentator remarks, 'they shut them off from import by sea.'

But the most striking example of this terrorisation is the Athenian decree of 426/5 B.C. concerning her ally Methone (*S.I.G.*, 75 [H.H. 60, Tod 61]): 'The Methonæans may import corn from Byzantium up to . . . medimni yearly. The officials at the Hellespont shall neither hinder them nor allow others to hinder them, under penalty of 10,000 drachmæ. The Methonæans shall on each occasion give written notice to the officials.' This inscription shows that Athens controlled the entire corn traffic from the Black Sea to the Ægean, and could permit or forbid passage as she wished. The Methonæans were allowed to load a limited supply of corn at Byzantium, but not to sail into the Black Sea. According to Wilamowitz,[1] entry to the Black Sea was normally barred; so that, without express permission, only Athenian ships could have brought corn to Methone. But this view is based upon the conception of 'national' trade and 'national' monopoly. Trade in those days was not national but cosmopolitan, and it mattered nothing whose ship it was that carried corn. What did matter was the destination of the corn. Athens in the Peloponnesian War controlled the entire export from Byzantium, that is from the Black Sea regions in general, so that only her allies were allowed corn, and that in limited amounts.

Thucydides in a famous passage [2] distinguishes the real causes of the Peloponnesian War from the legal pretexts. The direct occasions of rupture, he says, were the Athenian support

[1] *Gr. Lesebuch*, ii, 2, 249.
[2] i, 88 [*cf.* 23 and 118]. See v. Arnim (above, p. 134, n. 1), p. 12.

of Corcyra against Sparta's ally Corinth, and the affair of
Potidæa, which also brought Athens and Corinth into conflict;
but, in fact, the Spartans did not go to war for these reasons,
but out of fear for the growing strength of Athens. This was
not fear of the growing strength of a great commercial rival;
it was purely and simply the fear of an imperial power which
held the keys of its neighbours' granaries. The mastery of the
corn and timber lands and of the routes to them meant the
mastery of others' lives: no clearer indication of this could be
desired than the effects of the Megarian Decree.

Any power which controlled the routes of supply might
seize them without scruple when it so desired, and so cut off
its neighbours from their resources. After Chæronea, when
it was rumoured that Athens was invested and as good as lost,
'the Rhodians manned their ships of war and forced merchantmen to put in at Rhodes, so that traders proceeding to Athens
had to unload their cargoes of corn and other goods in Rhodes'
(Lyc., Leocr., § 18). 'At a time when corn was scarce and
public funds were low, the Byzantines forcibly seized ships
sailing out of Pontus' ([Arist.] Econ., ii, 1346b). Demosthenes
speaks of such seizures by the Byzantines in v, § 25, and again
in l, § 6, where he reminds his hearers how merchantmen about
to sail out of Pontus were seized in a time of dearth by Byzantines, Calchedonians and Cyzicenes—and prices rose in the
Piræus. Here once again it must be insisted that we are
concerned with necessary supplies and not with trade in
general.

The growth of Athens, which began with Peisistratus and led
on to the Empire, is at no stage a symptom of the growth and
expansion of general trading relations. The Black Sea policy
of Pericles had nothing to do with a desire to further Athenian
export trade.[1] The Athenians in the fifth century consolidated
the strong points gained by Peisistratus overseas, but not in
order to use them as trading outposts:[2] the wars against
Eubœa, Ægina, Chalcis, Cythera, were not waged to get rid

---

[1] As, for example, even W. Otto maintains, Kulturgesch. d. Alt., p. 85.
[2] Pöhlmann (G.G., p. 147) cites Potidæa.

of commercial rivals.[1] The occupation of Sigeum on the Hellespont, the settlement of Miltiades in Thracian Chersonese, the conquest of Salamis and, perhaps as early as this, of Lemnos and Imbros off the Dardanelles, the advances in northern Macedonia, the Thermaic Gulf and the lower Strymon, the setting up of Lygdamis as tyrant of Naxos,[2] these were no more prompted by commercial policy [3] than the expansion of the Corinthian sea-power or the growth of Samos under Polycrates.[4] When Athens had dealings in the West with Segesta, Rhegium, and Leontini; when an Athenian admiral defended Neapolis against barbarian inroads; or when Themistocles used his personal connections in northern Peloponnese, Corcyra, and Syracuse,[5] in the service of his city, there was no thought of building up commercial connections; [6] and, though historians have called it so, Thurii was not a Panhellenic trading station under Athenian leadership.[7]

Athenian thalassocracy was the handmaid of supplies. It set up purely military outposts in order to maintain its empire, and occupied points from which it could control and ration the supplies of others. It created dependencies which paid tribute and provided food, and it lived at their expense. It either exploited them directly or it used them for settling its surplus population in cleruchies. Pericles' intention in founding settlements in Chersonese, Thrace, Naxos, Andros, Thurii, was to rid the city of an unemployed and restless mob and to supply the needs of the people; and at the same time to have garrisons in the dependent territory and so prevent revolt (Plut., *Pericles*, 11).

When Rhegium and Leontini sought help against Syracuse at the time of the first Athenian expedition, the Athenians agreed 'ostensibly on the ground of their early friendship, but

[1] Büchsenschütz, *Bes. u. Erw.*, p. 404.

[2] Hdt., i, 61, 64 ; *Resp. Ath.*, 15, 2 ff.

[3] Meyer, *G.A.*, ii, 644, 774 ; Busolt, *G.G.*, ii, 249 ; the occupation of Sigeum is described as a trading link.

[4] See above, pp. 53 and 103. Meyer, *G.A.*, ii, 774.

[5] Thuc., i, 135 ff. ; Plut., *Themist.*, 24, 32.

[6] Zimmern, *The Greek Commonwealth* (2nd ed.), p. 373.

[7] Zimmern, *loc. cit.*

in fact, in order to prevent the export of corn from these regions to the Peloponnese, and, further, in the hope of making conquests in Sicily' (Thuc., iii, 86). The Sicilian expedition was an attempt upon the great corn lands: during it, says Demosthenes (lvi, § 9), the price of corn went down in Athens. The Egyptian expedition of Pericles was without question undertaken for the sake of corn;[1] and Nicias attacked Cythera because it was a port of call for vessels bringing corn to Peloponnese from Egypt and Libya (Thuc., iv, 53).

VI. *The Corn Trade*

In the primitive conditions of this age it was impossible to maintain the supply of necessities by trade alone. Trading was dependent not only upon the goodwill of stronger neighbours, but upon the goodwill of foreign traders. The Greek merchant was primarily a corn-merchant, as all the examples show; and the predominant importance of the corn trade is abundantly clear: Xenophon describes merchants as 'corn-lovers.'[2] Moreover, the overseas corn-merchant was almost without exception a non-citizen.[3] Hence the marked dependence upon the foreign trader and the need to conciliate him in every kind of way—by chief seats at the theatre, meals at the public cost, priority in the business of the law-courts—so that he should come 'not for gain but for honours, and as to friends' (Xen., *Vect.*, iii, 3–4). The various exemptions granted to these traders speak clearly enough. They were primarily in the interest of the city which granted them.[4] The importation of corn by private persons was always regarded as a special service, as a patriotic or a philanthropic act. It was a matter of boast in the law-courts (Dem., xxxiv, § 38);

[1] Otto, *Kulturgesch.*, p. 86, n. 166.

[2] *Econ.*, xx, 27.

[3] This has long been recognised ; see Gernet, p. 328 ; Meyer, *Kl. Schr.*, i, 132.

[4] See p. 116. We cannot, however, speak of any general exemption granted to traders, as Boeckh has shown (i, 107 ff. [pp. 85 ff.]). Resident alien traders enjoyed a certain freedom from military service, as was only natural, but this was their only general privilege.

and inscriptions show how highly it was honoured. In 330 B.C. Athens rewarded a Cypriot trader with a wreath, and granted him diplomatic assistance, 'because, being the first corn-dealer to reach Athens at a time of scarcity, he delivered 3000 medimni of corn at 5 drachmæ the medimnus, and further presented 3000 drachmæ as a freewill offering for the purchase of corn (*S.I.G.*, 304). The speaker in Demosthenes (*l.c.*) boasts that he not only imported more than 10,000 medimni of wheat at 5 drachmæ, but put one talent at the disposal of the State for the purchase of corn. Other examples could easily be added;[1] and with them may be classed the great gifts of corn from foreign princes, like that of Psammetichus of Egypt, who gave Athens 40,000 medimni of wheat in 445/4 B.C.[2] Not only regular traders, but private persons, who ordinarily had nothing to do with trade, gave their services in this way; and the cities, which honoured them in these ways, were entirely dependent upon their help, whether it was offered spontaneously or, like the special contributions of citizens in other emergencies, was called for by the State.

In either case it was the State which bore the responsibility. In Aristotle's time 'corn' was among the standing *agenda* of the principal ecclesia in every prytany;[3] and the corn supply was recognised as one of the main cares of a statesman (see above, p. 112). In Athens there was no trading class to take the business into its own hands;[4] and the State on occasion had to act for itself—to buy corn with money contributed by private persons, or to make arrangements to meet the purchase from public funds.[5] At a time of dearth in Clazomenæ[6] the

---

[1] Not all from the fourth century, however : *I.G.*, ii², 283, 342, 400, 407 ; *I.G.*, vii, 42, 62 (Oropus) ; *S.I.G.*, 354 (Ephesus), 495 (Olbia), 493 (Histiæa).

[2] Philoch. *ap*. Schol. Arist., *Vesp.*, 716. Francotte has collected the known instances in *Mélanges Nicole*, p. 145, n. 1.

[3] *Resp. Ath.*, 43, 4 (see above, p. 112).

[4] The foreign trader was, of course, not a citizen ; and in Athens, at least, it seems that the resident trader also was a non-citizen. See above, p. 7.

[5] *S.I.G.*, 344, ll. 80 ff. (letter from Antigonus about Teos and Lebedos, 303 B.C.).

[6] [Arist.], *Econ.*, ii, 1348*b*, 16 ; Riezler, *Finanzen u. Monopole*, pp. 20 ff.

government bought up corn in foreign markets, giving oil lent by private citizens as security for payment; and on this occasion it hired vessels for the purpose—that is, it took transport as well into its own hands. It need hardly be said that in such cases it drove the best bargain that it could. In Selymbria, for example, a law had been passed, at a time of scarcity, forbidding the export of corn; with the result that supplies were plentiful. The government then bought in all the corn—beyond the necessary year's supply for each citizen—at a very low price fixed by decree. It then repealed the law, and was able to sell at a large profit when prices rose with the opening of the market.[1] In other words, when the State took the corn trade into its own hands it was ready to exploit it in the interests of the treasury. On one occasion Leucon of Bosporus (Dem., xx, § 33) sent so much corn to Athens in time of scarcity that fifteen talents were over for the treasury; which can only mean that the State sold the surplus advantageously abroad.[2] It is to illustrate such public speculations that the *Economics* adduces the cases mentioned. A further example comes from Byzantium: the government secured corn on credit by forcible seizure of passing ships; when payment fell due and the merchants complained, the government paid them interest at 10%, and recouped itself by increasing the price to the consumers.[3]

The interest of the State in the corn trade is further exhibited in the care it took to safeguard transport. Athens intervened on behalf of a Cypriot corn-merchant whose sails had been seized by the Heracleots (p. 116); consignments of corn were escorted by battleships—Demosthenes (xviii, §§ 73 ff.) speaks of a convoy of twenty ships 'for the safe conduct of corn' (cf. *S.I.G.*, 305, and p. 107 above). So in Demosthenes (l, §§ 17 ff.) we have a convoy for corn-ships which the Maron-

---

[1] [Arist.], *op. cit.*, 1348*b*, 33 ; Riezler, *op. cit.*, p. 22. See also below, p. 154. [Reading with Keil <τοῖς ἄλλοις>ἐν in l. 34, the Oxford editors translate : ' They had a law which forbade the export of corn to another state which was suffering from famine.']

[2] No other interpretation is possible ; see Fränkel, Boeckh, ii, *Adn.* 154.

[3] [Arist.], *op. cit.*, 1346*b*, 29.

eans and Thasians also claimed to use; and at viii, §§ 24 ff.
Athenian trierarchs receive payment from the Chians, Ery-
thræans and other sea-coast cities of Asia Minor for the protection of their merchantmen (though we must not conclude
from this that Athens had organised an international league
for the safeguarding of the corn-trade, and that this protection
had become a source of public revenue).[1] During the Peloponnesian War Athens fortified the promontory of Sunium to
ensure safe transport of corn;[2] and Chabrias fought a sea
battle with the Lacedæmonians to the same end.[3]

The activities of the Athenians against the pirates had no
other purpose than to maintain order in the empire and to
secure the transport of food. (Such were Cimon's expedition
against the Dolopians of Scyros; the dispatch of triremes
against pirates in 335/4 B.C.; the decree of Mœrocles; Philip's
proposal to police the seas in concert with Athens.[4]) For the
seizure of corn-ships was not confined to the professional
pirate; it was the normal and traditional method by which the
State itself secured its food supply. Piracy and privateering
were practised under the State protection—as is shown by the
examples of Byzantium, Chalcedon, and Cyzicus.[5]

In addition to military action the State frequently took
legislative steps to guard its supplies. It might forbid export,
as in Athens,[6] of all produce except oil, or, as in Selymbria,[7]
of corn. In Teos a curse was laid upon those 'who hinder
the importation of corn by land or sea, or re-export imported
corn.'[8] There was a law that two-thirds of the corn which
entered the Piræus must be brought to Athens;[9] no resident
in Athens might carry corn to any other port, under penalty
of death;[10] no Athenian might lend money to a trader carrying

---

[1] As Gernet does, pp. 361 and 364 (see above, p. 22, n. 1).

[2] Thuc., viii, 4.   [3] Xen., *Hell.*, v, 4, 61 ; Diod., xv, 34.

[4] Plut., *Cimon*, 7 ; *I.G.*, ii², 1623, Bb. 276 [*S.I.G.*, 962] ; Dem., lviii,
§§ 53, 56 ; Dem., vii, § 14.

[5] See above, p. 144.   [6] Plut., *Solon*, 24.   [7] Above, p. 112.

[8] Collitz-Bechtel, iii, 5632 [*S.I.G.*, 37, H.H. 23, Tod 23].

[9] *Resp. Ath.*, 51, 4.

[10] Dem., xxxiv, § 37, οἰκῶν 'Αθήνησι (*i.e.* a metic) ; Dem., xxxv, § 50 ff. ;
Lyc., *Leocr.*, § 27.

corn to any other port;[1] and, to prevent accumulation of stock and holding back for the market, no dealer from abroad was allowed to buy more than the legally fixed amount of 50 phormi (Lys., xxii, 6).

The food-supply was controlled by a body of corn-police. It was the task of these *sitophylakes* in Athens to secure that the unmilled corn which came into the market was sold accord-ing to the law; that the miller sold his meal and the baker his bread in accordance with the prices of barley and of wheat, and at the weights laid down by them; and to see that the measures taken by the State to guard against artificial rise in the price of corn were duly observed.[2] For the last-named purpose they kept lists from which the amount of imported corn could be ascertained (Dem., xx, § 32). On the occasion of extraordinary purchases a board of so-called *sitonæ* was entrusted with the management and distribution of the State-bought corn.[3] The government maintained granaries in which corn was sold or distributed free to the public.[4] A striking example is the proposal of Teos and Lebedos in 303 B.C. (*S.I.G.*, 344) that a sum of 1400 chrysi should be set aside from the public revenues and entrusted to a private individual for the purchase, storage, and sale of corn.

This kind of intervention was not confined to times of scarcity, nor was State aid restricted to the proletariat. In the ancient view it was the duty of the State to feed its citizens; and this duty dominated its economic policy throughout.[5] Public purchases of corn were to assume gigantic proportion in later times, when Rome was able to rely on her provinces for supplies.

---

[1] Dem., xxxv, § 51. These two laws—one affecting the trader, the other the lender of capital—must be distinguished from each other, and each from a third (see below, p. 170), which deals not only with corn but with other goods. Lipsius (*Att. Recht.*, pp. 97, 312) confuses all three.

[2] Arist., *Resp. Ath.*, 51, 3 ; Lys., xxii, 5 ff.

[3] Busolt, *Gr. St.*, i, 433, n. 1.

[4] Dem., xxxiv, § 37 ; Schol. Ar., *Eq.*, 103 ; Thuc., viii, 90, 5.

[5] Gernet (see p. 22, n. 1) ; Francotte, *Le pain à bon marché et le pain gratuit, etc.* (*Mélanges Nicole*, Geneva, 1905.) Boeckh, i, 97 ff. [pp. 77 ff.] ; Busolt, *Gr. St.*, i, 429 ff.

B. Commercial Policy and the Treasury

I. *Economic Tyranny*

Practically no Greek community was self-supporting; and consequently it was the need of securing food supplies and other elementary necessities such as shipbuilding timber, which in the first place determined the relation of the State to trade, and created a conscious and deliberate policy in this regard. But besides the policy which looks to supplies, there is another which looks to the interest of the treasury, which seeks to secure that whatever trade there may be within the boundaries of the State shall make for its enrichment. With this aim in view the government was ready to intervene with all the means at its disposal, regardless of the effects such intervention might produce: it was concerned with nothing except to fill its granaries and its treasury. Any attempt to foster national trade and production was foreign to its purpose. It was this intervention of the all-powerful State which as much as anything else hindered the growth and development of commerce. It limited and constricted all free economic life; and created that insecurity and uncertainty and lawlessness which accompany a permanent state of war. The Pseudo-Aristotelian *Economics* (ii, 1347*a*, 32) gives an example which throws a crude light on the situation. In Lampsacus the government decreed an advance of 50% in the price of oil, wine and corn—in order to divert that 50% into the treasury. The State did not act on behalf of a class of traders with whose interests it identified itself. On the contrary, it intervened in its own interests whenever opportunity offered, taking commercial enterprises into its own hands and seizing the profits for the treasury. Burckhardt's phrase, the 'economic tyranny' of the Greek city, hits the mark; and it loses little of its point by the fact that commercial activities were normally in the hands of non-citizens. For this tyranny did not stop short of its own citizen body. The State interfered not only in commerce, but in the whole economic life of the city. Property, money, credit, every kind of pecuniary transaction, were at its mercy.

There was no demand for service which it could not make upon the individual. It is well known how ruthlessly it interfered with the property of its citizens (p. 88). Expropriations, confiscations, redistribution of land were ordinary occurrences. And the cause is everywhere the same: the ancient city never had a regular budget. When normal revenues failed, it was bound in self-preservation to fall back upon violent means. It must be remembered that owing to lack of security no policy of State loans had been developed: what is commonly described as borrowing amounted in fact to reduction of capital, or robbery, or voluntary aid by individuals, or forced loans.[1] The examples in the Pseudo-Aristotelian *Economics* shows how the State fastened upon every possible form of property, with more or less inadequate guarantee of repayment to the owners: land, slaves, privateering rights, property of orphans, outstanding debts, golden ornaments, precious metals and money.[2]

In fact, State and individual were openly at war. This led to the most elaborate concealment of wealth,[3] to hoarding, and to the flight of capital abroad. The less a city was in a position to maintain itself at the expense of the foreigner, the keener, necessarily, became the struggle between it and its own citizens; and this struggle was bound to produce a citizen body which was concerned not so much to increase its wealth, as to maintain it. Things went so far that all possessions were a danger. 'When I was a boy it was not dangerous to be called rich, and a man was proud of it; to-day he does all he can to hide the amount of his possessions, for it is more dangerous to pass for wealthy than to break the law.'[4] In conditions like these it was impossible that there should grow up a class of citizen-merchants like those of the Middle Ages or of modern days. It is the necessary consequence of these conditions—and of the Greek attitude to any technical occupation—that those classes whose wealth fitted them best to form

---

[1] Riezler, *Finanzen u. Monopole*, pp. 56 ff.
[2] Riezler, *Finanzen u. Monopole*, p. 58.   [3] *Hermes*, 1920, pp. 156 ff.
[4] Isoc., xv, 159 ff. ; *Hermes*, 1920, p. 156.

a merchant-class stood aside from commerce and devoted themselves to the business of money-lending. This offered every opportunity of enrichment, and was relatively secure from the rapacity of private adversaries or the State. The curious division of all private property into 'visible' and 'invisible' (p. 88) was entirely due to this ruthless attitude of the government. To the former class belonged all property which any man could see, which could not be denied, and which, therefore, was taken into consideration when the State demanded services; to the latter, such property as was not immediately demonstrable, so to speak—for the most part such as was out on loan. Hence the enormous importance of all kinds of speculation. In addition to speculation and hoarding there was considerable investment in land: this continued to be the safest form of property; and at this period agriculture was the natural means of livelihood. The wars of the Greek world, in which each state thought to find its safety in the downfall and exhaustion of its rival, where the victor only spared the economic resources of the vanquished if he could find his own advantage in so doing, had their counterpart in every city in the war between city and citizen. It was a state of war of all against all: there was no chance there for the development of an even moderately regular and stable trade.

II. *Monopolies*

The second book of the Pseudo-Aristotelian *Economics*, with its examples of noteworthy financial devices of governments and rulers, is the most convenient source-book for the conditions described above. We are here concerned only with cases of State intervention in commerce; in particular with monopolies, which, even in classical times, are not infrequent. Of monopolies in general Aristotle writes in the *Politics* ($1259a$, 20): 'Some states when short of money create a source of revenue by establishing a monopoly of goods for sale.' We may fairly deduce from this passage that in classical times monopolies (*a*) were temporary, not permanent; and (*b*) were monopolies of sale, not of production. There is no indication

of standing monopolies except that of money-changing [1]—
another proof of the lack of certainty, security, and foresight
in the commercial life of the time: measures were taken for
the moment only. Of monopolies of production there is no
trace.[2] Aristotle says (*Politics*, 1267*b*) that in Epidamnus the
workers who laboured for the community were public slaves;
but it by no means follows that the State sold the products of
this slave labour and made profit from the sale. On the
contrary, Epidamnus, no doubt, made its profit by hiring out
its slaves to individuals, as private owners did, and as the
author of *de Vectigalibus* urged Athens to do (p. 78). The
use of the sea, for making purple dye and salt and for fishing,
sometimes appears as a right vested in the State; [3] but even
here we cannot speak of a public monopoly of production.[4]
We nowhere hear that the State took the production of salt or
purple into its own hands, or managed its fisheries directly;
we hear rather of the cession of public rights to individuals:
the Byzantines, for example, compensated certain private cult-
associations by making over to them the rights of fishing and
of selling salt (Ps.-Arist., *Econ.*, ii, 1346*b*, 21). Elsewhere it
was merely a matter of letting out these rights. It appears,
moreover—in Athens it is certain [5]—that no State which
possessed mines worked them on its own account: the profit
which accrued to the treasury derived solely from leases. The
very idea of direct exploitation of public domains by means of
a standing body of State labour was so unfamiliar that the
author of *de Vectigalibus*, who is concerned to expound (iv, 13)
'how the mines of Laurium may be made most serviceable to
the State,' has no further recommendation than that the State
should acquire a large body of mine-slaves *in order to hire them
out to private individuals*, and so replenish its exchequer. The

---

[1] In spite of Riezler's contention the monopoly of Datames was a purely
war-time measure (Ps.-Arist., *Econ.*, ii, 1350*b*, 16, reading Datames for
Didales with Schneider (*cf.* Polyæn., vii, 21) ; see *Hermes*, 1920, p. 163, n. 7).
[2] Busolt's view notwithstanding ; *Gr. St.*, i, 607.
[3] Boeckh, i, 372, note c. [p. 303, n. 24, but the later (German) edition
is very much fuller] ; Busolt, *Gr. St.*, i, 607 ff.
[4] *Pace*, Busolt, *loc. cit.*   [5] Boeckh, i, 377 ff. [pp. 309 ff.].

same author must have been thinking of State leases when he points to the richness of Attica by land and sea—agricultural products, metals, marble, the gifts of the sea—as a fruitful source of public revenue (i, 2). It is a mistake to speak of State production or industry in the classical age.[1] The public *ergasterium* belongs to Hellenistic times.

On the other hand, temporary monopolies of sales are common enough.[2] An example from Selymbria has been cited above (p. 148). A similar device, by which the State secured the opportunity of buying cheap and selling dear, was proposed to the Athenians by Pythocles ([Arist.], *Econ.*, ii, 1353a, 15): all the lead from the Laurian mines was to be bought from the lessees at the market price, and sold for three times as much. Cleomenes of Naucratis, whom Alexander placed in charge of Egyptian financial administration, killed the entire private foreign trade in corn by prohibiting export, and concentrating it in his own hands.[3] The city of Heraclea ([Arist.] *Econ.*, ii, 1347b, 3) bought corn, oil, wine, and other commodities on credit from the foreign dealers, and sold them to its mercenaries in enemy territory. The profits were large enough not only to provide pay for the troops, but to discharge the debt on the goods purchased.[4]

These examples show that the State did on occasion play the part of a trader on its own account. But it is perfectly clear that its trading enterprises were irregular and impermanent. At bottom they were nothing more than ingenious speculations

[1] *Cf.* Busolt, *op. cit.*, p. 604 ; and Riezler, *op. cit.*, p. 50.

[2] For what follows see Riezler, *op. cit.*, pp. 51 ff.

[3] Dem., lvi, §§ 7 ff. [Arist.], *Econ.*, ii, 1352b, 14 ; Diod., xviii, 14, 1. *Cf.* Riezler, pp. 33, 53 ; Wilcken in *Schmollers Jahrb.*, xlv, 2 (1921), p. 79 ; Van Groningen, *Mnemosyne*, lxiii, 2 (1925), pp. 25 ff. On Cleomenes' further schemes for securing the highest prices for Egyptian corn in foreign markets see my remarks in *Hermes*, 1923, p. 415.

[4] Plutarch (*Q.G.*, 29) relates that the Epidamnians elected from their number every year a ' seller,' who was sent to the neighbouring people of Illyria to conduct all commercial dealings in the name of his fellow-citizens. In spite of Riezler (p. 54), I cannot bring this into the present context. There is no indication that this regulation of trade between Epidamnus and Illyria implied that the State had any share or any control of the resulting profits.

suggested by chance or some sudden constellation of circumstances, and resorted to when no other escape from bankruptcy presented itself. How unfamiliar to these days was the notion of genuine State enterprise in trade is shown by another proposal of the author of *de Vectigalibus*. Athens ought, he holds, to maintain public merchantmen as it maintains its men-of-war—not in order to conduct public enterprises, or to build up a national carrying trade, but in order 'to hire them out like any other kind of State property' (iii, 14), and so benefit the public treasury. Of banking monopolies we have two examples for the fourth century—from Byzantium and from Olbia. In Hellenistic times we meet them more often.[1]

'The Byzantines farmed out the right of changing money to one bank. No other person was allowed either to give or receive money in exchange, under penalty of confiscation.'[2] We have here a monopoly of foreign exchange only, not of banking business in general. The notice is short to the point of obscurity; but the sense must be that the government monopolised what had hitherto been an unrestricted business, and farmed out the monopoly to a private firm.

In an Olbian law, probably of the early fourth century (*S.I.G.*, 218), we read (ll. 6 ff.): 'Whoever wishes to exchange gold or silver currency shall do so at the stone in the Ecclesiasterium. Whoever shall do so elsewhere is liable to punishment as follows: the seller shall be mulcted in the amount which he sold, and the buyer in the price at which he bought.' It would appear that the State had its own bank of exchange; for it also fixes the rate—$10\frac{1}{2}$ (or $11\frac{1}{2}$) Olbian staters to the Cyzicene stater (ll. 24 ff.); the rate for other currencies is not fixed (l. 28). No special tax is imposed upon foreign exchange transactions (l. 29).[3]

The monopoly of foreign exchange was the more important

---

[1] References in *Hermes*, 1920, p. 163, n. 5. On the Ptolemaic banking monopoly see Wilcken in *Schmollers Jahrb.*, 1921, pp. 85 ff.

[2] [Arist.], *Econ.*, 1346b, 24.

[3] I have dealt more fully with this law in *Phil. Woch.*, 1926, 368 ff. See also *Hermes*, 1923, p. 410.

in that the State on occasion decreed that all buying and selling within its boundaries should be transacted in the local currency. 'Every purchase or sale within Olbia shall be in the currency of the city, in Olbian copper or silver' (ll. 13 ff.). So in the Middle Ages rulers derived large profits from exchange and from minting: they struck special coins for each market, and permitted currency to these alone. But the Greek city had a further important object in restricting currency to the local, or a particular local, coinage—namely, to keep the coinage above its intrinsic value. The area of currency of most coinages in this period was very limited; for their high nominal value was only artificially maintained (p. 84). The Pseudo-Aristotelian *Economics* gives many examples of cities which enriched themselves by debasing their coinage—a device which is quite in consonance with the generally primitive economic conditions of the time. Even Athens occasionally resorted to such devices. Aristophanes (*Ran.*, 720 ff.) contrasts the old silver drachme, which rang true and was accepted everywhere by Greeks and foreigners alike, with the base 'new gold.' This was an issue of gold staters heavily alloyed with copper.[1] The pure silver was withdrawn from circulation: 'We use the old money no more,' says the Chorus at l. 725. There is a lively allusion in the *Ecclesiazusæ* (ll. 815 ff.) to the subsequent repeal of this 'copper-money decree': 'I had sold my grapes and had a whole mouthful of coppers. Then, when I was on the point of buying meal with them, the herald made his proclamation: no copper may be accepted—henceforward we use silver.'

It is usual to consider the imposition of a currency by an imperial power upon its dependents as a maxim of commercial policy, and to interpret in this sense the action of the Athenians in compelling their allies to adopt Attic coinage.[2] But this

---

[1] Boeckh, i, 30 [p. 22 ; but the later edition contains much that is absent here].

[2] The imposition of Corinthian coinage is similarly explained. In Hellenistic times : Smyrna imposes its coinage upon Magnesia (Ditt., *Or. Gr.*, 229, l. 55 (244 B.C.)). See Th. Reinach, *Mém. de l'Acad. des Inscr.*, xxxviii, 2 (1911), p. 354.

view is wholly mistaken. Such measures were purely *financial*. They were designed to increase the revenues of the ruling State from the exchange transactions which they rendered inevitable, and to enable it to make further profit by debasing the coinage when it saw fit.[1] The Athenian decree of 420 B.C. (*S.I.G.*, 87) lays down that 'if any man in the allied cities coin silver money, or does not employ the Athenian coins, weights and measures, but foreign coins, weights and measures, he shall be punished according to the earlier decree of Clearchus. Private persons shall, when they will, hand over their foreign money; the city shall change it . . . they shall pay it into the mint, where the superintendents shall receive it.'[2] It has not hitherto been noticed, so far as I can see, that this is the earliest State monopoly of foreign exchange of which we have evidence.[3]

III. *Customs and Dues*

The great importance of custom duties in the economy of the ancient city is in keeping with this universal view that trade must be made a source of revenue to the public treasury. As in the Middle Ages, so in classical times, these duties were only levied for excise purposes, and in both periods there was the same tendency to abuse. The state exploited commerce in the interest of its revenues, and the needier it was the fewer were its scruples. Other sources of revenue were uncertain and precarious. Taxation was the only relatively reliable source, and in theory it was inexhaustible. But direct taxation was avoided in all periods of antiquity; there remained, therefore, the method of indirect taxation.

The author of the Pseudo-Aristotelian *Economics* (ii, 1346*a*, 5) divides the resources of a city into three main categories: (1)

---

[1] The imposition of weights and measures is a wholly different matter. See below, p. 175.

[2] The text is mutilated, but the decisive words are certain : 1. 14, τὴν δὲ πό[λιν καταλλάττειν (A. Wilhelm) ; 1. 15, ἐπιστάτ[αι παραδεξάμενοι. See further : Weil, in *Hermes*, 1906, pp. 52 ff. ; 1910, pp. 351 ff. ; Hiller v. Gaertringen in *Zeitschr. f. Numism.*, 35, Heft 3.

[3] In the ideal city of the *Laws* (742*b*) the changing of Panhellenic into local currency is in the hands of the State (see above, p. 85).

domains; (2) taxes on sale and purchase; (3) income derived from 'the *emporia* and from transit duty.'[1] These categories correspond exactly to the normal views of the time. Isocrates (viii, 117) says of the Megarians that they became rich 'although they had no fertile land, no silver-mines, and no harbours'; Xenophon (*Hell.*, v, 2, 16), that the wealth of Olynthus depended, on the one hand, upon its shipbuilding timber, on the other, upon the revenues derived from many harbours and many *emporia*; and Isocrates again of Athens (viii, 21), that once peace is restored she will double her revenues, for the city will be crowded with 'traders and foreigners and metics.' Even metics are regarded from the fiscal point of view: 'Care for the metics,' says the author of *de Vectigalibus* (ii, 1), 'seems to me the best of all sources of revenue; for metics keep themselves, and are useful to the State without receiving payment from it—on the contrary, they pay the metic tax.' Towards the end of the fourth century the total annual revenue from the metic tax amounted to fully twenty talents (Busolt, *Gr. St.*, ii, 1222). It is only for the sake of revenue that the same writer (iii, 1 ff.) desires to attract foreign traders to the Athenian market, and enumerates the advantages which Athens offers them: 'the more they visit or settle in Athens, the more imports and exports, the more buying and selling; and in consequence the more will be paid to the State in rents and taxes' (p. 25). 'Only for profit and greed do cities throw open their market,' says Aristotle (*Pol.*, 1327a). Wealth and prosperity 'derived from trade,' meant wealth derived from duties imposed by a city upon the 'cosmopolitan' trade which came into touch with it. In order to create or maintain trade prosperity in this special sense, the city employed its resources to build and extend its harbours. It was for the sake of their *emporia* ('which they exploited') and their mines that the Thasians came to blows with Athens in 465 B.C. (Thuc., i, 100); the refusal of the Chians to sell the Œnussæ Islands to the Phocæans was due to the fear that the islands might

---

[1] For (2) see Wilcken, *Ostraka*, i, 182 ff. ; (3) reading διαγωγῶν with Boeckh, i, 370 [p. 300] for the corrupt διαγωνων of the text.

become an *emporium* (Hdt., i, 165), and so divert the excise duties which the Chians had enjoyed.

How important such profits were to the public revenue is shown by a number of data which chance has preserved for us. In Macedonia the harbour dues had been normally farmed for 20 talents; Callistratus brought the price up to 40 talents ([Arist.], *Econ.*, ii, 1350a, 16); in Rhodes they were worth over 166 talents (Polyb., xxx, 31, 12); Cersobleptes of Thrace drew not less than 200 talents a year from the *emporia* (Dem., xxiii, § 110); Boeckh (i, 384 ff. [p. 315]) has estimated the total of the 2% import and export duty in Athens at between 30 and 36 talents a year. In 413 B.C. the Athenians substituted a 5% import and export duty in the allied harbours for the old direct tribute, 'because they believed that in this way they would increase their revenue' (Thuc., vii, 28, 4).

In order to secure an easier and surer hold upon the traffic which visited its shores, the State concentrated it as far as possible in one or more fixed points. Obvious examples are Naucratis, Carthage, Bosporus, and Theodosia.[1] In the same way, if a whole city was not itself an *emporium*, the actual *emporium*, or harbour-market (for that is the real meaning of the word), was cut off from the rest of the city, and commercial traffic concentrated in it. This was the case in Alexandria,[2] in Chalcis,[3] and, above all, in the Piræus, where the whole district was marked out by boundary stones and cut off from its surroundings.[4] It was under the supervision of the 'overseers of the emporium,' who were responsible for the control of the customs. The idea of imposing duties upon the foreign trader is almost as old as trade itself. The foreigner arrives friendless and unprotected: the payment of dues secures him protection within the community with which he is trading. In early times it was the chieftain or prince who monopolised this source of revenue: the first known example is the fiscal exploitation of foreign trade by the Bacchiadæ

---

[1] See pp. 63 and 120.   [2] Strabo, 17, 1, 9.
[3] Dicæarchus, fr. 59, 29 (*F.H.G.*, ii, 260).
[4] Wachsmuth, *Stadt Athen.*, ii, 96 ff.

(p. 20). It is related of Periander that 'in all else he was moderate, for he imposed no taxes, and contented himself with market and harbour dues.'[1]

There were various types of duties; but since they were not protective, they did not vary according to the nature of the commodities. In the first place, land-borne traffic was unimportant, and duties levied upon it naturally played a very small part.[2] An export and import duty by land is recorded for some Cretan communities, as in the treaty between Olus and Latus.[3] According to the treaty between Gortyn and Lappa export by land was free, import subject to duty. Freedom from duty, then, is a matter of treaty agreement. In Crisa, about 600 B.C., a transit duty (see p. 164) was imposed on goods for Delphi: Crisa exacted extortionate dues from ships and pilgrims arriving from Sicily and Italy (Strabo, 9, 3, 4). So in Corinth dues were levied upon traffic passing between Peloponnese and Central Greece;[4] and a similar situation is revealed in the treaty between King Amyntas of Macedon and the Chalcidians (p. 114). As to the Athenian import and export duties on land-borne goods from Megara and Bœotia we have no information.

But the great bulk of such revenue was derived from duties upon sea-borne goods. Of the method of assessment we know nothing, even in Athens. The commonest tax upon imports and exports was the 2% *ad valorem*, the so-called 'fiftieth.' It is found—even in Hellenistic times—in Athens, Epidaurus, Trœzen, Cyparissiæ, Delos, Halicarnassus, and Atarneus.[5] In Athens all incoming goods, including grain, and all outgoing goods were subject to it. The officers charged with the collection were known as the *pentekostologoi*. Demosthenes on one occasion appeals to their books in order to prove the value of

---

[1] Heraclides, fr. 5 (*F.H.G.*, ii, 212).

[2] For what follows see Busolt, *Gr. St.*, i, 613 ff. *Cf.* Bücher, *Beiträge*, pp. 19 ff. For Athens : Boeckh, i, 382 ff. [pp. 313 ff.].

[3] Collitz-Bechtel, iii, 5075.   [4] Strabo, 8, 6, 20.

[5] The evidence is collected in Busolt, *Gr. St.*, i, 614, n. 4. Outside of Athens there is only inscriptional evidence. For Athens, see Boeckh, i, 382 [p. 313].

a cargo carried by a certain ship from Athens (xxxiv, § 7). This shows that the tax was collected in money, not in kind.

The tax collected in 413 B.C. from the allied states of Athens was one of 5%. This charge upon all goods entering or leaving the *emporium* of each dependent state took the place of the old direct tribute. It was simply the expropriation by the stronger power from the weaker of one of its main sources of revenue, and may be compared with Philip's exploitation of the harbour and market dues of Thessaly.[1] There is no question of *imposing* a 'twentieth' upon the dependent communities, as modern commentators would have it, postulating a corruption in the text.[2] This is to misunderstand the situation. 'The Athenian substituted the "twentieth" for the tribute' is what Thucydides says. The dependent cities had hitherto collected import and export duties like every other maritime city in Greece; and all that Athens did was to appropriate these duties to herself and to increase the rate; for it is unthinkable that these smaller cities had been levying duties more than twice as high as those of the Piræus.[3]

A $3\frac{1}{3}$% export tax on corn was levied by the princes of Bosporus. If the corn was destined for Athens this was reduced to $1\frac{2}{3}$%. The same privilege was enjoyed by the Mytilenæans up to a total of 100,000 medimni (p. 115); corn exported above that amount was subject to a tax of $1\frac{1}{9}$%. [*S.I.G.*, 212.]

Besides duties upon imports and exports, the State derived revenue from transit dues.[4] Taxation of this kind (we have seen examples of its use in overland traffic) has lent itself at all times and in all places to arbitrary abuse, as in the system-

---

[1] Dem., i, § 22.

[2] Thuc., vii, 28, τὴν εἰκοστὴν . . . ἀντὶ τοῦ φόρου τοῖς ὑπηκόοις ἐποίησαν. Stahl, Classen, and Hude read ἐπέθεσαν or ἐπέταξαν,—'they imposed.' [The Oxford text retains ἐποίησαν.]

[3] The 5% import and export tax in Ægina has nothing to do with the measure of 413 B.C. See Boeckh, i, 396, and Fraenkel's remarks, ii, *Adn.*, 537.

[4] Polyb., iv, 47, 3 : 52, 5, and Pollux, ix, 30 ; Strabo, 4, 3, 2 ; [Arist.], *Econ.*, ii, 1346a (though corrupt in MSS.), and *S.I.G.*, 135 [H.H. 95], l. 15 (see p. 114).

atic and oppressive application of the mediæval transit tolls; and it was not unnatural that Greek sea-powers found it a profitable method of adding to their revenues. A typical example is the Athenian toll set up at Chrysopolis, opposite Byzantium, in the year 410 B.C. Every vessel proceeding through the Bosporus to the Black Sea or the Ægean was subject to a 10% duty; and to carry this out, thirty men-of-war under two commanders were stationed there, a 'tithe-house' was built, and the town itself was fortified.[1] In the third century the toll was revived by the Byzantines, which brought about war with Rhodes.[2]

It is one of the most regrettable gaps in our knowledge that we have no information in regard to transit dues in Athens itself. Boeckh maintained (i, 76) that the Piræus was a free harbour, and Wachsmuth,[3] Beloch[4] and others have followed him. On this view only such goods would be taxable as crossed the boundary of the *emporium*—that is, passed into the town or the country, or alternatively came into the *emporium* from the town or the country, and were exported thence by sea; the *emporium* itself would be a free harbour, and transit goods (for example, that third part of the imported corn which might legally be sold abroad) would be tax-free. Francotte[5] has expressed his doubt; and later Bücher most emphatically urged the possibility of the contrary view.[6] An exact demonstration based upon the ancient sources is impossible, and we are forced to fall back upon general considerations.

Boeckh argued that the *emporium* was separated off from the

[1] Xen., *Hell.*, i, 1, 22 ; Polyb., iv, 38, 43 ff.

[2] Polyb., iv, 38 ff., 52. We hear elsewhere of tithes, but in the absence of detailed information it is impossible to decide in each case whether it is a transit, import, or export tax ; *e.g.* in the psephism of Callias (*S.I.G.*, 91 [H.H. 49, Tod 51]) ; in Harpocration, *s.v.* δεκατευτάς ; and the tithe raised by Cersobleptes of Thrace (Dem., xxiii, § 117), which Boeckh explains as a duty on all commodities (i, 405 [p. 334])—for tithes appear frequently in other connections, *e.g.* as a tax on produce and estates (Boeckh, i, 398 [p. 327]).

[3] *Stadt Athen*, ii, 96 ff. ; *R.E.*, v, 2532.

[4] *Jahrb. f. Nat. u. Stat.*, 3rd Series, vol. 18 (1899), pp. 626 ff.

[5] *L'Industrie*, ii, 131.

[6] *Beiträge*, p. 19 ; see also Oertel, *Anhang*, p. 521.

rest of the Piræus, and that such a demarcation would be idle except on his view. I believe that a general consideration of the Greek attitude to trade as one of the main sources of public revenue shows Boeckh's contention to be impossible. Crisa taxed goods which passed through her territory on the way to Delphi, Corinth taxed the traffic across the Isthmus, Athens that of the Bosporus. The elastic use of the word 'exploit' (καρποῦσθαι) is an indication of the readiness of the State to turn any conceivable group of circumstances to its fiscal advantage.

Boeckh holds that in the Piræus transit goods were subject only to special 'emporial dues.' Now we frequently meet in Athens and elsewhere (Crete, Macedon, Panticapæum, Delos, Rhodes) (references in Busolt, *Gr. St.*, i, 614, n. 3) the word ἐλλιμένια or 'harbour-dues,' and a board of collectors called ἐλλιμενισταί. The word, as the examples show, frequently means import and export duties; but it is clearly susceptible of other meanings. For the lexicographer Pollux (viii, 132) distinguishes between the collectors of the 2% import and export duty and the collectors of these 'harbour-dues'; and Eupolis (Pollux, ix, 29) speaks of a 'harbour-due' which must be paid 'before one goes on board.' This points to the existence of other levies besides that on imports and exports. What Eupolis is referring to is not clear. An ἐπιβατικὸν is mentioned in inscriptions, but we have no precise clue to its nature.[1] Ἐπιβάτης can mean a passenger;[2] and it seems likely that Eupolis is alluding to a payment to which any passenger, unaccompanied by goods, was subject on entering or leaving the harbour. In the Xenophontean *Respublica Atheniensium*, I, 17, we read that the compulsion upon the allies to come to Athens for law-suits increased the yield of the 1% tax. Now we have no right to assume that this is some export tax which for a time took the place of the usual 'fiftieth,' or 2% tax; and although there were quite a number of 1% taxes in Athens, the nature of which we cannot accurately determine (Arist.,

---

[1] Gilbert, *Staatsaltertümer*, i², 392, n. 2.
[2] *Hermes*, 1923, p. 398.

Vesp., 658), we should not reject off-hand the possibility that we have here to deal with this 'passenger-tax.'[1] Nevertheless, it is not likely that a levy bearing the name of 'harbour-levy' was nothing more than this supposed passenger-tax; it should be regarded, therefore, as has been done since Boeckh, as a general charge for the use of the harbour.[2]

In his programme of reform the author of *de Vectigalibus* writes (iii, 12 ff.): 'It would be a useful measure to build for the shippers additional berths for their vessels; for the merchants, places where they may buy and sell their wares; public hostelries for passengers; accommodation and stalls for traders in Piræus and the city. That would not only be an adornment of the city but would be a rich source of revenue.' Again at iii, 5 (see p. 25): 'The more foreigners settle in Athens or visit it, the more goods will be imported and exported, the more bought and sold, and consequently the more will be paid in rents and dues.' There can be no manner of doubt that such conveniences, which were almost all in the port, already existed before the proposals of our author; and Boeckh is therefore right (i, 388 [p. 319]) in connecting these 'harbour-dues' with a payment 'for permission to deposit commodities in the warehouses and magazines.' In the same way landowners in the Middle Ages profited from the rent of stalls and booths on their land.

The existence of special harbour-dues in Athens and elsewhere cannot be doubted. Nevertheless it must not be supposed that transit goods were liable to these special payments only. Athens was a great centre of import and export; but besides that it was the distributing centre for the whole Greek world: the mass of goods which passed through the Piræus must have exceeded the Athenian imports and exports. In later times Rome made Delos the centre of distribution for the eastern Mediterranean and at the same time declared it a

---

[1] But we cannot then speak—as Boeckh would have us do—of a 1% tax upon cargo and upon whatever a passenger brings in or takes out with him, for this is covered by the regular ' fiftieth.'

[2] It cannot, however, have been expected to cover all the vast public expenditure upon the harbour, as Boeckh maintains.

free harbour—which amounted to exempting it from any dues whatsoever. 'You have exempted Delos from taxation,' said the Rhodian Ambassador in Rome (Polyb., xxx, 31, 10); and the result of this exemption was that the whole traffic of the Rhodian *emporium* was concentrated in Delos, and the yield of the Rhodian dues fell from 1,000,000 to 150,000 drachmæ. But it cannot be maintained that conditions were the same in the fifth and fourth centuries, and that Athens would have proclaimed freedom of transit as a means of attracting to herself all the commerce of the Greek world. The author of *de Vectigalibus* is concerned to enumerate every thinkable advantage which Athens offers to commerce; but these advantages are not such as depend on favourable tariff conditions: 'One might think that Athens had been built upon the central point of Greece or of the world itself; every man who will go from one end of Greece to the other must pass by water or by land through Athens as through the centre of a circle' (i, 6). Besides the favourable geographical position, he points to the excellent sheltered harbour of the Piræus, and to the advantage which the purity of the Athenian coinage brings to the foreign trader (iii, 1). He is concerned to discover every conceivable untapped source of revenue which trade could yield; and if the transit traffic had been exempt in his day this obvious source would scarcely have escaped his search. Nowhere in the many panegyrics upon the singular readiness of Athens to welcome goods from all the world is there any mention of such hospitality to the foreigner as consists in special exemptions from duty;[1] nor in the detailed discussions of the relations between Athens and the other states of Greece is there mention of any relation which corresponds to that between the free port of Delos and Rhodes. On the contrary; in Athens, too, the revenues from transit dues must have been of great importance to the treasury, probably of greater importance than those from the *emporium*, in view of the fact that the *entrepôt* traffic exceeded that of import and export proper. The attempt of the moderns to belittle the transit traffic in comparison with

[1] See p. 122.

exports and imports is based upon the false assumption of a highly developed export industry in Athens. If Athens cut off its *emporium* from the rest of its territory, it did so in order to secure a concentration of commercial activity, and that from what may be called policial motives—as a town tries to concentrate the sale of goods in its market.[1]

In regard to the method of collection, it appears that the State did not work through its own officials, but followed the regular practice of ancient taxation, and made over the duty of collection to farmers or companies of farmers, in each case to the highest bidder. A foreign state or ruler might on occasion fill the part, as in 390–89 B.C. when the 10% toll at the Bosporus was farmed by Thrasybulus to the city of Byzantium.[2] The separate farming-out of the duty on imported corn in Athens (Dem., lix, § 27) shows that the taxation of different classes of goods was separately arranged.

It remains to discuss the market dues. The Scholiast on Aristophanes (*Ach.*, 896) speaks of these as an ancient institution, and it is told of Periander that he drew his revenues not only from the Corinthian harbour but from the market (p. 161). This market tax[3] was not a mere stall-rent, but an excise duty upon all goods exposed for sale. In Athens there was a legal tariff for different kinds of goods, *e.g.* for fish and for eels. The tax was normally levied at the city gate or in the market itself. A Greek city was as prompt to exploit its markets as its *emporium*. The author of *de Vectigalibus*, in the passage where he proposes intensive exploitation of the Laurium silvermines, does not forget the business which he believes will develop in the local market—and will provide the state with a further source of revenue (iv, 49). Towns where festivals were held turned the markets associated with such festivals to the advantage of the public chest (*I.G.*, ii², 1245).

Boeckh (i, 382, 395 [pp. 313, 323]) appears to assume that,

---

[1] *E.g.* in Thurii : Theophr. *ap.* Stob., *Flor.*, 44, 22. Cf. *S.I.G.*, 344, l. 95.

[2] Xen., *Hell.*, i, 1, 22 ; Diod., xiii, 64, 2.

[3] Boeckh, i, 393 ff. [p. 323] ; Büchsenschütz, *Bes. u. Erw.*, pp. 556 ff. ; Busolt, *Gr. St.*, i, 616 ff.

in addition to the market-tax, a 'purchase-tax' (payable by the buyer), which is found almost everywhere in the Greek world (ἐπώνιον, ἐγκύκλια), was levied upon goods sold in the market. I cannot believe this to be true: such a double imposition would have rendered business impossible. The Greek 'purchase-tax,' wherever we encounter it, relates to purchase of land, farming of taxes, purchase of State property, priesthoods, and so forth.[1] It appears that it is not to be regarded only as a source of revenue; it served also to document contracts of purchase.[2]

C. STATE CONTROL OF COMMERCE

I. *Legislation*

It remains to deal with the legislative and political control exercised by the State over commerce. This has already been discussed so far as it relates to the supply of necessities; but even the pre-Hellenistic State went further, and took steps to ensure the regular and orderly conduct of commerce in general within its territory. It is true that 'cosmopolitan' trade in the Greek world, as elsewhere, influenced the development of law, and brought into being certain legal principles and usages relating to trade, which conflicted with the separatism which otherwise determined international relations; but it is impossible to speak of commercial law as a special branch of law before the time of Alexander, and in view of the Rhodian Sea Law I believe that even for Hellenistic times the utmost reserve is necessary. In the classical age [3] there was no separate merchant class, there were no gilds possessing the right of jurisdiction and self-government, no great trading companies like those of the later Middle Ages and modern times—in short, all those factors were absent which in later times contributed

---

[1] Boerner, *R.E.*, vi, 243 ; Busolt, *loc. cit.*

[2] The Pseudo-Aristotle (*Econ.*, ii, 1351a, 8) records a proposal made by Chabrias to Tachos, the King of Egypt, that for every *artabe* of corn sold a tax of one obol should be levied from buyer and seller alike ; but this appears to be quite exceptional.

[3] See Goldschmidt, *Universalgesch. d. Handelsrechts*, i, 53 ff. ; Ehrenberg, *Handb. d. Gesamten Handelsrechts*, 1913, i, 70.

most to the formation of a special code of commercial law. Commercial methods in this period were still primitive, they conformed to no legal norm; business was conducted by word of mouth, the notion of credit was undeveloped, there was no legal rate of interest, the validity of contracts was sanctioned by no fixed forms. Nevertheless, it is possible to distinguish certain common usages in Greek commerce, notably in the body of detailed regulations which Plato has drawn up for the 'second-best' State of the *Laws*—and which must conform very closely to the actual practice of his time.[1]

The legal rules which relate to foreign trade and to the activities of *naukleroi* and *emporoi* are, in Athens at least, concerned only with bottomry loans—if we exclude those which deal with the supply of food and other necessities. They are the so-called 'emporial laws,' and suits arising out of them are 'emporial suits' (δίκαι ἐμπορικαί). These laws by no means include all the enactments concerning freedom or restriction of trade: it must not be supposed that all regulations governing import and export, corn-supply, and provision of other necessities are subsumed under them;[2] nor, though it is commonly assumed,[3] is 'emporial suits' a general term for

---

[1] We are not concerned here with the general principles of the Greek law of property and contract in relation to trade.

[2] As Thalheim holds (*R.E.*, v, 2531).

[3] Boeckh, i, 64 [p. 50] ; Platner, *Der Prozess und die Klagen*, i, 290 ff. ; Büchsenschütz, *Bes. und Erw.*, p. 531 ; Thalheim, *R.E.*, v, 2530 ; Beauchet, *Histoire du droit privé*, iv, 90 ff. Lipsius (*Att. Recht und Rechtsverf.*, p. 632) repudiates the extension of 'emporial suits' to *all* cases at law involving commercial matters ; but even he has failed to recognise their exclusive application to bottomry contracts, as is clear from his assertion (p. 721, n. 162) that they are *mainly* concerned with such contracts, and from his language elsewhere (pp. 86 and 632 ff.). On p. 633 he further maintains, on the authority of Lysias (xvii, 5), that in *earlier times* the competence of the 'commercial courts' was wider. To this it must be objected that the fact that the ναυτοδίκαι dealt with a dispute about landed property which has been dismissed by another court is only indirect evidence for emporial suits, since they had jurisdiction also in cases of citizen birth (Lipsius, p. 86). Hitzig (*Zeitschr. der Savigny-Stiftung*, 1907, p. 227) supposes in Dem., xxxii, § 1, a second category of covenants not directly involving foreign commerce. This view has already been rejected by Lipsius (p. 632, n. 18).

all suits involving *emporoi* and *naukleroi*. In the one passage which remains to us where emporial laws are expressly named (Dem., xxxv, § 3), the matter at issue is a bottomry loan made in accordance with these laws. It is of these same laws, though he does not expressly name them, that Demosthenes says (xxxiv, § 52), 'they offer many and powerful aids to the bottomry business.' In short, we have in them a body of law designed exclusively to safeguard this particular interest. The 'emporial suits,' of which we have details in five Pseudo-Demosthenean speeches (those against Zenothemis, Apaturius, Lacritus, Phormio, Dionysodorus),[1] are all concerned with the bottomry business, with suits by or against *naukleroi* and *emporoi* arising out of 'written contracts from and to Athens' (*Zenoth.*, § 1). At a time when business was conducted by word of mouth only contracts for such loans were committed to writing (p. 89). It should be noted, of course, that the nature of the particular breach of the law which gives rise to such suits varies from case to case.[2]

We possess only fragments of these emporial laws, and are compelled to confine ourselves to scattered notices in our authorities.

1. Demosthenes, *Dionysodorus* (lvi), § 10: 'The laws which lay down that *naukleroi* and *emporoi* must proceed, under the severest penalties, to the *emporium* to which they have contracted to proceed.'

2. Dem., *Phormio* (xxxiv), § 50: The death penalty is decreed for a trader who shall borrow on already mortgaged security.

3. Dem., *Lacritus* (xxxv), § 50; *Dionys.*, § 6: The law which forbids the lending of Attic capital for trade in foreign markets.[3]

---

[1] Lipsius, *op. cit.*, pp. 631 ff.

[2] In the five known cases there is a δίκη ἐξούλης, a δίκη βλάβης, and a δίκη χρέως.

[3] *Hermes*, 1920, p. 135. According to Isocrates (xvii, § 42) it was forbidden in Athens at the time of the Corinthian war to lend money on a ship which 'belonged to a Delian.' From this Lipsius concludes (p. 312) that Delos was hostile to Athens in the war. Büchsenschütz (p. 531) is

4. Dem., *Theocrines* (lviii), §§ 10, 54: The law which safe-guards *naukleroi* and *emporoi* against frivolous and oppressive suits by imposing as penalty for subsequent withdrawal of the charge a more serious degree of *atimia* than in ordinary public suits.[1] This, too, can only apply to suits which arise out of bottomry contracts.

The difference between emporial and other suits consists, according to Attic law, in this, that the former were heard before a special court, originally by the *Nautodikai*, and from the middle of the fourth century onwards before the *Thes-mothetai*. Both these boards occasionally heard suits 'con-cerning the status of foreigners,' that is, cases of illegal claim to citizenship; which is an indirect proof that the emporial suits had to do with foreign merchants, and that Athenian trade was carried on almost exclusively by non-citizens. In fact, without exception all the cases which have come down to us concern foreigners. Further, these cases belong—from the middle of the fourth century onwards (Dem., vii, § 12)—to the class of 'monthly suits' which enjoyed the privilege of a shortened and accelerated hearing and were only brought before the courts in the winter months, when seafaring was at a standstill (Dem., xxxiii, § 23). This was also to the advantage of the foreign trader only temporarily resident in the city, and has its parallel in the swift procedure of the mediæval merchant law.[2] Both there and here this marks one of the more advanced stages in the development of law as it relates to foreigners, and is one of the most notable modifica-tions of the principle that the foreigner has no rights. The author of *de Vectigalibus* emphasises the fact that rapidity of

vague : 'A ship from a country which at that time had no free inter-course with Athens.' For myself, I can see nothing in the passage except the law quoted above from Demosthenes.

[1] So Lipsius rightly (p. 328, n. 39) with Haffter and Platner. We must not, however, with Büchsenschütz (p. 530), bring into relation with this the decree of Mœrocles against those who 'violate the rights of merchants.' This had to do with piracy (Dem., *Theocr.*, § 53). *Cf.* § 56, where the Melians are fined ten talents under this decree because they had harboured pirates.

[2] Goldschmidt, *loc. cit.*, p. 120.

procedure is to the interest of the foreign, not of the citizen trader, and that at a time when 'monthly suits' did not yet exist: 'If prizes were offered to the courts for the justest and swiftest settlement of disputes, so that a litigant anxious to sail could do so without delay, this, too, would encourage traders to come more readily and in greater numbers to Athens' (iii, 3).[1] Finally, the penalties for either party are more severe in these than in other cases. The law prescribes imprisonment for the defendant until he shall have discharged the payment imposed on him, whereas in ordinary cases he was only liable to distraint upon his property (*Apat.*, § 1); and similarly for the non-suited plaintiff in respect of the *epobelia* due to the defendant (*Dionys.*, § 4; *Lacr.*, § 46).[2]

Legislation, then, so far as it relates to foreign trade and finds expression in the emporial laws, was designed exclusively for the safeguarding of the bottomry business. The State concerned itself particularly with this business, and it looked to the interests both of the lender, or capitalist, and of the trader. At a period when the distinction between capitalist and trader was absolute, trade was wholly dependent upon loans, and that form of speculation became a favourite method of investment. In fact this legislation is the clearest possible expression of the dependence of all Greek trade upon borrowed capital.

The only known law affecting local trade—apart from mere police regulations—is the Attic law which prescribes that to the 'monthly suits' shall belong also suits for the recovery of a loan 'if a man shall have borrowed capital in order to set up a business in the market' (Ar., *Resp. Ath.*, 52, 2). In view of what has been urged with regard to the character of emporial legislation this is extremely significant, and indicates that local trade also was in part carried on without capital of its own. 'Banking suits' also enjoyed the legal privilege of

---

[1] Only traces survive of a similar procedure out of Athens ; in *Zenothemis* (§§ 5–9 and 14) there is mention of a bottomry case in Cephallenia, where the courts decide that a merchantman must sail for Athens, and, as the context shows, without delay.

[2] *Cf.* Lipsius, *op. cit.*, p. 633.

a shortened procedure. These were suits brought by or against bankers in respect of loans, usually of loans made at rates above the normal 12%: other suits in respect of loans enjoyed this privilege only if the loan had been made at that rate or below it.[1] The State thus gave its protection to all foreign and local trade and to money-lending in the matter of legal procedure; this, however, must not be regarded as protection of trade as such, but as protection of the lending business which was necessarily involved in trade.[2]

The whole body of commercial legislation of this age, so far as it was not concerned merely with police regulations, is thus to be regarded as the protection by the State (*a*) of its necessary supplies, and (*b*) of the money-lenders who provided the capital indispensable to the existence of trade. The majority of the emporial laws and the local trade law cited above show very clearly how this protection favoured the capitalist: 'Many and powerful aids to the bottomry business' (above, p. 170). For the capitalist alone was a full member of the citizen community. The trader was either a foreigner out and out, or he was a metic; and even as a metic he had only an incomplete share in the privileges of citizenship and in many respects was not even a legal person.[3]

II. *Market Police*

For the rest, the State exercised control over inland trade through police regulations for the market. These aimed at ensuring the regular conduct of business and at maintaining order: 'The first consideration is to secure the necessary order in the market, and for that purpose there must be a magistrate to supervise the business carried on and to see that everything is done in order and as it should. For the exchange of the necessities of life by sale and purchase is indispensable to any city' (Ar., *Pol.*, 1321*b*).

[1] Billeter, *Gesch. d. Zinsfusses*, pp. 26 ff.

[2] Much the same is true of banking ; the Greek banker usually had no capital of his own, but operated with the moneys of his clients (*Hermes*, 1920, p. 165).

[3] Ar., *Pol.*, 1275*a*, 1278*a*.

The laws in question are grouped under the general name of market laws,[1] and with them are included regulations governing market dues.[2] The following examples, which could be supplemented from inscriptions, indicate the nature of these provisions.

1. Ar., *Resp. Ath.*, 50, 1: Only pure and unadulterated wares may be put on sale.

2. Dem., xx, § 9: Both to buyers and to sellers 'all deception is forbidden.'[3] So Plato in the *Laws* (917*b*) proposes the rule that the seller must never demand two different prices for his wares.

3. Xenarchus *ap.* Athen., vi, 225*c* [Kock, fr. 7; Pickard-Cambridge, fr. 2]: It is forbidden to fishmongers to sprinkle their fish with water.

4. Dem., lvii, § 30: 'He has slandered us not only in defiance of the decree which relates to the market, but of the laws which ordain that a case for "evil speaking" shall lie against anyone who shall defame the market trade of a citizen male or female.' We must distinguish here. Within the body of market legislation, about which we have no further information, there is first a *decree* against bringing a man's trade in the market into disrepute, no doubt with business rivalry in view. (We hear of 'defamation in the emporium' as a feature of commercial life even in those days.[4]) Secondly, there is a *law*, protecting a citizen who plies his trade in the market against contemptuous comment upon his means of livelihood—for such a livelihood was universally despised.

In Athens it was the board of *agoranomoi* who saw to the observance of these rules and were responsible for the orderly conduct of business. This board is found in all Greek states: it is mentioned in inscriptions of no less than one hundred and twenty communities.[5] To these overseers of local trade correspond, for foreign trade, the 'overseers of the *emporium*,' who have the duty of general supervision and in particular of

---

[1] Lipsius, *op. cit.*, pp. 93 ff.   [2] *Cf.* Schol., *Iliad*, xix, 21, 203.
[3] *Cf.* Theophr. *ap.* Harpocrat., *s.v.* ; Hyperides, *Athenog.*, 14, 6.
[4] *Cf. Hermes*, 1923, p. 418.   [5] Busolt, *Gr. St.*, i, 491.

securing observance of the law (above, p. 163) that two-thirds of all the corn brought to Piræus must be sent to Athens (Ar., *Resp. Ath.*, 51, 4), and of the other law (p. 149) that no Athenian may lend money to a trader conveying corn to a foreign harbour (Dem., xxxv, § 51). That their competence extended to the administration of the other laws governing corn supply is not recorded, but is probable. They had nothing to do with the observance of the 'emporial laws.'

Finally, one of the most important tasks of State supervision was the control of weights and measures. The special officers entrusted with this duty were called in Athens the *metronomoi* (Ar., *Resp. Ath.*, 51, 2).[1] The Greek State, like the mediæval, claimed for itself the right of authorisation and control in this matter; but we hear of no such attempt to exploit this right in the interests of revenue as we meet in the Middle Ages, unless indeed the charge for the use of the public scales in Cyzicus in the sixth century is to be so explained (*S.I.G.*, 4). State supervision of coinage has already been discussed (p. 157); here it need only be added that the universal penalty for false coining was death.[2]

D. Commerce in the Ideal State

Finally, it remains to examine the political and economic theories of the fourth century as they are presented in the Ideal States of Plato and of Aristotle. Hitherto these have been for the most part considered and judged on the assumption that the fourth century had reached an advanced stage of economic development; but when they are compared with a relatively primitive stage of development it will be seen, as in Xenophon's *de Vectigalibus*, that the discrepancy between theory and fact is considerably less, and the ideas less Utopian, than is commonly supposed. They are seen not to be 'a reaction against an advanced national-economic civilisation'

---

[1] Boeckh (ii, 318 ff.) has provided a commentary to the large fragment of an Athenian decree relating to weights and measures, probably of the year 330 B.C. (*I.G.*, ii², 1013).

[2] Fourth century : Dem., xxiv, § 212 (Athens) ; *I.G.*, xii, 2, 1 (Mytilene, Phocæa). Hellenistic Age : *B.C.H.*, 31 (1907), p. 37 (Delos).

(Pöhlmann), comparable to the modern reaction against capitalism to which socialism gave the first impetus, but rather to be a mark of the very primitiveness of contemporary economic conditions and a symptom of the unique importance of the citizen body.

It was a natural consequence of the actual conditions that the Ideal State was an agricultural state, in which for the full citizens commerce and trade were out of the question. To the citizen of the ancient state commerce and industry existed primarily as a means of ensuring the existence of the state, particularly its food supply, and of filling the public purse; beyond that they existed only as a field for investment and speculation. And the position of commerce and industry in these Ideal States corresponds to this fact. Both in the real and in the Ideal State the leisured class of full citizens is dominant, and exists by force at the expense of an unprivileged class; what is Utopian in the ideal projects is simply that the economic independence of this leisured class is more complete —and that the activities of public life are made to conform to an ethical pattern: moderation in material demands is insisted upon, and life is to be given up entirely to the highest philosophic activities of the *homo politicus* in the widest sense. To attain this, the ideal citizen had to be relieved from all striving after material gain. If he is not denied private property altogether and made to live entirely on systematised contributions from others, he is at least limited to landownership; money must be done away with entirely, and an end thus put to every form of pecuniary transaction.

But it is only for the upper class of full citizens that wage-labour and business is to be abolished. In Plato's 'best state' the leisured class depends not, as in the world of fact, upon the normal revenues of the State (warfare, domain lands, customs, levies) and of the individual (land, house property, speculation of all kinds), but on the contributions of the wage-earning or trading class. In this way the citizens can dispense with private property and lead the ideal life of unhampered devotion to the service of the State; they have neither wives nor children of their own, and are concerned only to maintain the numbers and the quality of the ruling class in consonance with the rigid exclusiveness of the actual citizen state. The counterpart to the economic life of the actual state is rather to be found in the 'third class' alone:[1] the land-workers, house-builders, weavers, shoe-makers, carpenters, smiths, herdsmen and the rest; and the local dealers and merchants, which last 'are needed to convey from another community what the state lacks at home' and are the 'servants who attend to export and import' (*Rep.*, 370). These share among themselves the products of the special art of each by buying and selling to each other; they have their market and a 'currency as the accepted token of exchange' (371*b*).[2] But all these workers live apart from the independent ruling class, which dwells together, like a military unit, in its 'camp,' from which it can best beat off its foreign enemies and control its native country population. So it was in Athens: the city was primarily the seat of the citizen body, the Piræus the centre of trade and industrial life—carried on for the most part by resident aliens.

In the 'best state' the workers, though they lived apart, were still members of the citizen body; but in the 'second-best state' the separation is carried further, and they, with their slaves, are treated as foreigners or metics, and excluded

[1] Whether Plato meant the third class to be included in the communism of the first and second classes or not has been in dispute since Aristotle ; it is now generally held that he did not (see Pohlenz, *Staatsgedanke*, p. 88 ; Oertel, *Anhang*, p. 560). Understanding of the economic organisation of the Ideal State seems to me impossible except on this assumption. The main argument is Plato's precept about the use of money (see next note) ; further, see 417*a* and 419, where the guardians are contrasted with the 'others,' who can only be the workers. Besides, as I indicate above, I believe 369 ff. to refer to this class—which seems to me conclusive.

[2] That Plato denied the use of money to the ruling class only is shown by the words of the *Republic* itself : ' To them alone in the city is contact with gold and silver forbidden ' (417*a*). It is commonly held that we must suppose a contradiction, since we read in 422*d* : ' We use gold and silver in no form, and it is forbidden to us.' But the speakers are ambassadors addressing members of a foreign state—that is, they are members of the ruling class.

12

altogether from the community. The city workers live apart, 'outside the city and round about it'; only in the country do workers live together with citizens, since there their services are needed on the spot. But in its economic aspect the 'second-best state' is less Utopian, in that the leisured upper class more nearly approximates to that of existing cities. Unlike the citizens of the 'best state' they do not depend upon a working-class to supply their needs; they are themselves productive, and live on their produce. They have personal and real property, a family, and slaves: they possess at least one parcel of land, assigned to them by lot; all allotments are of equal value, and are divided into two parts, of which one is near the city, the other in the country. They are 'farmers, cattle-breeders, bee-keepers' (*Laws*, 842*d*). But they do not work themselves; all productive work, including agriculture, is made over to their slaves (806*d*, *e*) and to non-citizen hired labourers (742*e*). Their produce is saleable. Two-thirds, it is true, of the total yield and stock is public, and goes to meet the consumption of the citizens (who have a common table) and their slaves; and every citizen has the right to distribute as much of this as he thinks fit to slaves and freemen (848*c*); but the rest is assigned to the non-citizen workers, to whom it is *sold* (848*a*), whereas no citizen may buy from another. The sale takes place in the 'strangers' markets'—corn, fluids, cattle, hides, clothing, textiles, felt are enumerated at 849*b*. On the other hand, the citizen may (within legally prescribed limits, 850*a*) buy from the workers at the 'common market' anything which he needs over and above his own produce. For this unavoidable traffic with the workers (742*a*) the citizens have a coinage (though not of gold or silver); for in the 'common market' 'wares are exchanged for coin, and coin for wares' (849*e*). Coinage is further needed in order to pay wages to craftsmen and other hired workers (742*a*, 847*b*). This coinage, however, as in many real cities (see p. 156 above), has no exchange value outside the city.

Since the citizen in his capacity of landowner and producer might on occasion increase his wealth by business activities or by 'treasure trove or gifts or other windfalls' (744e), and since, on the other hand, the stability of property must be maintained, any surplusage has to be made over to the state treasury or to the gods (745a). 'The law-giver must watch over the citizens' revenues and expenditure of whatever sort' (632b). This stability of property takes the form of a fourfold classification of the citizen body according to wealth. The citizens may, of course, enter the ideal colony bringing greater or less possessions with them; but the State sees to it that upper and lower limits are observed: the minimum for the first class is the parcel of land which each citizen receives by lot; the maximum of the fourth class is four times that allotment (744). This property classification may not be disturbed by buying and selling (850a). The citizens must be 'well-off' or possess 'moderate means' (806d) in order to devote themselves at leisure to public business (763d); but any alienation of property (beyond the sale of the third part of their produce), and in particular of landed property, is forbidden. Gold and silver are banned; 'vulgar money-making and usury and discreditable cattle-dealing' are forbidden, and the citizens must live on the produce of the land. No citizen or his slave may be a handicraftsman (846d); he is forbidden under penalty to ply a skilled trade (847a); and neither freely nor under compulsion may he become a merchant or a dealer (919d).

Aristotle's economic theories follow similar lines. Money serves solely to facilitate exchange of goods and must never be the instrument of enrichment, for money-making—'chrematistic'—is contrary to nature. And most important, 'the best state will not admit the worker to citizenship' (Pol., 1278a). How Aristotle conceived the translation of his theories into practice, and how he pictured to himself the working of such an economic organisation, we do not know; but this at least is certain, that his ideal too was an agricultural state, with stable equality of wealth, and stable population; and a system of common housekeeping and common tables.

The 'banausic' population of Plato's 'best state' is left to itself and leads the economic life of reality. But the metic traders in the 'second-best state' are in many ways limited in their economic activities, since they exist solely to supply the citizens with what they need beyond their own agricultural produce. This population and its slaves are permitted to engage in buying and selling even of wine and corn, and that as local dealers (849*d*); but trading 'for the sake of enrichment' is forbidden throughout the whole state (847*d*), where, indeed, there is no money except the local medium of exchange (p. 156).

Trading is regulated by an ordinance of which the following are the principal clauses (915*d* ff.): 1. All buying and selling must take place in a fixed place in the market. 2. In any cash transaction over 50 drachmæ the vendor must remain for ten days in the city and inform the buyer of his place of residence in case of subsequent dispute—especially in selling of slaves. 3. Adulteration of wares or of currency is forbidden. 4. The number of local dealers must be kept as low as possible. 5. Only those men who can be specially vouched for are allowed to become dealers. Special steps are to be taken to safeguard dealers from 'degeneration into shame and infamy.' 6. All prices are fixed by law. 7. Delivery and payment must be made punctually. 8. Financial transactions in money or credit are forbidden, even to non-citizens (921*c*; *cf.* 849*e*, 915*d*). 9. Foreigners engaged in trade and paid occupations may reside in the city for not more than twenty years, after which time they must leave the city with all their possessions (850). (These last are registered by the State and must never exceed twice the value of the citizen's parcel of land.)

Commercial policy in the *Laws* is concerned solely with supplies. It fulfils the Aristotelian rule: 'a city must engage in trade for its own interests alone, never in the interests of others,' and 'must not make itself a market for all nations for the sake of gain' (*Pol.*, 1327*a*). There are, therefore, no duties on export and import (847*b*), no tax on sales, no taxation of metics (850*b*). It is only to secure the necessities of existence that this state has dealings with the world about it. 'The sea is a "salt and bitter neighbour," as Alcman calls it; it brings trade to a city and the squalor of merchandise and money-making' (705a). The ideal city therefore lies some ten miles from the sea. It secures its supplies from its own lands so far as it can, and needs no laws regarding shippers, merchants, dealers, innkeepers, customs, mines, or money-lending (842). It forbids the importation of all unnecessary goods—incense and spices for the gods, purple, dyes, and 'everything which any craft may need for the production of superfluous things'— and the export of anything which ought to remain in the country to meet its unavoidable needs. Export and import of war-material are, however, permitted (847b, c). The city produces nothing beyond its own needs: 'though it yields all things it does not yield in great abundance; else export would become possible and the city would be filled once more with gold and silver coin' (705b. Cf. 949e). The public treasury alone possesses money which has exchange value abroad— this is necessary for the conduct of war and in dealings with other states—and any citizen who leaves the country (which he may not do until he is forty years of age, and then only as a herald, ambassador or religious representative of his city, 950d), must change his local currency at the treasury and change back on his return (742a, b).

In spite of all, trade in articles of necessity must remain; the city cannot dispense with the foreign trader. As it must receive foreign visitors to festivals, ambassadors, and travellers who come to see the country, so it receives the merchants who 'swarm over the seas each summer, ply their trade for profit and pass on to other cities.' The traders are received in the markets and ports and are put up by the proper officers in public hostelries outside, but near, the city; it is the duty of these officers to see to it that the traders make no disturbance, and if need arise, to settle their dispute at law—but for the rest to have as little to do with them as may be (952d ff.). The trader is one of those foreigners with whom the state must necessarily reckon: he resides temporarily in the city with his slaves for public or private ends (848a), and mingles with the permanent working population.

It is clear, then, that there is no indication in the theorists of a desire to abolish trade as the intermediary between production and consumption, just as there is no such indication in the tendencies of the actual cities of the classical age (see p. 4). Plato expressly recognises that the class of traders is indispensable, and nothing to the contrary can be proved in Aristotle. The activity of the dealer is a 'service' which he renders to the producer (*Rep.*, 371*c*; above, p. 2); merchants and dealers confer a 'benefit' upon mankind in that they 'transform an unsymmetrical and uneven distribution of goods into a symmetrical and even distribution,' and 'supply all wants and make for equality of possession' (*Laws*, 918*b*, *c*). Aristotle takes an even kindlier view of foreign trade than Plato, as his discussion of the geographical characteristics of the best city shows (*Pol.*, 1327*a*). But trade, indispensable as it is, must never go beyond the limits of its function, which is to link production with consumption. It must not serve the end of enrichment, but serve only to secure necessary supplies. For that reason the 'second-best state' has no money, and does not even exploit commerce for the benefit of the public purse. For the privileged citizen body of the Ideal State such exploitation of private trading is of no importance: their material welfare is secured in other ways, and to them such matters as shipping loans and customs duties are things of no concern.

INDEX OF SUBJECTS

INDEX OF PROPER NAMES